Nurturing Sanctuary

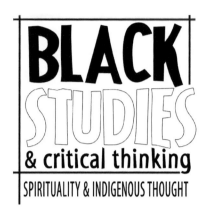

BLACK STUDIES
& critical thinking
SPIRITUALITY & INDIGENOUS THOUGHT

Cynthia Dillard, *Series Editor*

Rochelle Brock and Richard Greggory Johnson III
Executive Editors

Vol. 67

The Black Studies and Critical Thinking series
is part of the Peter Lang Education list.
Every volume is peer reviewed and meets
the highest quality standards for content and production.

PETER LANG
New York • Bern • Frankfurt • Berlin
Brussels • Vienna • Oxford • Warsaw

TOWNSAND PRICE-SPRATLEN

Nurturing Sanctuary

Community Capacity Building in African American Churches

PETER LANG
New York • Bern • Frankfurt • Berlin
Brussels • Vienna • Oxford • Warsaw

Library of Congress Cataloging-in-Publication Data
Price-Spratlen, Townsand.
Nurturing sanctuary: community capacity building in African American churches /
Townsand Price-Spratlen.
pages cm. — (Black studies and critical thinking; v. 67)
Includes bibliographical references and index.
1. Service learning—United States. 2. Communities—United States.
3. African American churches. 4. Social justice—United States. I. Title.
LC220.5.P74   361.3'70973—dc23   2015016452
ISBN 978-1-4331-2598-0 (hardcover)
ISBN 978-1-4331-2597-3 (paperback)
ISBN 978-1-4539-1642-1 (e-book)
ISSN 1947-5985

Bibliographic information published by **Die Deutsche Nationalbibliothek.**
Die Deutsche Nationalbibliothek lists this publication in the "Deutsche
Nationalbibliografie"; detailed bibliographic data are available
on the Internet at http://dnb.d-nb.de/.

The paper in this book meets the guidelines for permanence and durability
of the Committee on Production Guidelines for Book Longevity
of the Council of Library Resources.

DEDICATION

This book is dedicated to my mother, Dr. Lois Price Spratlen. Mom passed away on Holy Saturday, hours before Easter Sunday of 2013. Professionally, Mom's many achievements are far too numerous to list here. Among those of note is that she was the University Ombudsman and Ombudsman for Sexual Harassment at the University of Washington for over 20 years. Among her many gifts, Mom was an amazing leader and collaborator and she had an intense dedication to excellence. I deeply value how she nurtured the professional development of others while also nurturing social justice. And Mom encouraged—in fact, demanded—no less of the same from my family and from all those whose lives she touched.

When I first spoke with Mom and Dad about the genesis of this book, we talked about their childhood memories of church and faith. At one point we were trying to recall the biblical definition of faith that is often quoted. After a bit of struggle and moving on to other topics, Mom shouted out, "The substance of things hoped for! The evidence of things not seen! Hebrews 11:1. *That's* it. I'll tell you. That Baptist Training Union sticks *with* you even after all these years." Our shared laughter followed. And somewhere in the Spirits, Ora Price, my maternal grandmother, had to be smiling. I am grateful to be one of her sons and to be living in the Ancestral Echoes of her Calling. Mom, your smile and laughter echo in my Spirit. May this book do justice to your childhood memory and to the ever-presence of your life and legacy.

TABLE OF CONTENTS

Part 2
Tensions of Faith

Conclusion

ACKNOWLEDGMENTS

First and foremost, I give thanks to the God of my understanding, whose Grace enriches each breath and whose gifts lead me to seek the best of myself in fellowship with others. I give thanks to my Ancestors, the known and the unknown. I am especially grateful to the many that were forced to take the journeys across the Atlantic Ocean against their will. I am grateful to be the product of those who lost their lives on the ocean's waters and those who survived and flourished beyond bondage. My faith includes the belief that I was in my Ancestors' dreams then. And I hope this exploration of faith is a worthy expression of their hopes and prayers for a better life.

My thanks go to Professor Cynthia B. Dillard. Her interest in the idea for this book began with notes on a napkin during a coffee shop conversation we shared in 2010. I thank her for her belief in the contributions this book could make.

I give thanks also to my "sanity sistas" of professional development. The sistas of our African American Graduate and Professional Student Association (especially Drs. Carlene Brown, Debra Greenwood, and Eileen Hayes) made the vagaries of graduate school move from tolerable to almost fun given the fellowship we shared (along with Ernest, Kevin, and the "brothas"). We did good work then, and we continue to do so across the years. I give thanks to

Dean Linda Burton, whose guidance, along with Professor Barry Lee, helped make my Penn State postdoctorate years productive. Linda, you opened me up to the value that can result when multiple methods of qualitative research are put to good use. Thank you for sharing your craft and friendship. And I give thanks to my sanity sista extraordinaire, Professor Emeritus Ruth D. Peterson. Thank you, Ruth, for all that you give to, and share with, so many. The quality of your life and career is a model for what sociology can do when done well. As I said in *Reconstructing Rage*, "perhaps the only thing greater than the quality of your scholarship and willingness to support the growth of others is your humanity." I am so grateful to know you as mentor and friend, and I would not be sane without you. And Professor Lauren J. Krivo, thank you for all of your thoughtful critiques, feedback, and friendship across the years and for your ongoing support of my possibilities.

I share many thanks for the lives, voices, and thoughtful contributions of the Caring Congregations for Healthy Youth (CoCHY) project participants. I give thanks to Professor Kenneth Steinman, who invited me to participate to manage and take full responsibility for the qualitative methods and data the CoCHY project produced. I give thanks also to my colleagues, Professors Linda James Myers, Elizabeth Cooksey, Randi Love, and Korie Edwards, for their efforts to help produce good data, and to my former doctoral students who were research assistants on the project, Professors Kosi Kubeka and Jason Whitesel. Their contributions and leadership were extremely helpful throughout their CoCHY experiences. I share a very special thank you with the parents, pastors, service learning volunteers, students, and especially, the African American teenagers who provided the honesty and experiences reflected in these pages. The project was challenging for many reasons. Yet throughout, their sustained participations made the many hours worthwhile. Without their willingness, there would have been no project and no book. I hope the participants feel that I have done justice to their commitment to share their faith so thoughtfully.

For their thorough transcriptions, my thanks go to Maren McDaniel and especially Ingrid DeHaan for their high-quality attention to detail and also to Muge Galin for her helpful copy editing throughout the production of this manuscript. I give thanks to William Goldsby, Pastor Orinda Hawkins Brinkley, and Eric Harper for their friendship and thoughtful reflections on the challenges of faith leadership during our discussions in the spring of 2014.

Finally, I share thanks with my family: to my sister Pamela, U.S. Ambassador to Uzbekistan. Holding our grandfather's Bible from the 1920s as you were being sworn in at the State Department was among the great Blessings of my life. Her professional excellence is mixed with the depth of her faith search, and I am grateful to have shared in both. Pat, as a public health practitioner and scholar, I appreciate your willingness to recreate yourself in so many ways. This, all the while growing and raising your family, is a testament to your flexible excellence. Paula, I have been amazed at the depth of your faith since I was a kid and you were in high school. You have done Goodwill Baptist Church proud across the years. And I very much appreciate how you and Pat use sports in your lifework and many ways of mission. I give thanks to my brother, Khalfani, who dedicated his life to Pan-African devotion many years ago. Khalfani, I continue to appreciate you as an *eniyan ti igbagbo nla* (Yoruba for "person of great faith"). Thanks also go to my Mom, Dr. Lois Price Spratlen, to whom this book is dedicated. With each sunset's arrival I am reminded of our conversation about faith, as we sat at the kitchen table at 809 many years ago. When I asked her if she believed in God, she paused and said, "God for me is in the beauty of the sunset. In the Olympic mountains, the Puget Sound, and in the evergreens. God is in the dogwood tree leaves and in the memory of my mother. God for me is so many things." Mom, I love you always. And finally, thanks go to my father, Professor Emeritus Thaddeus H. Spratlen. Dad, you are a pastor's son and a person of profound character and spiritual depth. I think I appreciate your patient kindness and passionate sense of justice most of all. Your support and encouragement across the writing of this book were vital. I love you, Dad, and admire you in ways beyond words.

INTRODUCTION

· 1 ·

COMMUNITY CAPACITY BUILDING IN AN AGE OF FAITH?

Pedagogy and Tensions of Nurturing Sanctuary

Culture comes from the Latin word *cultus,* which means "to care for." At its heart, it has to do with growth: of crops (as in the word "cultivate"), or of peoples. Culture is a set of [symbolic and material] ideas, practices, and rituals that help human beings develop morally, intellectually, and spiritually.

— Terrance MacMullan[1]

The Negro of America needs an Age of Faith. All great ages are ages of faith. It is absolutely necessary for a new people to begin their career with the religious verities.... Christianity is contrary to the spirit of caste—spiritual kinship transcends all other relations.... No matter what destiny awaits the race, religion is necessary either as a solvent or as a salve.

—W. E. B. Du Bois[2]

One of the most vivid memories of my childhood is being four or five years old and sitting with a longtime family friend during a December church service. My mother was nearby but occupied with music, playing her guitar at the front of the church. There was an excitement in the chapel. It was the holidays, and Santa Claus was going to make an appearance. The anticipation of gifts was the preoccupation of every child in the church. We were an African American family and were members of an overwhelmingly white Unitarian Church in a small, college town in northwest Washington State. And yes, soon, Santa Claus was going to make an appearance. At OUR church! Before Christmas!! I remember thinking to myself, "What made us so special?" Then, just when us small kids were about to burst, from the entryway just outside of the chapel, we heard the familiar sound of "Ho! Ho! Ho! Meeerrrrry Christmas!" The chapel doors opened, and in walked... my father in a Santa Claus suit. Tall and calm, with pillow padding to pudge up his frame, there he was with his kind brown face and unmistakable eyes giving candy bags to all of us kids. "Well wait," I said to myself, still very much a believer in the Santa Claus myth. "That's not Santa Claus. That's Dad in a Santa suit. What gives?! Santa Claus couldn't make it, and Dad was willing to stand in for him?" That's what seemed to make the most sense to the 5-year-old me. Our family friend leaned over and asked me, "Do you recognize Santa Claus?" "Yes," I calmly responded. "That's my Dad dressed up as Santa." I was at once surprised and proud—and annoyed. It was one of my first moments of youthful spiritual dissonance. In that moment, there was a significant distance between my ideal and lived experience of spiritual well-being, brought about by an uncomfortable tension in a place of faith. It is one of my very few church-centered childhood memories. I cherish it to this day.

Many people have special church-centered memories from their youth. These are often among the most vivid and valued aspects of their formative faith and Sacred socialization. And for the vast majority of African American children, raised with some form of religious affiliation, this socialization most often takes place in predominantly African American settings. In one's childhood and for many years thereafter, meanings given to those moments matter. This book explores those moments and meanings to enrich our understanding of faith-health pedagogy and tensions of nurturing sanctuary.

Echoes of W. E. B. Du Bois

In 1903, W. E. B. Du Bois felt that Christian religious adherence was a means to proactively challenge both the structure and "spirit of caste" to enrich an African American citizenship. So he emphasized the need for an "Age of Faith." Then and now, what does it mean to be in one? What is the current culture of religious verities (i.e., enduring truths) for African Americans today and into the future? More specifically, how do pedagogy and tensions inform Sacred socialization and the answers to these questions? Living in this period in which religious organizations openly solicit African American men to "come back to the Church," and during the apparent decline of formal religious affiliations,[3] how is sanctuary being nurtured by and with African American teenagers?

Nurturing Sanctuary answers these and related questions using data gathered from a collaboration of nearly 20 predominantly African American churches in a large, Midwestern city. These churches were brought together as part of a multiple-methods, longitudinal, faith-health research project to explore relationships between faith and health in the contemporary socialization of African American teens. Despite increasing secularization, "religious service attendance [is] one of the most popular activities in the United States. In a typical month… half of the U.S. population attends religious services at least once."[4] Among these many, rich, religious affiliations that remain, exploring how they inform health and wellness is an increasingly important concern. "The incorporation of faith-based organizations [into] health and welfare… [is] a sensible move [because] religion-based communities are considered to be exemplars of social capital ideals of reciprocity, integration, socialization, activism, and volunteerism. [These] are thought to solidify the community and benefit the individual."[5] How these capacity-building ideals matter, and the outcomes they are creating, are the central contributions of this book.

Collecting the Data

As I entered the basement room of yet another church as a co-investigator on this research project, I became more conscious of the need to connect with these African American teenagers willing to share the details of their lives for the sake of this research project and $20 in compensation. Several teenagers had arrived early and were already in the room well before their survey time was to begin. These teens had come to share their experiences of faith, health, risk, and erotic decision making for the project: Caring Congregations for Healthy Youth (CoCHY, pronounced "KO-chee"). The CoCHY project successfully brought together 18 predominantly African American churches of various sizes, neighborhoods, denominations, and sensibilities in a Midwestern city. These churches partnered with health department units at the city and county levels. This included a county health initiative that predated the CoCHY project, called FaithWELL. The "well" (as in the holder of holy water) of shared faith nurtured the wellness in the county's outreach to congregations. The goal was to bring them together to address racially informed health disparities at the local level. FaithWELL was led by Mr. Robert Marstone, a minister and clinical social worker at the county health department. Beginning with the contacts the FaithWELL initiative had established, the CoCHY project had been initiated by an interdisciplinary team of researchers from three units of the local university: public health; African American Studies; and urban, religion, and life-stage researchers in sociology. At its narrowest focus, CoCHY was an interdisciplinary exploration into why the "protective" influence of religious participations did not seem to reduce the likelihood of first sex among African American teenagers, when compared to other religious teens.[6]

In that moment of entering the church basement room, my goals were simple: Provide a caring affirmation of shared respect for these African American teenagers as they shared details of their lives through the privacies of an anonymous survey using a PDA device (i.e., immediate electronic entry and anonymizing of the data). The paradox of a church basement and potential spaces of socialized silence, the electronics of privacy, and the request for them to be as open and honest as possible while in the company of fellow teenage church members was a helpful one: a paradox of public privacies, and helpful because these data—the faith-health risk relationship among church-affiliated, African American teenagers—could assist in the enrichment of health promotion and strategies of youth religious participation. As I looked over the room, I assessed the "fit" of these teens in being there. Do they all seem to be at least 13 years old? Yes. Next, assist the research assistant in administering the surveys, in the uncertain silence of this church basement.

Findings from the Survey Data

In the first year of the CoCHY project, 496 African American teenagers from 18 churches completed the survey. Three-hundred sixty-five youths repeated their participations in each of the three years of the project. This was two-thirds of all eligible teens from the convenience sample of predominantly African American churches.[7] That percentage was reduced by the disproportionately poor turnout of teens from two of the three largest churches in the sample. Removing them, 81% of eligible teenagers from among the remaining churches participated. This demonstrated the willingness of these teens to engage with technology (i.e., using the PDA devices) to share their lives in a privately public setting.

CoCHY survey respondents were both similar to, and different from, their local and national peers. According to data from an internal project memo, CoCHY youth were slightly more likely to live in married, two-parent homes compared to their local peers. And CoCHY participant teen births were virtually identical to other African American teenagers, compared to their local and national peers. The most striking difference was in household structure. While more than 50% of U.S. African American teens lived in female-headed households, and more than three of every five local African American teens did so, just over one-third of CoCHY teens lived in that family structure. At first glance, church affiliation made a sizeable difference, with a much lower prevalence of female-headed households.

Table 1. Comparing CoCHY Survey Participants.

Characteristic	CoCHY Data	Local County*	United States*
Ages 15–19 years, living in married households	31.3%	30.3%	35.6%
Ages 15–19 years, living in female-headed households	35.1%	60.9%	54.0%
Percentage of 15-to-19-year-old women who gave birth in the past 12 months	5.1%	5.0%	4.9%

*2005 American Community Survey (African Americans only).

Beyond these statistics, regarding risk behaviors, CoCHY teens were comparable to their national peers. Fifty-nine percent reported having been intimate in some way. This was comparable to the 58% of "nonvirgins" reported in the nationally representative Adolescent Health Study[8] and ever having had sexual intercourse is consequential regarding engaging one's faith. Compared to their nonsexually active CoCHY peers, sexually active teens were 14% less likely to attend church regularly, 29% less likely to feel close to God, and 33% less likely to participate in a church-centered youth group.[9] While the causal inference cannot be made from these cross-sectional associations, sexually active CoCHY teens engage their faith differently from teens who have not yet been sexually active. Fifty-one percent of the teens felt their church was a very good place to discuss serious issues, 56% found church never or rarely boring, and nearly two-thirds of surveyed teens have had a moving spiritual experience. And while 68% reported attending religious services one or more times each week, nearly three of every four teens had "made a personal commitment to live their lives for God."

While the percentage of youth who liked church varied a great deal (0% to 72% among churches with ten or more youth), overall 42% of CoCHY teens did so. And those who did (a) attended religious services and participated in youth activities more often, (b) privately practiced their faith more frequently (e.g., praying alone), (c) felt closer and more similar to friends at church, and (d) reported feeling closer to God. And perhaps most heartening, 87% of the respondents reported that if the decision to attend church were entirely up to them, they would attend at least as often as they now do. This is comparable to the 84% of U.S. religiously attending teens regardless of race who said they would do so if the decision was theirs alone to make.[10] Religious settings were also associated with enriching social ties, as 56% reported having a close church friend they could tell anything to. And regarding religious leadership, 44% of CoCHY youth reported having spoken with their senior or youth pastor. Of these teens, 46% said their pastor was the first adult they talked to about a serious concern, and more than two-thirds of these teens felt doing so was a good experience.

But these faith engagements do not mean all things are well in these teenagers' lives. Yes, feeling closer to God and more frequent church attendance did significantly reduce sexual permissiveness, cigarette smoking, and depression. These two indicators of religiosity also increased educational aspirations for the future.[11] And on the "lighter" side of concerns, nearly half of CoCHY teens think their pastor would disapprove of most of the television and movies they watch, with nearly three-fourths of them watching three or more hours of television each day. More seriously regarding health and wellness, 9% of them report having smoked marijuana in the past month, 10% have carried a gun in the past year, 11% are current cigarette smokers, and 17% have gotten drunk in the past year. These percentages are well below national averages for all U.S. teens,[12] which is hopeful regarding religious affiliation as a protective resource in the lives of African American teenagers. Yet perhaps most distressing regarding faith and psychosocial well-being, one in five CoCHY teens had thought about ending their life in the past year. This is substantially higher than the recent national averages of 17% for African American high school girls and 9% for African American high school boys.[13] In addition, this CoCHY percentage of teens with suicidal thoughts is nearly twice the 13% of CoCHY teens who would describe themselves as being "very spiritual." Clearly, this suicidality/spiritual perception ratio of nearly 2:1 is cause for concern. There is a marked disconnect between presence at, and participation in, religious activities, and a socialized resonance that leads such teens to value themselves enough to not consider taking their own life. How did systems of shared information between Sacred and secular settings (pedagogy); the understanding of passionate purpose and shared intimacies, sexual and otherwise (erotics); and exchanges among persons borne of different eras (generations) matter in nurturing sanctuary? In the pages that follow, answers to this vital question are explored by recognizing and valuing tensions within two primary "institutions of refuge" in the African Ancestry experience: families and churches.

From National Data Recommendations to Local Elaborations

The 2005 book *Soul Searching* is perhaps the single most comprehensive analysis of the religious and spiritual lives of American teenagers. In it, Professors Christian Smith and Melinda Lundquist Denton analyze data from the National Study of Youth and Religion (NSYR) to explore "the character of teenage religion, the extent of spiritual seeking among youth, [and] how religion affects adolescent moral reasoning and risk behaviors… to foster discussions in families, religious congregations, community organizations and beyond."[14] The NSYR is a nationally representative sample of nearly 3,300 U.S. households with one or more teenagers. Consistent with additional prior research considered throughout the book, recommendations for future research extend from Smith and Denton's extensive analyses and five vital conclusions. In *Nurturing Sanctuary*, each of these conclusions and related recommendations is directly addressed. As a result, it enriches these prior contributions by analyzing data from a longitudinal project exploring three generations of African American church affiliates. These conclusions and how they are addressed are briefly considered here.

Conclusion 1: Better Engagement and Challenge—"Parents, pastors, religious educators and congregational leaders concerned with youth largely need simply to better engage and challenge the youth already at their disposal, to work better to help make faith a more active and important part of their lives."[15] *Nurturing Sanctuary* analyzes the how and how much of these engagements and challenges presented to, and with, religiously affiliated African American youth. It does this using multiple methods to analyze the content and contributions of six faith-health workshops from a service-learning research project conducted in collaboration with African American churches in a large, Midwestern city. These workshops went beyond the Sunday school model of the Christian tradition to focus on a diverse set of faith-health topics. And each of them was designed to better engage and challenge church-attending youth, while also reaching out to interested other youth and parents in adjacent neighborhoods and those with common faith and social spheres of interest.

Conclusion 2: Teaching Teens—Consistent with much research, *Soul Searching* suggests that, "Parents and faith communities should not be shy about teaching teens [because] most teens are teachable. [Adults should] make themselves available in times of trouble and crisis, to work toward becoming models and partners in love and concern and sacrifice... even if teens themselves do not let on that they are interested."[16] The teaching of teens is explored in two primary ways. First, in Chapter 2 as noted earlier regarding Conclusion 1, the teaching of teens is analyzed using external resources from a university-sponsored, faith-health, service-learning research project. Second, to better understand how independent church resources are being used, what congregations are doing in their regular, self-funded, faith curricula to engage youth is analyzed in Chapter 4.

Conclusion 3: Social Awareness—The teaching of teens can be understood as something much more than faith engagements toward an enriched sense of the Sacred. Consistent with Smith and Denton, Professors Shawn Ginwright and Julio Cammarota emphasized that service learning is typically too pedestrian and charity-oriented and does not foster anything more than very limited outcomes. For them, the goal of these teachings should be social awareness. "Social awareness places an emphasis on community [capacity building] through critical thinking that raises questions about the roots of social inequality."[17] The service-learning research project was designed and developed to do the very thing Ginwright and Cammarota emphasized, believing that service-learning can engage, and be a valuable means toward, social awareness. The service-learning sociology undergraduates contributed to the teaching of church-affiliated teens and other youth in several ways. They also enriched the social awareness of others and themselves by completing four critical reflection assignments about community, their service-learning course, and the Service Learning Initiative (SLI) workshops in which they participated. To understand how these faith-health experiences of civic participation mattered, these critical reflections of student volunteers for each of the service-learning workshops are analyzed. As a result, in Chapter 3, their formative social awareness is explored.

Conclusion 4: Intergenerational Relationship-Building—"Better adult teaching of youth will require stronger adult relationships with youth… another important general way religious congregations may better engage youth is through simple, ordinary adult relationships with teenagers."[18] How this is being done in African American churches creatively, and perhaps even controversially, is explored in Chapter 5. This chapter includes the analyses of intergenerational resource exchanges shared by parents of teenagers, youth pastors and senior pastors, teenagers, and young adults who have recently aged out of their teen years and into sustained faith affiliations of their young adulthood.

Conclusion 5: Youth Articulation—"A major challenge for religious educators of youth, therefore, [is] fostering articulation, helping teens to practice talking about their faith… to help youth learn to speak [the] language of faith."[19] *Nurturing Sanctuary* analyzes how youths' language of faith is being fostered through the structure, content, and contributions of faith-health, service-learning workshops (Chapter 2); the formative social awareness of service-learning student volunteers (Chapter 3); the successful and sustained regular programs, practices, and curricula of youth church affiliations (Chapter 4); and how Hip Hop and other largely beneficial tensions inform interactions among generations (Chapter 5). By doing so, this book documents and analyzes ways in which the language of faith is being practiced within and beyond church settings, of, by, and among youth and three generations of faith.

Institutions of Refuge

Families and churches are perhaps the two most vital institutions in the past, present, and future of the Black experience. African Americans, in particular, who report going to religious services and praying daily more often than the general U.S. population, or any other ethnoracial group in the United States,[20] are the focus of *Nurturing Sanctuary*. The positive relationship between an active faith life and improved health has been well-established in prior research. In general, religiously affiliated persons report better mental and physical health, a higher quality of life, and a longer life span.[21] What are the faith-health pedagogic, erotic, and intergenerational resources of community capacity building with and for church-affiliated African American youth? How do these faith-health capacity-building resources matter? *Nurturing Sanctuary* uses unique data from a longitudinal exploration of African American faith to answer these and other related questions. By doing so, it explores the role of spiritual dissonance—tensions between one's ideals and values and the life practice of those ideals and values—in the "Black Sacred Cosmos; [i.e.,] the religious worldview of African Americans."[22]

Extending from cognitive dissonance theory,[23] *spiritual* dissonance is any tension between a professed value or ideal of faith and the lived expression of that faith. Spiritual dissonance results from "distinct differences between ideals and lived experiences in four domains of spiritual health... [and] is indicated by a difference in mean value of greater than 1.0 between the 'ideal' and 'lived experience' in any domain of spiritual well-being."[24] Yet to understand what it is and how it matters, much lies beyond a scaled, quantitative measure. The Black Sacred Cosmos is reflected in and beyond "the institutionalized staying power of a human community that has been under siege for close to four hundred years"[25] and the demonstrated priorities and domains that contribute to—and challenge—the wellness and wholeness of church-affiliated African Americans. Despite the sustained rise of secularization and uneven church attendance, especially among African American men,[26] churches continue to be valued institutions and means of affiliation for many. In addition, churches are sites in which any number of social justice and other beneficial initiatives take place. And, in many African American churches, this increasingly includes public health initiatives to enrich the relationships between faith and health. In the Christian tradition, faith is understood as "the substance of things hoped for, the evidence of things not seen."[27] This definition in the Letter to the Hebrews provided Christians with strong encouragement to persevere in the face of persecution. Faith is a belief beyond unseen truth, grounded in a sense of the Sacred, and informed by a code of ethics. It is reflected in a trust and demonstrated both publically and privately in one's daily walk.

Health is "a dynamic state of well-being of the individual and society, of physical, mental, spiritual, economic, political, and social well-being—of being in harmony with each other, with the material environment and with God."[28] Faith *and* health are "domains that traditionally have been viewed as separate [yet] are coming together in new ways [and] in recent years there has been a surge of interest in relationships between [them]."[29] Amidst the challenges and changes of today, many innovative expressions of faith are being nurtured. Faith has long been a capacity-building resource, a means to improve the assets and enhance the well-being among a particular group of people or a community. For African Americans, faith is often viewed as being among the most vital means for wholeness and flourishing beyond survival and over time. Wholeness is the symmetry among physical, emotional, and spiritual health or "the integration of body, mind and spirit"[30] with one's environment. It can also be understood as the presence and pursuit of a spiritually grounded and undivided life and as one of the outcomes of using faith as a capacity-building resource, even when a dissonance remains. In short, faith and wholeness nurture one another, and when they do, capacity-building outcomes often result. How they nurture one another in contemporary African American churches—and how spiritual dissonance informs the reciprocity between them—is the focus of this book, through analyses of the lived expression of spiritual dissonance in the capacity building of parents, pastors, and teenagers in African American churches.

How faith and spiritual dissonance engage in a reciprocity, or pattern of Sacred exchange, and how that reciprocity was reflected in, and emerged from, health-wellness in-services, focus groups, and other collaborative events, are analyzed. To better understand the "how" of contemporary faith and wellness, this book furthers our understanding of belief systems, behaviors, leadership collaborations, and health interventions of parents, pastors, and youth affiliated with a diverse group of collaborating congregations in a large Midwestern city.

A Conceptual Foundation

My research analyzes the dynamics of African American community formation. My historical work has shown how civic, political, and religious community organizing shaped the "Great Migration" of African Americans' movement into U.S. urban areas of the South and the North across the 20th century.[31] And predominantly African American churches were among the institutions whose influence on urbanward migration I evaluated. They informed the attractiveness of potential destinations for prospective migrants and their families. The gendered significance of the religious effect (i.e., statistically significant on women's urban in-migration during the 1930s, but not for men) stuck with me. What goes on in these African American churches? And how does that matter in the lives of their church members? To answer these questions as a foundation for what follows, I bring together three conceptual strands: community capacity building, reciprocities between faith and health, and pedagogy as a "practice of freedom."[32] Each is briefly introduced here.

Community Capacity Building

Faith is a capacity-building resource. Capacity building is "maximizing the local area assets of individuals, families, organizations, and others, to share in and collectively nurture an improved quality of life within that local area [through] fellowship with others."[33] Relationships, collaborations, and consensus building are among the aspects of this approach that are very much in keeping with the Christian sentiment and idealized striving to realize beneficial outcomes toward an improved quality of life. This can include partnerships across the "three-legged stool" metaphor of faith-centered entities (i.e., churches), service providers (e.g., government health units), and academic researchers sharing resources to collaborate and realize mutually beneficial ends. Given its fit with this project and book, the faith-health-research trio is emphasized here. "A rhetorical divide has emerged between community *builders*, who emphasize bonding and bridging social capital, and community *organizers* who work with disenfranchised communities to make demands on the existing power structure through confrontational actions."[34] Both sides of this supposed divide focus on the value of relationships between social and structural capitals and how their interdependencies can nurture quality-of-life outcomes, for individuals, organizations, and communities, that is, across the micro-to-meso-to-macro continuum. And both sides of the supposed capacity-building divide often agree that a focus on assets and asset maximization—regardless of how overt or hidden said assets may appear to be at the outset—is central to a capacity-building paradigm.

Critiques of this approach emphasize its fit with the Horatio Alger "bootstraps" myth-making and convenient blaming-the-victim sentiments.[35] But the strengths emphasize values agency and assets *in partnership with* a full consideration of structural constraints and how best to navigate strategies of action within and beyond them. This is significant, especially when it comes to realizing the potential of a would-be collaboration and research project funded through a health agency (Centers for Disease Control and Prevention), initiated by and through university researchers, that then reaches out to African American churches and other community partners.

Faith-Health Reciprocities

It has long been understood that expressions of faith in various forms (e.g., private actions of valuing Sacred things, public religiosity of institutional participation) are a valued element in the lives of many persons and especially in the lives of African Americans. Prior research has documented the importance of the Sacred and the diverse roles it plays in African American lives.[36] Its presence, the roles it plays, and its many outcomes make up the Black Sacred Cosmos. "The Black Sacred Cosmos of African Americans is related both to their African heritage, which envisaged the whole universe as sacred, and to their conversion to Christianity during slavery and its aftermath."[37] Though given the African origins of Christianity itself,[38] the conversion process Lincoln and Mamiya wrote of is the more Caucasian-inspired "Western" variation of Christianity associated with more recent centuries that were informed by the transatlantic slave trade. But what is most vital is their recognition of a "Sacred Cosmos" among African Americans across the wide spectrum of religious affiliations.

"The communal sense of freedom has an internal African heritage curiously reinforced by hostile social convention imposed from outside on all African Americans as a caste."[39] So strong is this African-grounded communal sensibility that "freedom has always meant the absence of any restraint which might compromise one's responsibility to God… [so] in song, word, and deed, freedom has always been the superlative value of the Black Sacred Cosmos."[40] Extending from that history, and the bridge of time and change between then and now, what contemporary ways of faith and freedom are reflected in the socialization practices of African American churches within and between generations? This book focuses on how these ways of faith are understood and enacted by African American youth and how they are informed by dialogues across racial, institutional, and generational differences.

It has also long been understood that expressions of faith shape a variety of life outcomes, including health and well-being. A negative faith-health relationship, no relationship, and a dissonant relationship (i.e., both negative and positive, simultaneously) between religiosity and general health have also been reported.[41] And the direction of effects between them may be more reciprocal than linear.[42] Still, the overwhelming majority of studies report a positive association between religiosity and health outcomes. *Nurturing Sanctuary* enriches a dialogue within and between the various strands of faith-health relationships. It extends from the CoCHY, community-informed, collaborative research project.[43] The CoCHY project was initiated to explore how religiosity among church-affiliated African American teenagers informs their sexuality and risk-related decisions and actions. In addition to being a co-investigator on the larger CoCHY project, I was also the principal investigator of a related SLI. The SLI was internally funded by the university. And those SLI data, along with data from the larger CoCHY project, are brought together to explore a variety of faith-health relationships among church-affiliated African Americans across the Christian continuum.

Inspired by the biblical injunction to "heal the sick" and "cleanse the lepers," Christian religious institutions built the first hospitals, and early physicians and nurses were often clerics, monks and other religious orders.... [Churches] share a legacy of caring for the sick, the elderly and the needy with the public health community... [and are] uniquely positioned to help bring health care to people that are in the most need of care.[44]

Because of sustained affiliation with them, African American churches are understood as an important presence in nurturing the health and well-being of African Americans across the life course. This book explores systematic patterns of information sharing (i.e., pedagogy) within and across generations and their perceived contributions to well-being. Youth engagement in church has long been understood as a fundamental element in the socialization of children, especially African American youth. In 1899, W. E. B. Du Bois noted that most Black Churches had programs geared toward the young. In the 1930s, Mays and Nicholson found that at least 65% of African American urban churches sponsored such programs. And in 1990, Lincoln and Mamiya found that similar efforts were (still) common. Similarly, in his study of the northeast United States, Billingsley showed that 57% of Black Churches in that region had developed networks with local youth groups, and 77% had developed alliances with local schools. And in a national analysis from just over a decade ago, Barnes showed that over 91% of Black Churches surveyed offered various programs geared toward youth.[45]

This racially informed faith-health relationship has also been shown to be important in the lives of various life-stage subgroups, including teenagers. Systematic reviews of research have shown that, despite often uncertain theoretical foundations informing the research, faith as religiosity and spirituality has consistently been shown to have positive effects on the health attitudes and behaviors of adolescents.[46] This research has shown that religiosity is positively related to overall and psychological health, prosocial values and behavior, and negatively related to substance abuse, early sexual activity, and various less prosocial (i.e., "delinquent") behaviors.[47] With African American adolescents being more religiously engaged than other groups, and given the centrality of churches in their lives, exploring how the faith-health relationship is lived and tensions that exist within it among African American adolescents and their families is an important extension of this research.

A Pedagogy of Sacred Service

Consistent with the legacies of John Dewey and W. E. B. Du Bois, the education-for-liberation sensibilities of Paulo Freire are also central to this book. Freire's legacy enriches pedagogy that I join with capacity building and the faith-health nexus as the primary conceptual foundations of this text. In *Reconstructing Rage*,[48] William Goldsby and I analyzed Reconstruction, Inc., a learning organization founded by, and focused on, former felons and their post-incarceration lives. We demonstrate how the organization shapes, and is shaped by, the family, community, and organizationally collaborative experiences of these returning citizens. Central to their principled transformations is their vesting faith in the Sacred nature of being of service to and with others.

Similarly, in *Nurturing Sanctuary*, Sacred service is explored through the active faith lives of church-affiliated parents, pastors, and teenagers—and secular university students working in collaboration with them. "Instead of being a form of charity which impoverishes the recipient, where active work is going on… helping others is an aid in setting free the powers and furthering the [motives] of the one helped."[49] When merging learning with service, "when the school introduces and trains each child of society into membership… saturating [them] with the spirit of service, and providing the instruments of effective self-direction, [there is] the deepest and best guarantee of a worthy, lovely, and harmonious society."[50]

Consistent with these ideas, Paulo Freire stated that "education either… facilitates the integration of [people] into the logic of the present system and brings about conformity to it, or it becomes the practice of freedom, the means by which men and women deal critically and creatively with reality and discover how to participate in the transformation of their world."[51] Others have called this "teaching for transformation," "teaching for critical citizenship," or other similar terms intended to recognize the Deweyian truth of the vital role of educators in enriching a possibly progressive curiosity among those they teach.[52] Like Dewey and Du Bois before him, Freire's pursuit was the use of education to enrich justice outcomes by openly acknowledging and addressing social ills of all forms. "Overcoming social ills through the creation of social intelligence was the process…. One reason Dewey wanted to democratize the schools was to have students experience the mutuality of social life through service."[53] To most accurately understand and then address social ills is the fundamental reciprocity between thinking and action that Dewey, Du Bois, and Freire all saw as inextricably linked. Dewey consistently emphasized the following in his work: (a) the need to abandon either/or thinking; (b) the direct links between educational experiences and the formations of democracy, in the most holistic sense of the term, as in communitarianism; and (c) the value of combining (a) and (b) with movement well beyond didactic banking in education, to give rise to more equitable community formations or the "good community." Some have suggested that "there is currently insufficient information to determine if service-learning outcomes of faith-based service projects are actually realized."[54] Part 1 of this book shows how service-learning outcomes of faith-based service projects are being actualized to the shared benefit of all those in collaboration. Learning through service informed by the Sacred is quite consistent with the Dewey-defined foundations, its theoretical roots, and its beneficial engagement for 21st-century students of a global world. Rather than a dismissible legitimation of what has conveniently come to be known as "middle class guilt," this is where social responsibility is instead understood as a socialized life praxis. The pedagogy that made up the foundations for the service-learning and focus group portions of the project extended from this libratory pedagogical ideal. Because there was, in its design, an intended and overt exchange among its service-learning, research, and faith-affirming motives, it was, in practice, a community-engaged pedagogy in the traditions of community-based participatory research.[55]

Overview of the Book

This book is organized in two parts. Part 1 focuses on pedagogy as the practice of faith and freedom by analyzing the interdependence of faith, health, and youth in a service-learning project. Chapter 2 discusses what happens when funding is made available for churches to define for themselves how the faith-health-youth intersection is to be engaged, the topics that are prioritized, the strategies of action used, and the collaborative processes that were and were not valued. The six projects of the SLI engaged multiple reciprocities—patterns and processes of Sacred exchange, among disciplines, denominations, the Sacred and the secular, faith-health priorities, and so forth. The projects took place in and through a graduate level Public Health course and an undergraduate sociology course taught by the author. The value, experience, and contributions of each project are analyzed and compared. The SLI projects addressed various topics, including mental health, abstinence, sexual decision-making among teens, sexual abuse prevention, virginity pledging in faith-led teenage intimacy, physical activity in whole health, and "having fun in the name of the Lord," while engaging in health assessments and a dialogue between religion and science. In three collaborative and three single-church initiatives, various complexities arose. All projects achieved success even as they were challenged by limited funding and various paradigm tensions as old-school faith socializations of adults met with second-generation Hip Hop's worldview and expectations. What resulted were valuable and instructive interactions across the Sacred-secular bridge. Some best practices for multiple methods projects that bring service learning together with a participatory research framework emerged to enrich relationships among faith, health, and the sharing of quality information within and beyond the church sanctuary and the classroom walls of higher education.

In Chapter 3, reflection is central to the process of quality information exchange and takes on an especially valuable meaning in service-learning courses. Chapter 3 follows from the sentiments of John Dewey regarding the essential role of reflection in valuing experience and education as an ongoing dialogue in the learning process and in democracy itself. This chapter focuses on the journaling of students in the undergraduate sociology service-learning course from their expository, free-form writing as a course requirement. Students' willingness to risk in their writing in a variety of ways—symbolically, materially, emotionally, spiritually—allowed the reflection process to succeed. The course helped move students beyond the typical cultural invasion of "poverty tourism" such a course often fosters. Across a range of the variables of risk, uncertainty, and short-term growth, the student reflections demonstrated an important element of reciprocities among faith, pedagogy, and the capacity-building process of civic engagement central to being within and beyond the service-learning classroom. Through their writings, students made meaning of their experience and began the long, often slow process of moving from a problem-based, "we are better, and they are the other," approach of privilege to a more, "we are each other's collaborators" capacity-building learning model and practice. Perhaps more importantly, students were introduced to, and many of them internalized the lessons of, reflection as a necessary skill for active participation in a democracy.

In Part 2 (Chapters 4 and 5), the erotics of faith are explored. Chapter 4 is based on data from 10 focus groups and 2 focus group follow-up sessions I co-facilitated. They explored how faith informs the sex-, and sexuality-related parenting of African American teenagers. We asked, "What is safe relationship-building among African American teenagers? More specifically, how and when is it safe for interactions between the Sacred and the sexual to be realized?" Parents and pastors' answers to these questions inform the risk environments, decisions, and outcomes of teenagers. It explores how a reciprocity can occur, between faith (a sense of the Sacred within and beyond religious institutions) and the erotic (spaces of passion and purpose within and beyond the sexual). Chapter 4 answers these important questions of contemporary parents and pastors. These groups identified the values, strategies of action, and assessments of African American faith leaders. What emerged was their sense of erotic messaging that works, what (else) works less well, uncertain inclusions (e.g., teens displaying same-sex desire), and evangelical empathy toward genderqueer others who have lapsed due to various factors, including alienations from within churches. From these faith leadership contributions, best practices within and beyond the contemporary erotic socialization of African American teenagers emerged.

In Chapter 5, interactions between generations are analyzed to specify how they are shaping the present and future of African American faith. Focusing on the presence, expressions, and outcomes of spiritual dissonance, the chapter analyzes focus groups in which multiple generations of church affiliates considered the faith socialization of Black youth. Contributions from these data are then triangulated, bringing them into dialogue with data from feedback and follow-up sessions, along with findings from in-depth interviews of African American teenagers. From these three groups of data (intergenerational focus groups, focus group feedback sessions, and in-depth interviews of youth) several telling findings emerged. Among the most engaging were new interpretations of *The Prodigal Son* parable in 21st-century youths' lives, using intergenerational collaboration to respond to challenges in Black youth ministry and domains of spiritual dissonance as a *beneficial* resource in the faith of an increasingly secular age.

Nurturing Sanctuary concludes with Chapter 6. In it, the two parts of the book are summarized, "best practices" emerging from these summaries are specified, and next steps in the pedagogy and tensions of faith are also detailed. By doing so, Chapter 6 describes a formative model of resource reciprocity and collaboration toward improved faith-led capacity building and sustainable health equities. These reciprocities include those that are conceptual (e.g., capacity-building spiritual pedagogy), institutional/communal (e.g., faith community-university resource sharing), strategies of action (e.g., traditional

COMMUNITY CAPACITY BUILDING IN AN AGE OF FAITH?

"versus" Hip Hop religious services), and others. Throughout Chapter 6 and this book, faith socialization is recognized to be a generally beneficial, though incomplete, resource in enriching the quality of life among the parents, pastors, and youth who nurture sanctuary through the faith-centered and principled transformation of their lives.

PART 1

PEDAGOGIES OF FAITH

· 2 ·

SERVICE LEARNING IN THE FAITH AND HEALTH OF AFRICAN AMERICAN YOUTH

We hope to give the teens information to make decisions considering how God wants them to mirror their lives. The program will give them [accurate] information to make better life-choices, and will be based on the premise of "restoration." As we prepare the teens to do the right thing, we will also let them know that if you have made poor decisions in the past, it doesn't end there…. So they know they can still make the best of the situation and move on to have a fulfilling life with the Lord.

—Alicia McGregor
Youth Ministry, Grace Cathedral Church[1]

Where the school work consists in simply learning lessons… [it] becomes a clandestine effort to relieve one's neighbor of his proper duties…. When the school introduces and trains each child of society into membership, *saturating him with the spirit of service,* and providing him with the instruments of effective self-direction, we shall have the deepest and best guarantee of a larger society which is worthy, lovely, and harmonious.

—John Dewey[2]

Introduction

How does reciprocity between faith and health matter in the lives of African American youth? Defined biblically as "reaping what one sows,"[3] reciprocity is the expression of shared norms of Sacred exchange. It is giving without an expectation of return and the Grace-affirmed receiving that often occurs in having gifted another in this way. "True" reciprocity is far less about "the expectations and obligations of mutual aid which it engenders"[4] and much more about "harmony bonds governed by the search for fairness, rhythm, equity… and the motivation for justice, fairness and balance."[5] Sacred and secular, adults and youth, Black Churches and university departments: these are multiple expressions of reciprocity in the harmony bonds between faith and health among church-affiliated African American youth.

How is a faith-health reciprocity expressed in the lives of religiously involved African American youth? When adult youth leaders in Black Churches collaborate with university researchers and city and county health service providers, how might that reciprocity be enriched? Alicia McGregor spoke of the reciprocity between teenage risks and choices and information to enrich an understanding of "God's mirror" in their lives. At the turn of the 20th century, Professor Dewey emphasized that the best way for lessons of worth to be learned in schools was for that learning to be "saturated with the spirit of service" toward better citizenship and a better society. Wellness is a product of many things and one's most immediate environment of support matters. Wellness is often spoken of in nods and whispers of uncertainty regarding how someone is doing. Churches are a place in which those whispers may be exchanged. But what wellness is being nurtured beyond the less visible concerns?

The SLI of the CoCHY research project sought to answer these and other related questions. A collaboration of 14 predominantly African American churches, three units at a local university, and both city and county health department representatives were brought together to complete a strengths-based, "community-engaged pedagogy involving diverse stakeholders in research partnerships."[6] The "heart" of the SLI was an interdisciplinary partnership between a sociology undergraduate course that was preceded by a graduate level public health course. The courses assisted CoCHY congregations in designing youth-centered, church-initiated, faith-health projects that could help improve the short- and long-term wellness of their youth. Twelve churches put together internal youth leadership groups to submit preapplication letters of interest. The letters clarified how the project would address a youth faith-health topic of their choosing and how the small but valuable funding ($1,000 maximum) would be used. From these, six projects were funded. Three of them were single church projects, and three were collaborative, bringing together as many as four churches. With the assistance of the public health graduate students, each of these participating congregations' youth leaders designed the projects for the youth of their congregations, friends of those church youths, and youth from neighborhoods adjacent to the churches. With a dialogue between youth faith and health at its core, what follows is an analysis of these layered reciprocities.

Churches are an enduring institutional affiliation in African American culture, history, and life. Given the African origins of all three major Western religions,[7] it is these Ancestral Echoes that informed the CoCHY SLI project. And it is these very Ancestral Echoes that informed how these young people moved within and across the differences of race, gender, class, and community context to explore how faith and health can be understood as a Sacred reciprocity of spiritual praxis among African American teenagers. Within them, a transitory yet beneficial reciprocity emerged between largely White university students and leadership and youth from predominantly African American churches, especially those in The Community in Action sociology course.

Service learning made vital contributions to both the learning process in higher education and to nurturing faith-informed, health-wellness community outcomes, this in a city marked by severe racial health disparities.[8] The SLI of the CoCHY project, through its participatory research framework and patterns of engagement, required the undergraduate service learning course to directly contribute to the logistics and facilitation of each SLI project. Students nurtured course-guided risks in their learning as a practice of freedom. They engaged in a reciprocity beyond the university's more and less visible walls, with the course curriculum inside and beyond the classroom and with those on their service-learning volunteer teams.

Managing Motives: Initiating the Service-Learning Process

The SLI was a product of a number of factors. One, the larger CoCHY project's engagement with the participating congregations was originally very stratified and alienating. It was stratified in being oriented toward senior church leadership to the exclusion of the actual critical mass that often is central to the work of mission actually getting done. Two, the original and ongoing steering committee structure brought together church leaders, health service providers, policy affiliates, and university researchers, yet it was deemed incomplete as a means of engaging collective leadership. Three, the data productivity and analysis process was moving at the pace of academic research and productivity, but it did not translate in a timely fashion into congregational benefit in ways the churches could access and value. This in turn led many church leaders to express concerns regarding a true reciprocity of church-level benefit within the research collaboration. And four, all of these issues were informed by uneven and ethically challenging academic project leadership that led to "nods and whispers" of uncertainty about the project as a whole.

All of these factors were made worse when a central figure of the academic project leadership made a racially and culturally insensitive joke regarding the larger CoCHY project's focus on the faith and sexuality of African American teenagers. After the said person's initial denial of any need for an apology to anyone, this person's apology to the project's steering committee was a non-apology. It perpetuated an environment of misinformation by intentionally "blurring the nature of the offense... [and engaging in] the discourse of minimizing responsibility"[9] for actions and outcomes both significant and subtle. The larger project, and even the SLI project within it, was negatively impacted with a wound that never fully healed across the subsequent project years. The SLI project was an outgrowth of all of the above. And unlike the larger CoCHY project, I was the principal investigator of the CoCHY SLI. As a result, each process of the SLI was led in a fundamentally different manner of equity and participatory engagement.

The University Initiative and the Proposal

The primary goal of the university's SLI was to provide leadership and coordination "for development of service-learning courses and service-learning partnerships, [have the] courses incorporate a method of teaching and learning that connects academic content and community service [to] make academic learning come to life [and] create windows to understand the community and open doors to make a difference in education and life." As the project description of my SLI grant proposal stated, the project's purpose was to provide a better understanding of the relationship between religiosity and risk-related behavior among African American adolescents [by] providing community-oriented university students to help… reduce their risk of involvement with [negative health outcomes, by] furthering a model of faith-based prevention…. The expected outcomes include: a) improving the relationship between the [university] and African American congregations throughout the city; b) individually and collectively enhancing the resource and empowerment levels of these congregations; and, c) increasing the awareness and wellness outcomes of youth, their parents, their congregations and their community.[10]

The risk-related focus was later changed as an expanded scope of youth faith and wellness relationships became the larger mission of the researchers, church leaders, and health service provider project affiliates. The community-engaged pedagogy of the SLI grant and how it was led nurtured sanctuary to address the substantial race-informed health disparities between African American teenagers and non-Black others. As a result, the SLI created an equity-driven structure for predominantly African American churches to define for themselves the focus and means of addressing the faith-health exchange among teenagers.

The Requirements

The proposed initiatives needed to be strengths-based and relational, that is, informed by, or a beneficial departure from, any existing youth initiatives already taking place at one or more of the churches involved. Each of them engaged diverse stakeholders, including church youth in the development and design of the workshop(s). They were relational by either bringing multiple churches together for a single common goal or nurturing other forms of collaboration (e.g., a resource exchange between a youth science center and the church, exploring both faith and science in youth well-being). The collaborative teaching and applied learning domains of community-engaged pedagogy were demonstrated in the diverse forms, voices, and experiences of instruction or facilitation within each individual initiative, in the involvement of youth leadership in the designs of the project(s) and in the "hands-on" curriculum and activities that each of the initiatives built into their design(s). The applied learning domain also came into play, since the goal was for the public health graduate student teams to mentor the collaborations and individual churches in moving from this small grant initiative to then pursue a larger, external grant to expand the project or otherwise move the SLI initiative forward on a larger scale.

The Goals of the CoCHY
Service-Learning Initiative[11]

The SLI project extends from the Dewey foundation of educating for effective citizenship within a democracy. The reciprocity between a Public Health graduate course and a sociology undergraduate course demonstrated how learning can be saturated with service to the benefit of both interdisciplinary exchange within higher education and for the community collaborators participating in the CoCHY SLI project. Thus, to do so within the framework of participatory research enriched each of these benefits. Participatory research is typically grounded in community capacity building—that is, "maximizing the local area assets of individual[s], families, organization[s], and others, [which] can then be brought together to share in and collectively nurture an improved quality of life within that local area."[12] The SLI was a capacity-building research initiative that was participatory in its process of collective decision making and emergent equity in its use of resources and their implementation. The Community in Action (sociology) course helped students move from a "doing for" approach toward others as charity to a "doing with" approach in a reciprocity of resources for mutual benefit. Reciprocal learning leads "both students and community people [to] act as partners in an educational process."[13] And its reciprocal learning contributed to the enrichment of both faith and health in the community and the enrichment of the students' understanding of themselves as scholars with careerist plans and as agents of change toward affecting a transformed world.

Table 1 presents the five primary goals of the SLI, grounded in community-engaged pedagogy. Goal 1 of the SLI project was to repair and enrich the collaboration of the larger CoCHY project. The collective interests were demonstrated when the churches defined for themselves what they perceived to be the most vital topics of youth faith and health they desired to address in their SLI project(s). Preapplications created an initial opportunity to gauge the level of interest across participating churches and to provide a preliminary screening of the various topics of interest. They also furthered collaboration among congregations whose preapplication shared a focus similar to that of others. Mini-collaborations within the larger collaboration furthered the participatory project intent. From the 14 participating CoCHY congregations, 12 preapplications were submitted.

Table 1. The Five Primary Goals for the Caring Congregations for Healthy Youth – Service-Learning Initiative.

- Goal 1—Create Access for Church-Defined Youth Health Initiatives

    - To enable 10–15 local staff, parent, and youth participating groups at 10–15 local congregations to identify a health issue that (a) is relevant to teenagers in their congregation(s), and (b) can be improved through congregation-based programming.

- Goal 2—Fund Worthy Projects

    - To fund the most promising projects that understand and address a health issue that meets the criteria of Goal 1.

- Goal 3—Enact Multiple Collaborative Domains of Reciprocity

    - To enable students in two different disciplines (public health and sociology), courses (Public Health and Community Initiatives, Sociology of the Community in Action), and student levels (public health graduate students, sociology undergraduate students) to participate in a service-learning experience that (a) illustrates the relevance of health promotion and sociological theory to real-world settings, (b) provides substantive, regular interaction with congregational staff and/or lay leaders, (c) provides substantive, regular interaction with university faculty and other students working in other congregational settings, and (d) results in each student team completing a discrete product (e.g., a grant application [at the graduate level], an assessment report [at the undergraduate level]).

- Goal 4—Nurture Congregational Praxis

    - To help publicize, design, and implement the funded congregational projects in local congregations to most effectively act on CoCHY's commitments to research *and* action.

- Goal 5—Explore Congregational Praxis

    - To analyze factors that facilitate as well as hinder congregations' ability to use theory and research to develop their health promotion activities for youth.

Explicit in Goal 2 was the desire to fund the most worthy projects. Implicit within this goal was the likelihood that not all of the proposed projects would be defined as "most promising." Also, a hierarchy would inform the collaborative suggestions made and the funding pool upper limit for any individual SLI project. This goal informed both the collaborative and participatory goals combined with the fact that a total of (only) $6,500 was available to fund all of the SLI projects viewed by the author and the research staff as "most promising." Reciprocity as Sacred exchange and the recognition that various expressions of reciprocity come together in a project grounded in participatory collaboration was the focus of each, especially the SLI project's third goal. In 1899, in *The Philadelphia Negro*, W. E. B. Du Bois devoted an entire chapter to "The Health of Negroes." In the chapter, he began, "The characteristic signs which usually accompany a low civilization are a high birth rate and a high death rate; or, in other words... neglect of the laws of physical health."[14] In this seminal work central to the founding of American sociology, Du Bois articulated an analytic appreciation of anthropology, demography, history, and the health sciences.

With these words, Du Bois instigated an interdisciplinary reciprocity between sociology and public health. Three generations later, David Mechanic wrote that "much of the content of sociology directly concerns man's adaptation to his changing environment, thus this field has important implications for public health practice."[15] More recently, the Institute of Medicine grounded the present and future of public health. Its aim "was to generate organized community effort to address the public interest in health by applying scientific and technical knowledge to prevent disease and promote health."[16] Informed by these motives, the SLI of the CoCHY research project was a dialogue between multiple elements, including its Public Health-sociology two-course planning and participation structure.

Goal 4 recognized the guiding presence of praxis in all that the project was and could be. Any practice of community-engaged pedagogy has no meaning without the dialogue between theory and action, and so was the case with each individual SLI workshop, as well. This goal was also informed by the goal of critical awareness of resources and resource use within the participating churches. It raised questions about the efficiencies of resource use that can best lend themselves to "the most effective actions" of exchange between faith and health among church-affiliated youth from within the churches themselves.

Goal 5 focused on the evaluation phase of the SLI projects. Analyzing how churches engaged Goal 4 and the outcomes sought and achieved was central. As did each goal, Goal 5 recognized whole health as a multilevel resource across individual, familial, congregational, communal, and generational expressions. More broadly defined, this goal was much more than assessment alone. Like the four prior goals, Goal 5 recognized whole health as a multilevel resource across individual, familial, generational, congregational, collaborative, and other communal expressions.

Saturating Learning with Service: Public Health and the Community in Action

Refining the designs of the SLI projects took place during Public Health in Action, a graduate course in the local university's School of Public Health taught by Dr. Randi Love. Consistent with the SLI project's second goal, the course "illustrated how an appreciation of sociological variables can assist the public health practitioner."[17] Defining health as a public interest placed value on the interdependence between individual and communal wellness and emphasized the reciprocity between disease prevention and health promotion as an extension of applying scientific and technical health knowledge.[18] The course's "Rationale" summary statement presented on the syllabus emphasized how it

> utilizes the case study approach… integrated into the classroom experience. [It] seeks to bring understanding to a complex issue by emphasizing a detailed analysis of the context of a limited number of events and their relationships… [to] encourage independent thinking, bridge theory and practice, encourage reflection and decision making, and approximate the professional environment of public health professionals.

Each of the projects was guided by an "action-oriented community diagnosis [AOCD] to indicate that when public health professionals engage communities in assessing their strengths and problems, they are ethically bound"[19] to use AOCD to engage in beneficial transformations toward greater health and wellness outcomes. The input the Public Health graduate students provided SLI project design refinements improved the quality of the contributions made by these church-initiated projects and the guidance of the church leaders of youth. Together, they (a) placed each SLI workshop in a foundation of prior research, (b) grounded each in research questions of faith-health interaction, (c) specified outcomes for improved well-being, and (d) provided a plan of action for future grant-worthy projects extending from the current initiative.

The Community in Action

I taught The Community in Action undergraduate sociology course. These undergraduate students were the on-site service-learning volunteers for each of the SLI projects. Groups of six students assisted church leaders and outside consultants in the implementation of the initiatives. The course was grounded in my interests in having the students engage in a dialogue among the history of cities and the urban form, their patterns of change over time, current makeup, and relationships to contemporary health and well-being. An additional goal was for students to appreciate the use-value of sociology as an applied discipline. Toward that end, the two required texts of this primarily junior and senior year's class addressed these themes,[20] and the "scope and expectations" emphasized the following:

> This course introduces you to the main concepts, theories, and methods of urban sociology. [You will]: broaden your understanding of the processes that shape urban life and neighborhood change; make individual and collective contributions to community as a process of social change (i.e., the *praxis* of sociology)... [and learn] to think more critically—assessing conceptual strengths and weaknesses and understanding both.

Both course descriptions shared a common emphasis on the role of praxis, the importance of community context beyond the classroom, and critical reflection as being central to them. As noted earlier, through the course, the CoCHY SLI project contributed to the enrichment of faith and health in the community and students understanding themselves as scholars with careerist plans and as agents of change toward a transformed world.

The course engaged the reciprocities of the SLI grant project, and the classroom engagements bridged community beyond the classroom. To clearly demonstrate how the process of community is driven by choice and structure, students had to prioritize their first three SLI workshop topics and teams. Because there were six groups, and no group could have more than six members, it was unlikely that every student would be able to participate in their first-choice topic and team. Each of the workshop themes were introduced to the students (see Table 2). In the end, just over half of the students were able to participate in their first-choice team, and only two students participated in their third-choice team. "The school of action research that [Kurt Lewin] developed stressed the active involvement of those affected by the problem in the research through a cyclical process of fact finding, action, and reflection, leading to further inquiry and action for change."[21] The division of labor among team members was quickly specified within the first week. Outreach of the groups to their church adult and youth leadership was done, and preliminary meetings soon followed. Then, students studied the grant proposal and project overview completed during the Public Health in Action graduate course the previous quarter, and they prepared for their on-site service experiences. The six individual SLI workshops took place, and the students' term papers were completed. Because the six faith-health SLI workshops were placed within the context of urban sociology, students experienced the variety of course themes in various ways. Toward the end of class in his fourth required critical reflection, one student, Edward K., remarked as follows:

> At first, I admit I was truly oblivious as to what I should expect, as the concept of a class structured around the community seemed rather broad and vague at first glance. It seems rather difficult to believe that any social observer could truly come to fathom the myriad of relations between individuals, others, and the community at large…. [Now], I find myself coming to sense the painstaking processes with which social observers have analyzed complexities in the urban arena…. Little did I realize I would be informed on a topic I did not fully understand prior to entering this course…. I make no claims of being any sort of outspoken advocate to end urban health problems. But I realize now that the movement to end [them] is one I truly support.

The academic side of the history, structure, and process of urban areas was partnered with both the practice of sociology in community settings and the value of exploring how faith and health interact with one another. The Community in Action course brought together these three strands to simultaneously achieve its service, teaching, and research goals. As Edward K.'s course summary and evaluation demonstrate, the course enriched these relationships. It used the information and experiences toward the engaged citizenship of students, church leaders of youth, and the primary target audience of the church-affiliated youth themselves.

The SLI Projects: Faith-Health and Community-Engaged Pedagogy

Before the service-learning projects began, preapplication letters of interest were screened and collaboratively merged based on comparable topics and possible church resource sharing to maximize the capacity building intent of the CoCHY SLI. Leaders of youth from 12 congregations submitted SLI letters of interest. Of the 12, nearly half (5) of them were for abstinence promotion initiatives. Church leaders (understandably) prioritized this more often than another topic and twice as often as any other single theme. The choice of topics likely grew out of the intent of the larger CoCHY project, which focused on faith and the sexual decision making of African American teenagers. This was consistent with the moral-ethical-scriptural ideal that informs sexuality in the Christian tradition in general and with youth in particular. Though "the words of Jesus are neither extensive nor detailed on sexual matters,"[22] great investments regarding the moral boundaries and uncertainty regarding all things erotic idealize a chaste choice for all of those outside of marriage and especially for teenagers. "Christians are to restrict sex to marriage not simply because God or Jesus said so—they did—or because Bible stories always honor marital sexuality and disparage other sexual relationships—they do not—but because doing so reflects God's promise-keeping nature."[23] These SLI church leaders prioritized being the keeper of promises and using the SLI resources to assist youth in the late-adolescent process of keeping theirs.

Other workshop preapplications focused on a wide range of topics, from fostering fellowship in a congregation-wide "lock in" slumber party, to an exploration of diabetes and its prevention, to cheerleading and dance squads, and basketball teams. All 12 churches listed a diverse set of prior or ongoing youth initiatives within their congregations, and all but one demonstrated how youth were to participate in the design and planning process of the project. Consistent with the SLI's community-engaged pedagogy, a clearly demonstrated intergenerational leadership needed to be in place as refinement of the preapplications took place. In short, the letter of interest process enriched multiple elements of the SLI project's reciprocity between community-engaged pedagogy and participatory action research. "Engaging communities has the potential to reduce the cultural distance between academic researches and the communities in which they work, improve the relevance of research questions to a variety of community needs… and increase the uptake of research findings."[24]

The preapplication not only reduced the cultural distance of the research process among the churches but did so among the various denominations of collaborating churches as well and the doctrinal differences among the increasingly nondenominational religious marketplace. Nurturing collaboration is an important element in community-engaged pedagogy and participatory action research: "Collaboration gives rise to a variety of issues causing concern and anxiety [and] the issue of trust in particular has been reported repeatedly to be significant."[25] The SLI preapplications screened projects to merge those that were topically comparable and enrich between-church collaborative ties. An SLI review committee evaluated them, and from the 12 church-specific preapplications, 6 fundable SLI projects emerged.

Table 2 shows the details of each of the six projects. The symmetries among them were a product of thoughtful and effective collaboration and capacity building. All six projects used one or more outside "experts," and all six managed to have some ways of congregational teenagers and younger children

Table 2. CoCHY Service-Learning Initiative Project Overview.

Service-Learning Project	Church Leadership	Focus: Faith and…	Presentation Structure	Intended Intervention	Resource Presentation
The Spirit of Body and Mind	Single Church	Mental Health	One-Day event; expert intervention	Wellness Awareness Workshop	Therapist, social service employee, and a person with mental illness
Generations of Wellness	Collaborative	Intergenerational Movement	Multiple weeks; shared walk day as closure event	Step monitoring, food monitoring, Intergenerational pairs	Pedometers, fitness consult, goal mapping as acts of faith
Precious Patience	Collaborative	Abstinence Promotion (innovative curriculum, goal of understanding one's sexual self)	Multiple weeks; ending with Sacred certification	Overt, faith-informed sexual socialization	Role playing, talk show framing, teen parent testimony
The Way of Active Faith	Single Church	Sciences and Services of Health	One-Day event; health fair with a variety of health evaluations, change suggestions	Health assessment "Fun Day" resources	Youth science socialization, fire safety, poison center
Keepers of Sacred Youth	Collaborative	Preventing Sexual Abuse (especially the victimization of children)	One-Day event; expert intervention, emergency counseling was available	Sexual abuse awareness and proactive resilience	Sexual assault resource network program
Sacred Liberty	Single Church	Abstinence Promotion (traditional curriculum, virginity pledging as closure)	Multiple weeks; Bible study curriculum, virginity pledging, ring ceremony	Traditional, faith-informed sexual socialization	The Bible, abstinence-only brochures

both being the information recipients of greatest priority and involved in the presentations. Three of the SLI projects were collaborative, and three were single-church-organized events. Three of them were multiple-week initiatives that were to have kickoff and closure events, with biweekly fellowship among them. Three of the projects were one-day workshops marked by expert intervention and recommendations for behavior modification to enrich the faith-health reciprocity. Three of the projects addressed overtly sexual themes, developed to address ways in which the Sacred and the sexually erotic inform one another. The three others addressed one or more behavior changes toward faith as "whole health."

Two projects were perhaps the most "brave," because they were willing to directly address taboo topics: *The Spirit of Body and Mind* challenged silences associated with mental illness. And *Keepers of Sacred Youth* informed those in attendance about child sexual abuse, its prevention, and, for those who have been victimized, how to enrich faith of resilience as a survivor of that childhood trauma. The projects moved from formative development to collaborative and/or more cohesive foundations. Across the diverse themes of focus and wellness intentions, the SLI project-wide expected outcomes of improving the ongoing relationship between the state university and African American congregations throughout the Midwestern city and the others presented earlier remained.

In the Field of Faith

What contributions did the SLI projects make and to whom? What emerged within the initiatives and beyond them in the process of community-engaged pedagogy and participatory action research? Table 3 summarizes answers to these and related questions.

The Spirit of Body and Mind

When one African American church was willing to explore the stigma of mental illness from a faith-based perspective, other churches were hesitant to collaborate with it. In the end, because of this hesitation and the uncertain flexibility in the willingness to incorporate other wellness themes, Mount Sinai Baptist was the sole church in the leadership of this initiative.

Table 3. CoCHY Service-Learning Initiative—Project Outcomes.

Service-Learning Project	Church Leadership	Sacred-Secular Reciprocity Engaged	Faith-Health Emergent Outcome	Capacity-Building Assets Enriched	Long-Term Implications—Promising Practices
The Spirit of Body and Mind	Single Church	Across the Sacred-secular continuum, mental wellness can be informed by, and can influence, one's faith	-Faith-family connection -Faith as mediator in contexts of healing and mental health	-Healing toward an integrated self (*Leadership* as self-inclusion)	-Faith as a contextual resource for mental wellness over the life course
Generations of Wellness	Collaborative	Whole health wellness occurs through the body-mind-spirit trinity shared among generations	-Faith and fellowship in the motives of transcending technologies	-Healing toward interdependencies (*Interorganizational Networks* of health)	-Multiple Trinitarian collaborations (individual, generational, congregational, etc.)
Precious Patience	Collaborative	Sacred grounding in nurturing chaste/virginity expressions of Hip Hop in adolescent relationship building	-Being explicit is not "ungodly" -Dissonance between faith and erotic social spheres	-Healing toward collective self-worth (*Values* with and beyond a dissonant youth)	-From shame to sharing to erotic and other sacrifices

Service-Learning Project	Church Leadership	Sacred-Secular Reciprocity Engaged	Faith-Health Emergent Outcome	Capacity-Building Assets Enriched	Long-Term Implications—Promising Practices
The Way of Active Faith	Single Church	The dialogue between the Sacred and scientific knowing nurtures both as the joy of whole health wellness	-Spontaneity is valuable in a moment -Fictive kin as a faith-health resource	-Healing toward a scientific Sacred (*Sense of community*; fictive kin)	-Surprising benefits of fundamentalist reciprocity
Keepers of Sacred Youth	Collaborative	"It Takes a Village" to keep youth free from the sexual violation of them, and to heal childhood wounds as an adult	-Whole health in challenging painful prevalence -Intergenerational resilience	-Healing toward erotic safety (*Skills* of prevention and redemption)	-Collective faith investments getting to zero demands movement beyond sharing shame
Sacred Liberty	Single Church	Virginity pledge as a secular act that reifies the intensity of one's Sacred affiliation	-Ritual adherence as health outcome -Meanings of a ring (symbolic interaction in faith-health reciprocity)	-Healing toward one's brother's keeper (*Resources* toward valuing chaste adolescence)	-Strategies and uncertain flexibilities for traditions of future past

SLI Impact. Despite these and other challenges, *The Spirit of Body and Mind* SLI workshop was successful in having engaged in capacity building (i.e., using local-area assets toward the improved quality of life of persons) to the benefit of multiple participating groups, including the intended participants, the church, and the service-learning students. Youths in the church were provided with a greater appreciation of mental health being a part of the church mission. If they were concerned about their own mental well-being, they could understand seeking support for it as an affirmation of their faith, rather than a testament to sin or weakness. Shame or other stigma due to a family member or friend's challenges need not be experienced in silence. Exploring family dynamics of mental wellness in some detail is useful, and a life course process of worth, rather than a one-time event of hypervisible shame. And perhaps above all, participants need not feel alone in their experiences of these faith and mental wellness dynamics. According to one of the organizers, Arthur W., a youth participant said, "I always thought my uncle was just a bit 'touched in the head' like Nana [grandmother] say. Now I sorta see that he just a little bit not well up there and stuff. And now he's gettin' the help he needs.... We in the church and all can help. And I'm glad of that."

The church was provided a valuable lesson of mission: At times, one's calling for doing what one's mission demands will place one in a position of isolation, even in a circumstance where others similar to oneself are fellow participants in something larger than themselves. All of the churches were participants in a collaboration to explore faith-health reciprocity within and beyond church walls. Yet, the absence of interest in joining could be navigated successfully to the benefit of mission. A dialogue of other present silences of stigma informing the lives and faith of those in the church might also be addressed in the future.

The service-learning students benefitted in several diverse and interdependent ways. First, consistent with the larger intent of the SLI project, students participated directly in bringing together faith, health, and pedagogy. In a course "designed to introduce [them] to the main concepts, theories, and methods of urban sociology," engaging the sociological imagination to the urban form was the foundation on which an understanding of how faith informs health and how the students could be and were direct participants in teaching and learning that is "saturated with service" to the mutual benefit of themselves and others. They were also presented with the opportunity to engage that faith, health, and pedagogy relationship through challenging stigma associated with a silent and highly marginalized wellness struggle in the United States and beyond. Students were also presented with the demand to engage the utility of introspections, both in their lives and in the lives and life stages of others. Two students, Ashley U. (first quote) and Bradley H., observed the following:

> The biggest thing for me was helping to move something from being hidden to being unhidden, or known more. There's a lot of judgments that go along with "being crazy." So I get that. But we helped make those kinds of simple ideas seem more silly. And we helped the church build a stronger service relationship for mental health.

> It's still real hard for me to think about. But I think one piece of being a part of this service-learning team has kinda helped my understanding of my own cousin's suicide. Not that I get it, really. But, still it sort of makes more sense to me. And I think I helped the parents and the kids of the church know that kinda heavy stuff better also.

Generations of Wellness

Perhaps the single most ambitious SLI project was *Generations of Wellness*. Its goal was simple: Bring different churches, generations, and activity groups together to enrich ongoing dialogues regarding whole health and physical activity. What are churches doing to challenge the dual epidemics of obesity and diabetes among African Americans? To answer this question, this project was grounded in a Statement of Need that focused on the American Heart Association and American Obesity Association, estimating that (a) 30% of school-age children in the United States are overweight or obese, (b) nearly one of every six adolescents in the state of Ohio is overweight, and (c) African American children are at greater risk for obesity compared to Whites and others. Each of these findings was supported in meta-research on this topic.[26] A variety of negative health outcomes are associated with these trends. While being overweight is far more behavioral and contextual than genetic, these characteristics and their health outcomes are intergenerational, and early intervention through multiple institutional means is an important resource in creating change by challenging these negative health characteristics.

Generations of Wellness was the most collaborative SLI project; it included four churches, three denominations, and at least two different relationships to cultural competence and Africentricity as part of one's faith mission from among church leadership. Communicating across equity-informed bridges of shared respect, this project was informed by several variations (church investment, parent and youth participation, relationship to technology, record keeping, linking of steps to whole health [i.e., diet/nutrition, other behaviors]). Among the six SLI projects, this was the only one to develop and be guided by a Vision Statement and Mission. Its Mission Statement was, "Enhancing the lives of all involved in the program by providing physical activity opportunities and nutrition education for adolescents and their guardians belonging to the four churches." This statement corresponded well to the project's Mission: "To educate and prepare adolescents to maintain physical activity and healthy eating for a lifetime of healthy living." Secular goals and a life course perspective grounded the project. The statement had an implicit recognition of 1 Corinthians 6:19, recognition of one's body as one's temple, which is vital to the interdependent reciprocities of faith and health, parents and children, and one's senses of God's Grace and oneself. *Generations of Wellness* was the only project to be guided by a conceptual foundation (social learning theory) and then made the link among context, physical activity level, and whole health outcomes.

SLI Impact. Participants, churches, local health service agencies, and service learners were impacted by their different participations. A bond across generations was enriched among participants. This is especially reflected in the fact that among the four adult-youth pairs that provided near-complete information across the project data points, three had "church family" ties and were otherwise not related by blood. Though actual numbers limit the strength of conclusions one might draw, it appears that a bond of faith affiliation across generations was the strongest resource in nurturing follow-through in the documentation of behavior changes among the participants. Second, the metaphorical relationships between one's figurative or Sacred faith walk and one's actual, physical steps across the days and weeks of participation were enriched. Participants experienced their relationships with one another as a reciprocity of Sacred wellness. There is currently only a small number of studies exploring this relationship. But this research is favorable. For example, a study also found that "a faith-based physical activity intervention may be an appropriate strategy for increasing physical activity among sedentary black adults."[27] For one participant pair, their bond as "followers of the Lord [their] love was made stronger." Donna H., a grandmother and church mother who was paired with a teenager, suggested, "Even when the Lord was willing, my desire was kind of up and down. But Alexis kept me goin' in ways I didn't want to sometimes. I wasn't sure about this project. But I trust her as a child of Christ even more now. I'm grateful for that."

The churches were impacted by the adult leadership galvanized by the project. And the sense of agency in the change, both for individuals within the church and for the church as a whole, was enhanced by the *Generations* SLI project. This influence included refining leadership goal setting and program management. And perhaps most vitally, the churches were given a healthy example of their ability to knowingly and beneficially collaborate across multiple church differences (size, denomination, leadership style, etc.). By doing so, they too contributed to the essential transformation of silence into speech and action, anchored in a Sacred—and interdenominational— exchange. Service-learning students could appreciate the multiple meanings of the term "urban social movement." Without trivializing larger social justice initiatives of the past and present, the faith-driven social movement of this SLI was not lost on them. Second, because the project organizers grounded it in social learning theory, students were able to place their course and SLI participation in a conceptual context. They participated in a direct demon- stration of the praxis of social theory, that is, what works more and less well in the reciprocity between social environments that reward adaptive behaviors in the complicated process of sustaining behavior change.

Precious Patience

Strongly demonstrated over time is the protective influence of the church in the lives of African American children. With the larger project's focus on faith and health, leaders of youth in 6 of the 12 churches that submitted pre- applications in the SLI project included some aspect of abstinence, HIV/STI (sexually transmitted infection) prevention, or other sexually related theme. Not surprisingly, this was the most frequently mentioned single theme. The *Precious Patience* project brought three congregations together for an all-day retreat grounded in a more culturally competent alternative to other more mainstream, abstinence promotion teenager curricula. One nondenomina- tional church that was Holiness in its style of doctrine and participation and two Baptist churches responded to the "elevated rate of unwed teen preg- nancies and young single-mother households in the [predominantly African American] neighborhood" of a Midwestern city. In it, the number of births to unwed African American mothers is twice as high as in the urban county as a whole. Responding to this disparity, the project goal was promoting a faith-based abstinence. This was because, as stated in the proposal, "school sex education programs are available to teens in the neighborhood, but focus on the importance of safe sex and HIV/STD prevention. These views do not fit in with those of the neighborhood churches."

The day-long workshop included three sessions. The first session was a discussion led by church elders focusing on the spiritual aspects of abstaining from sex. It focused on adolescence as a faith mission of restraint and moral expression. It was less an acknowledged dialogue on tensions of erotic motives and much more a recitation of the "old stories" of Biblical assertion reinforcing the idealized decision to remain chaste outside of marriage regardless of one's age. The Sacred nature of one's wedding night was emphasized. The second session was a slide show about potential negative consequences of sexual activity, anchored in health department images of severe outcomes of STIs. It conjured fear as it was intended to. However, just as with the "Scared Straight" juvenile delinquency prevention initiatives,[28] its success is, at best, unclear.

These two sessions were supplemented by a testimonial of a former teen mother, Deja, now 21, with two children born outside of marriage. Her testimony was grounded in love for her two children though also being regretful for what she wished she had done. Deja had also gone through a "revirginizing" ritual founded on the belief that "virginity is not so much a past sexual history as a present attitude [of] reinvestment in the posture of a child before reality."[29] This is a means of reinstilling one's faith in a new self unto God. Forms of this procedure exist in some of the more fundamentalist expressions of Islam and Christianity. Deja moved from the fear-of-disease presentation to the prevention of unsacred behavior and consequent need for faith renewal. The primary focus of her words was very much in the material sense of life outcomes, delayed college dreams, economic concerns, and the like. She expressed social psychological elements, including feelings resulting from imposing on her mother and becoming one of "those girls" that she never wanted to be. This combination resonated well among the large number of youth in this well-attended workshop.

The third session focused on group dating. Teens were presented with a set of lightly scripted skits and role-played based on suggested situations. This turned otherwise labored, fear-based exchanges into joyful and caring troubleshooting. The open discussion that followed provided the teens with still more opportunity to consider the information they had been presented with in a way that was lively, spontaneous, and heartfelt. Throughout the discussions, church youth leaders remarked that this workshop enriched their understanding and appreciation of the many circles of faith, of which they are a part.

SLI Impact. Beyond these challenges, there were many benefits of the impact of the workshop for the youth participants, the churches, and the service-learning students. Given the workshop's content and structure, participants were able to demonstrate their agency in the solution of erotic and sexual safety. Each SLI project had this element to some degree, given their intended sequence of desired change—that is, a) problem arrival, b) assessment, c) tentative strategy, d) initial response, e) longer-term resolution. *Precious Patience* attendees directly "participated in their own rescue." In addition, the project acknowledged the interdependence between sexual decision making and self-worth. The youths modeled for themselves the need to nurture improved self-perception as a vital resource in the promotion of sexual safety. One participant noted the following:

> I've always been told that all I needed as a woman of Christ [quoting Matthew 17:20] was the faith of a mustard seed. Now I sorta get how all this decision stuff matters. Letting the mustard seed grow in my decisions, and stuff. More, like, about how my faith and risk and all that stuff come together sometimes.... And that teen mother speaker. She remind me of one of my cousins, who's all got the child, and droppin' outta school. It was good for me and a couple friends of mine to hear.

The churches of the *Patience* project benefited as all SLI participants did, by participating in the intercongregational lines of communication, perhaps more critically among their youth, who seemed less invested in the reputational capital so vital in the contemporary religious marketplace. Youth who valued formative friendships between churches realized they were often the primary constructors of them. They shared the faith work of creating these cross-church friendships with their different churched peers. The church youth leaders were moved to new places of understanding as well. As one youth leader, Carlyle Hampton, observed, "It is such a disconnection that takes place between our faith and our lives. And that is where religion comes in. So [Black youth] just learn how to be religious and not deal with all the issues that they are going through. But I have that openness in my church. Even in the way of discussing sexuality." This project improved information sharing among youth, providing a rich diversity of group dating alternatives. By doing so, each church helped reduce any sense of isolation among teens within it who sought to be consistent between their religious socialized ideals and behavior.

Service-learning students were in service to their own erotic explorations, as they assisted the Sacred and secular presenters of this workshop.

They engaged in a dialogue between potentially Sacred meanings of a statistical prevalence and how that might be understood, and secular behaviors informed by, and beyond, a socialized ideal. These macro-to-micro and Sacred-to-secular exchanges helped refine their critical thinking skills emerging from their John Dewey-inspired experiences of education "saturated with service." In addition, because of the various forms of data among the presenters, students were also provided with visually ethnographic and multiple methods of the event. One service learner, Jon B., noted the following:

> The speaker was a woman from the county health department. She was very informed about sexually transferred diseases and she came prepared with a slideshow. The show included pictures of STD's effect on the human body and it was shocking. I really thought *this was an effective way of almost scaring straight the kids*. They were very grossed out and the speaker was able to get the point across that this happens to kids on a daily basis. The kids were totally affected by her speech and slideshow.

This dialogue among art, science, and service existed at every stage. From being the presenter's helper for a pastoral handout, to noting the reaction of youths to the outcome severity of sexually transmitted diseases, to helping youth participants on and off the presenter space as the role-plays and skits took place, the service learners were engaged at various levels with diverse data.

The Ways of Active Faith

On an April Saturday, the weather was unseasonably cold. The expected high was to be in the mid-40s, and the day began cloudy, with intermittent light rain. This was the day of the *Active Faith* SLI workshop. The goal of the project was to encourage adolescents to take greater responsibility for health care so that their ability to move from ignorance to information to informed health decision making would be improved. One particular church took the lead on this project and demonstrated rather early in the process a lack of willingness to affiliate with the perceptions or suggestions of any other church. "There still are some religious leaders who resist the use of social science research—whether applied or basic—for fear of what it might tell them."[30] Perhaps there are also congregations that seek access to leadership in, and use of resources from, an interdisciplinary and participatory research project of the social sciences, while at the same time resisting the affiliative tenet of the project for fear of what shared power in any form might tell them—about themselves, their affiliates, and their youth. Perhaps what appeared to be an unappreciative obstinance contributed in some way to this demonstrated resistance.

Perhaps the newness of a recent move to a new building and the associated stresses and necessary capital campaign within the church associated with the move led to a more cloistered and self-protecting position on the part of church leadership. Perhaps tensions among the associate ministry of the church that may have informed existing intergenerational leadership tensions within the family of pastoral leadership also contributed. Or perhaps the motive for not collaborating was simply in the history of their annual health fair, of having been enabled to limit full participation, having secured assurances from larger project leadership that funding for their health fair—and full control of it—would be forthcoming—given the level of other forms of their larger project contributions and/or other future projects then being considered. Many unknowns exist. Both the forced choice inclusion and resource denial due to inconsistent collaboration had strong disincentives associated with them. So the health fair proceeded as planned, as a one-church workshop on an unseasonably cold April day.

The underlying premise for the project is the shift in responsibility and nurturing of an increased consciousness and maturity of adolescence for their health. "Caregivers assume responsibility for physical health throughout adolescence [because] adolescents often do not possess the basic skills to take responsibility for maintaining their own health" (Project Proposal). The importance of the project was grounded in the presence of racial disproportionality in obesity, physical activity, and self-rated health among African Americans. These factors were then associated with two localized demographic factors: two-thirds of adjacent neighborhood residents are African American and two of every five children in the neighborhood live in single-parent homes that are at or below the poverty level. The church has recently initiated a youth outreach health initiative within its new neighborhood to call attention to the presence of the church as mission beyond its walls. And the overall project goal was "to improve the overall healthcare of adolescents in the congregation and in the community surrounding the church."

In the end, all seven external health initiatives were there, and the stations-of-wellness approach was used throughout the recreational and community rooms of the church. Three of the seven stations were to be positioned outside; two of those quickly moved inside because of the weather. Only a large, blow-up, play space sponsored by a local youth science organization remained outside. This play space was to be accompanied by two other exterior stations to promote cardiovascular activity and health. When the uncertain weather led to a disappointing early turnout from both within the church and the surrounding neighborhood, the staff of the science organization refused to fully assemble all of the activity resources. Despite the weather, uncertainties of outreach, uneven participation of the health providers, and other, more limited challenges, the whole-health approach of multiple stations engaged both the participating youth and their parents alike.

SLI Impact. Despite these challenges, there were many ways in which the *Active Faith* workshop benefited its youth participants, church, and service learning students. Given the workshop's content and structure, participants were able to begin, or further an understanding of, Sacred science as a life experience and reciprocity of comfortable engagement in their lives. Also, the relative insularity of their socialized church setting was caringly and beneficially broached by the presence and participation of the health service providers and the service-learning students, both of which were made up of persons whose race and class predominance were different from their own. One of the service learners overheard a church youth observe, "This is like bein' in one of those movies from way back when, or somethin', when doctors made house calls. Today, it's like we're more better than when we usually are." The church was impacted through the direct and indirect collaborative processes of SLI participation: providing collective leadership, having a willingness to research faith-related issues, prioritizing bidirectional learning, perceiving service providers and students in the light of equity and of nurturing cooperative exchange relationships. As with all capacity building, the seeds for all of these and more were already very much present in the leadership and context of the church. This SLI participation simply enriched each of these resource skills as a space of health promotion and a means through which Sacred science toward improved wellness was empowered.

Parents and youth from other SLI churches participated in the *Active Faith* event. Thus the church benefitted from the demonstrated healing toward an environment of shared respect. Regarding participating youth, youth minister Carol Campton noted, "I received a lot of feedback on their looking for more involvement in going into the colleges and seeing what other types of programs are going on where our church can go and be involved. I had a couple of youth that asked that question. And even them being speakers, to speak on the youth aspect of the church and what they're doing." Interacting directly with service-learning university students encouraged many of the youth to believe that they too are "college material" and that planning for that life stage can begin when and where they are now; that the church can take on leadership roles within, and beyond, public praise and worship, neighborhood loudspeaker evangelism, used clothing sales, and other regular activities for which it is known; and that youth within the church can understand their role as faith leaders in new ways.

Like the youth participants and the church leadership, the student service learners were impacted in many beneficial ways. *Active Faith* students gained a greater appreciation for the interdependent reciprocities (i.e., shared, Sacred exchanges) that informed the project, perhaps especially the fictive kin (i.e., nonfamily closeness that is stronger than blood ties) and the demonstrated relationship(s) among religious affiliation, fictive kin, and collective efficacy. Susan G. reflected as follows:

> What I also thought was interesting was their sense of family. Everyone looked out for everyone else, whether the kids were theirs or not. It didn't matter. It seemed as though they were one big family. The whole experience was quite different than anything I'd done. My church is very traditional and not too exciting. But this one was exciting and fun. *They made me feel more welcome than my own congregation has done to any outsiders.* All in all, I'm very grateful for the experience.... In the future I'd like to get more involved and volunteer in other community projects.

Keepers of Sacred Youth

Youth is understood to be a time of both vulnerability and protection, of possible mischief and punishment outcomes, of muted risk and manageable innocence. Spaces of safety are vital to this critical life stage. Yet many youth experience something very different. These differences may be shaped by extreme economic limitations and muted life chances. For others, they are informed by peer-to-peer victimizations and bullying, in and outside our nation's schools. Others experience perhaps the most troubling violation: sexual victimization long before puberty begins. *Keepers of Sacred Youth* addressed this challenging repetition.

A recent report of the Centers for Disease Control[31] estimated that local child protective services typically receives nearly 3.5 million reports of children being abused or neglected. Perhaps one of every five U.S. children experiences some form of child maltreatment, with approximately 1% being the victim of sexual assault.[32] African American children appear to have a higher rate of victimization. According to recent research, the vast majority of both female and male survivors of sexual assault were first victimized as children. Nearly half of all young males and nearly one-third of young female survivors told no one about their abuse.[33] In short, the prevalence is high, and African Americans appear to be overrepresented in this health disparity. Two churches, Faith Ridge Baptist and New Ways Christian Ministries, came together to explore the role they can play in the prevention of, and healing from, these assaults.

According to two data points Public Health in Action graduate students suggested as supportive for the SLI grant's funding, there were nearly 1,200 registered sex offenders the year prior to the project's proposal in the urban county in which the two churches are located. And more than 80 of those lived in the zip codes of the two churches, with more than 150 more living in zip codes adjacent to the local areas in which the churches are located. Due to this disproportionate concentration, the neighborhood rate was nearly twice that of the median rate (189%) across zip codes. Including the adjacent neighborhoods, more than 20% of the county's registered sex offenders resided within, or adjacent to, the blocks where the two churches are located. The critical element of this type of "stranger danger" frame popularized by media is that the vast majority of perpetrators are known and known well to the survivors. It is less about the stranger in the neighborhood with the lure of an ice cream cone and a teddy bear and much more about the person the would-be victim calls dad, or uncle, or neighbor.

Still, to nurture information toward prevention and contribute to the healing of survivors of sexual assault was deemed a worthy and supportable effort, although it was also viewed with stigma. Initially, no other church was willing to collaborate with New Ways Ministries, whose youth leadership initiated the project with its preapplication and was the only church in their thematic circle. Only when a new church was brought into the project by the youth leader at New Ways did the Keepers project become collaborative. This broadened the SLI project and mission; it also spoke to the management of stigma among the participating churches.

The workshop was led by clergy and two educators of the Keep Our Youth Safe project. In addition, representatives of Prevent Child Victims-U.S., the local children's hospital, and the Center for Youth and Family Wellness gave presentations. The workshop was very well attended, with more than 60 children and their parents present. Like most prevention initiatives, the project provided age-appropriate information that made the good touch/bad touch distinction. It began with a nationally recognized definition of sexual abuse:[34]

A—The employment, use, persuasion, inducement, enticement, or coercion of any
child to engage in, or assist any other person to engage in, any sexually explicit conduct or simulation of such conduct [to produce] a visual depiction of such conduct; or,
B—The rape, molestation, prostitution, or other form of sexual exploitation of
children.

Throughout the day, these definitions were brought to life and given strategy-
of-action clarity and urgency. Pinwheels for Prevention were created by the
children themselves. These pinwheels represent a bright future for both the
children and the community. They are founded on the desire for "all children
to live in stable, loving, and stimulating environments—at home, in school,
and in the community."[35] The dated yet thorough 1984 film, *The Most Unusual
Tale*, put the theme in a humorous light, without sacrificing the seriousness or
poignancy of adult responses to this severe problem. In it, the cartoon character, Felix the Cat, assisted persons of all ages in how to say "No!" to unwanted
touching. The faith context was supported by a brief presentation by the senior pastor at New Ways and the youth pastor of Faith Ridge. Both focused on
sex as a Sacred act shared between spouses.

Scriptural foundations were followed by stories of their violation, and
child sexual violation was presented as probably the most vile among actions
against God's Grace. Aspects of the critical differences between true and false
guilt were made, with emphasis being placed on the absence of agency to prevent victimization and the necessity for action if one has been, or is currently
being, victimized. The presence of forgiveness central to God's love was at the
core of these presentations, and any vengeance that may be felt was believed
to be best left in the hands of God, though the state may play a role in the
punishment process. The healing power of Christ was at the presentations'
core and challenging the abusive silence of ignoring the problem was something church leaders refused to participate in. Then links to, and handouts for,
resources addressing crisis intervention, signs and symptoms of victimization,
and a plan of action for prevention and for life as a survivor were among the
variety of community resources provided during the day-long workshop.

SLI Impact. Again, as with all SLI projects, despite these and other challenges, the *Keepers* workshop benefited its youth participants, church, and
service-learning students in many ways. Given the workshop's content and
structure, youth participants were given additional "good touch/bad touch"
information and quality examples of discernment in understanding relative
risk. They were presented with social service agency contact information if
they should ever find themselves sexually exploited. And they were presented

with specific strategies of action for saying no and other proactive responses to unwanted touch. Those that were survivors, both youth and parents, were presented with fellowship and an environment of support to challenge whatever silences or other stigma they may have experienced at some time in the past. The parents were presented with momentum toward more open dialogues, be they public discussions regarding the need for engaging the church in additional strategies of prevention or among the most intimate exchanges with their children in their efforts to keep them and themselves safer. Parents were given a recognition that this is a serious enough issue to warrant senior pastoral participation. "The way I see it," one youth survivor stated, "I'm still not sure what to do with the revenge. My real, real want for revenge. But I'm grateful to know that I'm not alone anymore."

The churches benefited in many ways. They enriched an individual and collective Sacred bravery within the project. This was demonstrated in their willingness to transform silence into language and action. They nurtured an otherwise isolating dialogue across the Sacred-secular bridge by engaging with the various service agencies—none of whom were religiously affiliated. Any perpetrators also were made aware of how to get help. The churches also initiated dialogues regarding policy and protection changes and challenged any collective shame that existed within them. Research suggests a multistage process in the willingness of churches to address sexual abuse.[36] This helps the church and all within it to move from Secret, to Discovery, then Polarization, then Recovery, to Transformation. The SLI workshop was one part in the participants' recovery, as church leaders reexamined their resources and responses that may have enabled prior abuse to occur, while also revising these same resources so that relationships in the congregation could be restored. Regarding the nature of congregational risks, one person among the church leadership groups was motivated to go to her senior pastor and eventually propose this project by her own truth as a survivor of childhood sexual assault. The reciprocity between her healing and that of the church richly benefitted both.

Service-learning undergraduate students were impacted in numerous ways by the *Keepers* project. Toward their understanding of sociology as a praxis, they had the opportunity to increase their comfort with moving from individual to society and back. Macro statistics were given micro life when individual survivors voiced their experiences, including their observations of how faith informs their lives beyond survival now. Also, students expressed greater appreciation for, and understanding of, many dialectics that inform this topic and project, including between the Sacred and the secular in the process of faithwork different from their own. As Adrian C. noted, contexts matter and inform the Sacred and the secular, victim and perpetrator, and environments of support that help heal:

> Prior to immersing myself in the world of sociological thought, I completed Ohio State's psychology major before drifting toward sociology as a second major. Henceforth, my analytical framework for interpreting society primarily focused on individual differences among persons as the basis for any one person's social and economic circumstances. I did harbor some speculation that the outer world did indeed play a role in one's socioeconomic status. But I now feel as if I *grossly underestimated the influential power of the world* outside one's everyday life. I've yet to abandon psychology as a means for analyzing society; I've come to believe that any individual's circumstance must be interpreted through more than one "social lens."

The *Keepers* project showed how the process of healing from sexual assault is comparable to other forms of societal trauma from which we all must heal. Not in an effort to minimize or silence. Rather, to better recognize how to respond and build capacity when dealing with abusive othering in various forms and the role faith can play in nurturing transformation.

Sacred Liberty

A single church prioritized a curriculum and emphasized the utility among its young people: "We are the church, trusting [only?] in each other, to model the marriage to the Lord we are asking of them" [as stated by a youth leader]. Reducing openness toward collaboration was a likely outcome. Encouragement to adapt the curriculum or otherwise collaborate was met with limited willingness. Not surprisingly, "the issue of trust in particular has been reported repeatedly to be significant in nurturing collaborative processes."[37] When steps toward trust are not demonstrated enough to bridge differences, a sense of emboldened othering may emerge. This is expressed almost as a paranoia and is perhaps especially present in religious contexts, even those in which one has come forward to engage in a collective effort to explore how faith matters in the health and wellness of African American teenagers.

Commonwealth Baptist Church directly applied Love's Truth Awaits (LTA). LTA is an international evangelical organization and a curriculum established in the early 1990s to encourage teens to abstain from sex and to do so by repopularizing the traditional "giving all of myself to my future spouse" idea. Marrying one's self unto the Lord in a shared ceremony, some of which mimics the trappings of weddings, is the means of affirming this commitment. The Silver Ring Thing is another organization that engages in similar events. Fervor of these types of organizations and curricula were probably at their peak during the 2004–2005 period in which the *Sacred Liberty* project was being planned and took place. The project was the recognition of living one's life—especially during periods of vital life-stage transitions—for the Lord, by embracing sacrifice for the Holy. *Sacred Liberty* was the recognition of freedom of choice and the power of using one's free will to serve God, especially concerning erotic choice making, harkening back to the values and narratives associated with the Garden of Eden—thus the project's title, *Sacred Liberty*.

Along with *Generations of Wellness*, discussed earlier, the *Sacred Liberty* project was also longitudinal. Over the six weeks of the program, 24 young people were introduced to, and explored, the biblical standards for sexual purity and then linked those standards to their lives. The church youth leadership adapted the national LTA four-week curriculum, adding an opening ceremony of introducing each other in pairs guided by a series of questions grounded in scripture. This included one's favorite Bible verse, church memories from childhood, and one reason why their sexual purity is something to be cherished. After each pair shared their answers with one another, they shared their answers with the entire group. These questions were then turned into discussion questions for the entire group, and the discussion was followed by a brief introduction to the LTA curriculum and related materials.

After the first week's introduction, the four-week national LTA curriculum was followed, guided by the following questions: (a) Week 1: "What is sexual purity?" (b) Week 2: "How is sexual purity experienced?" (c) Week 3: "What is Love's Truth Awaits?" (d) Week 4: "How is Love's Truth Awaits experienced?" Throughout, pen and paper activities (e.g., word searches, self-defining key terms, cut-and-paste word relationships) were then followed up with links to Bible verses, group discussion, and shared prayer as closure for renewed commitment to one's marriage unto the Lord. Session 4 supplemented this pattern with a guest speaker, a discussion on dating well (i.e., how to engage in intimate actions without increasing risk of sex), and a discussion on how to live one's teenage years with a daily commitment to Love's Truth Awaits. A pledge to do so was followed by a return to the renewal of one's favorite Bible verses. Two additional sessions were added to the LTA four-week curriculum, ending with a ring ceremony in the sixth and final week. At that final week's workshop, the senior pastor engaged the youth in a marriage ceremony modeled after one in the Black Baptist tradition. Vows were shared as a commitment between the youth and one of their parents. They were called up one by one and presented with their ring, which was placed on the ring finger by their parent. With all of the youth in their formal dresses and tuxedos, the ceremony was followed by finger food, music, dancing, and cake, similar to a wedding reception.

SLI Impact. The *Sacred Liberty* project successfully engaged a high percentage of the teenage youths in the church. Among those who regularly attend religious services, nearly half of all age-eligible teens of the church attended. The actual percentage was higher due to conflicting commitments of several teens (e.g., athletic team participation), and another group had already participated in a similar program at a previous time. The longitudinal framework of the project encouraged—and engaged—youth across an entire six-week period, with attendance being good throughout. Of the 24 teens that began the program, 22 completed it (92% completion rate); only 3 of those 22 missed one or more sessions, and only 1 youth missed two sessions.

As with all SLI projects, despite these and other challenges, the *Sacred Liberty* workshop benefited its youth participants, church, and service learning students in many ways. Given the workshop's content and structure, participants were given strategies of action to reduce the likelihood of their sexual activity. They have, and are encouraged to regularly look at, their commitment card, a "driver's license" affirming an abstinent life until marriage. They engaged in a right of passage and ritual that enacted a living faith toward desired outcomes. And in doing so, they nurtured a renewed investment in their faith affiliation. As one youth leader noted, regarding their commitment cards, the youth need to

> take it home and there are some steps you have to do when you do that. Okay? And the steps were they had to identify and understand their commitment and then they had to privately affirm the commitment with themselves and in their spirit. They had to spend time alone with God and allow the Holy Spirit to encourage them in their decisions.

The impacts of the project on youth participants included the following: solitude within the engaged Sacred; fellowship with their teen peers and dedication in their faith; reflection preceding, and in partnership with, prayer; a consideration of the meanings and demands of maintaining a faith promise, and the links among these and their motives, decisions, and actions.

The church leadership was presented with a challenge from a female survivor of sexual assault, who experienced her sexual debut at an early age and who had been a teen parent. The leadership was tepid toward her and her initiative. The youth pastor may have been threatened by this youth leaders' initiative or felt existing programming was enough. Whatever the motive, both the senior and youth pastor miscommunicated the information to the youth of the church, leading only girls to initially express interest in the project. The lay youth leader corrected that misinformation, which led to a predominantly female participation of 15 young women and 7 young men. *Sacred Liberty* also enhanced the willingness of parents to expose their children to a youth curriculum that is both outside of the traditional Sunday school framework and outside of their secular school settings. The church was gifted a model of parental initiative that became a program (i.e., the youth leader raising her daughter in this church). As a result, religious leadership was challenged to the benefit of all affiliates. Consequently, the church was overtly politicized, entering a dialogue with public policy. Title V, Section 510, of the state statute, along with Ohio Legislative Bill 189, were both considered within the SLI project and the church. A youth leader of the initiative suggested the following:

I made them think outside the [*Love's Truth Awaits*] box. And I gave them a scenario and asked them what they would do if a friend came up to them and said, "My mother's boyfriend is messing with me." What would you tell them? I was trying to get them away from the churchy answer of, "I'll pray for you." Because I told them a lot of teens may not go to church and may not understand what that means. They may not be able to go to church with you every time they kick out questions. And they was like, "What do you want us to say?" I said, "I don't want you to say anything because I know you don't have the answer. But I want you to think before you just blurt out something that's really not helping them. Just have an understanding for them." I focused on some of the key things they asked about. And then really discuss sex and not beat around the bush because they wanted some straight answers.... And I profiled the things I went through as far as rape, molestation, and other topics. So I wanted to show them that there are two sides to it. And now, if they fell into that category [of being sexually active], they won't feel like, "Well, I'm not like the other two ladies invited to speak [both virgins]." So we hit a lot of different areas.

Sexual honesty within the church was improved. This included the rigorous honesty of faith in the resilience of surviving sexual assault, the recognition that there is a continuation of life experiences and that one can learn from those experiences, and that the church can be enhanced through the active engagement of more informed parishioners.

The service learners were impacted in a variety of ways and were exposed to a great deal. There were rather apparent tensions between adult leadership (i.e., the youth leaders and the youth pastor), (even) in a faith-informed setting. Having their voice and visions muted through interactions with those same youth leaders, they experienced their own marginalization, a dialogue between Sacred symbolism (the rings) and ritual (the ceremony and pledge) and the praxis of secular service in the completion of a course requirement. And, for those students who were religious before their service-learning participation, there was a renewed appreciation of how each of these extend from the Sacred-secular reciprocity of this course. One student, Edward A., noted the following:

> I am grateful to see others be able to serve my Lord and Savior Jesus Christ through this pledge, and this Care-ring. I also care about myself. And I know my girlfriend cares about herself. And I'm glad that like the [Sacred Liberty] participants, we are also waiting. Even when so many of our friends in school—and in church—are not.

Many of the student volunteers experienced a "church effect" of (generally short-term) heightened investment in the formalized right of passage and everyday faith engagements. Through preparing their final papers, they were exposed to research challenging the relative utility of these types of programs and the likelihood of expressions of macro statistics that strongly suggest that the limitations of this type of curriculum increase the awareness of the students, both of the utilities of social science research and potential links between everyday teenager affiliations and behavior (in)consistencies following from them.

Faith, Health, and Reciprocity: Saturating Learning with the Spirit of Service

The CoCHY SLI funded six projects. Each project was a dialogue, a reciprocity of Sacred exchange among a number of interdependent resources and processes, the Sacred and the secular, faith affiliations and wellness actions, conceptual clarification and strategies of action toward change. All of these initiatives were informed by the relationships between service learning, community-engaged pedagogy and participatory action research. All were in an effort to build the capacity of local area churches collaborating with one another, health providers, and with three units of a state university to address challenges associated with relationships between faith and health among African American teenagers.

As in each of the SLI projects, in *The Spirit of Body and Mind*, the profound need for "transforming silence into language and action [as] an act of self-revelation that always seems fraught with danger"[38] was around issues of stigma within congregations. It was demonstrated through the brave actions of a church, youth leadership, and parents willing to engage youth in making visible the impact of mental health challenges in families and demonstrating the vital role of churches in addressing them. By doing so, they demonstrated that, even in a collaborative and highly participatory research project structure, multilevel individuality can have a place, when it makes a unique contribution that challenges the marginalization of others: "individual," in that the project was defined by singular effort and risked alienation; "multilevel," in that it was demonstrated by a youth leader and senior pastor, a member of the project's university research team willing to act against others who challenged the project's utility, and a church willing to persevere even when other churches were unwilling to share in the advocacy on behalf of this topic.

The scale of participation and intended outcomes is perhaps the single most salient lesson of the *Generations of Wellness* SLI project. The project spanned multiple churches, over multiple weeks, using multiple technologies, to record multiple life domain histories, in multigenerational partnerships. It ended in a culmination event ripe with opportunity for various forms of collaborative engagement and resource exchanges. Progress can be made toward disentangling the relationship between sex and shame, effectively and caringly (even) in an environment of the chaste ideal, where an abstinence until marriage mantra is the foundation of project organizers and participating congregations. The *Precious Patience* project demonstrated this. And, like the similarly themed *Sacred Liberty*, talking about sex and sexuality to teenagers in a religious setting can itself be a curricular choice and Sacred act, anchored in both a demonstrated ideal and engaged resilience after a life choice and outcome have occurred. These things can flourish when secular places become Sacred in their use and character, when a middle school becomes a space of shared neutrality different from the multiple congregations collaborating to complete the project. By demonstrating precious patience with one another, the churches institutionally modelled the same for the youths of each congregation that came together for the workshop.

The Ways of an Active Faith project essentially asked whether a one-church project can (still) be among the most collaborative initiatives. By bringing together a rich network of representatives from diverse health agencies and organizations, one can provide a helpful set of health initiatives under the whole health umbrella. The interdependence among the health stations allowed a collaborative wellness to clearly emerge. And yes, in addition to the interdependent resources and assessments, engaging the social scientific Sacred may make for a healthier future for both the scientific and the Sacred.

Similar to *The Spirit of Body and Mind* project, the *Keepers of Sacred Youth* project also provided a valuable model for successfully managing the faith-health-youth interaction with a highly stigmatized topic. Few people have reason to glowingly discuss the sexual exploitation of children within and beyond religious settings, while also considering the role of faith settings in healing from that present or prior trauma. This project was a dialogue about convenient engagements with youth and youth programming within churches and how they can be combined with the less convenient and stigmatized to the multidimensional benefit of all. In addition, as was demonstrated by this project, there are many potential benefits to collaboration in the contemporary religious marketplace between more commuter-oriented (generally) larger churches and more neighborhood and local catchment (generally smaller) churches.

In many respects, this project demonstrated how such alternatives might be thematically and procedurally designed. Unlike the single church organizing of *The Spirit of Body and Mind*, discussed earlier, the *Keepers* project showed how congregational collaborations could effectively contribute to the *collective* willingness of churches to transform silence into language and action.

And finally, the *Sacred Liberty* project demonstrated multiple reciprocities. When youth organizers are willing to violate a shared agreement hierarchy of church leadership to insure that a topic of need is addressed among a church's youth, faith-health reciprocity can be enriched. When a rather "boiler plate" and centrist curriculum with a "one-size-fits-all" arrogance and White suburban youth standardization is adapted with culturally competent activities and dialogue, balancing relationships between the required Sacred and the revised sexually secular for a "truer" faith is exemplified in healthy ways. Yet, even as these innovations unfold, given the religious structure and groundings in doctrine, hypertradition remains. This likely leads more traditional church leaders to not use more participatory strategies of action, being less willing to investigate how merging secular service-learning students may actually enhance their intended Sacred outcomes.

The CoCHY SLI was a collaboration between the Departments of Sociology and African American Studies and the School of Public Health. It used action-oriented community diagnosis (AOCD), and moved from outsider diagnosis to collaborative capacity building. Each of the projects was a product of church-initiated preapplications massaged into six workshops of collaborative design, intervention, and desired outcomes. And each project provided valuable lessons in the praxis of reciprocity.

The SLI was informed by Freire's vital observation regarding pedagogy, that is, that it can become "the practice of freedom... the means by which young women and men learn to participate in the transformation of their world."[39] The practice of freedom is about nurturing awareness and engagement and a just citizenship of shared investments across differences, desired equities, and mutually beneficial outcomes. The reward structure of intended outcomes clearly varied among participating subgroups, churches, and affiliated health agencies. Students desired a good grade. Church leadership desired an enriched religious bond to the Lord and church. Parents desired a reduced risk and improved well-being among their children, including an enriched religious bond. Youth desired new information and a church setting that meant more to them. And I and my research collaborators desired quality project outcomes and improved collective investments in the project's intended contributions. Yet, despite or perhaps because of these differences, shared investments between subgroups of the SLI project nurtured the individual projects and allowed the larger initiative to succeed.

"The school of action research that [Kurt Lewin] developed stressed the active involvement of those affected by the problem in the research through a cyclical process of fact finding, action, and reflection, leading to further inquiry and action for change."[40] Researchers are raising questions regarding this cyclical process and the viability of community-based, research-guiding service learning. This guidance is driven by the research project goals. Service learning could then serve the best interests of asking and answering useful research questions emerging from those goals. This allowed each of the five SLI project goals to be effectively achieved. An SLI project youth leader, Tracy Lowell-Bonder, aptly stated the following in her follow-up interview:

> I've talked to several teens and heard stories of different teenagers who won't come to church because they've been molested. Or they've been raped. Or they won't come to these groups because they figure "It's too late for me now," because they've already entered into some type of sexual relationship even though it wasn't the right type of

one. But [let them know they]... can come back and I think that gives [the teens] greater passion for people. Not just preach at others. But really tell them, "Look, I understand your pain." And for those who haven't gone through that, not giving them just a pretty picture of, "This is the way your life should be" because for all of them it's not.

The service-learning grant was my effort to participate in a more reciprocal pattern of relationships the larger CoCHY project was not achieving. This more participatory turn can help move service learning from academia, using communities to serve students, into more equitable engagements in which students are engaged both within and beyond the classroom to effectively serve communities.

One among the central means of exchange within a desirable community is reciprocity, forms of respected, equitable exchange, grounded in a shared sense of the Sacred. As noted elsewhere, reciprocity is a vital element of community. It "extends from a collaborative foundation, proactive strategies of cooperation, [and] relationships informed and enriched by respectful negotiation... within and beyond ritual in a spirit of equity."[41] Service learning refers to "reciprocal learning in that students apply theoretical knowledge to 'real world' situations, [to] connect the service experience to the course content."[42] Service learning is reciprocal learning, both inside and outside of classroom and service settings.

Required journaling engages reciprocal learning as explorations toward insight. It is an uncertain curious mixture of engaged curiosity at a leisurely pace and doing what is asked in pursuit of the desired "A" grade. It is a means of developing a new and uncertain understanding of one's self, as one also explores the undiscovered and rediscovered experiences that occurred just days or years prior to the reflection itself. For service learning students, reflection can enrich reciprocity, the nuances of willingness and risk, annoyance and discovery.

The six SLI projects were, in effect, three pairs of topically themed symmetry. One pair included projects addressing "irreligious" taboo (responding to mental illness and preventing and surviving sexual assault). Another pair prioritized the virginal ideal in nurturing late adolescent abstinence. And a third pair promoted whole health, furthering a place for the science of health to be understood as an act of faith in enriching one's body as God's temple. To explore more personal reciprocities in the pedagogy of faith and health, service learner reflections within each of these themes are analyzed in Chapter 3.

· 3 ·

REFLECTING FAITH

Service Learning and Community-Engaged Pedagogy

Before I left I went around and talked to some of the [health agency] volunteers. I thanked them for allowing us to participate. It was awesome to see how important the event—as well as the congregation and community—is to them.... What I also thought was interesting was the [church's] sense of family. Everyone looked out for everyone else. Whether the kids were theirs or not.... The whole experience was quite different than anything I'd done. My church is very traditional and not too exciting. But this congregation was exciting and fun. *They made me feel more welcome than my own congregation has done to any outsiders*. I'm very grateful for the experience.... In the future I'd like to get more involved and volunteer in other community projects.

— Susan G.
Active Faith SLI student volunteer

Effective citizenship should include an ability to analyze problems and engage in action.... Concrete experience moves to reflective observation... then to abstract conceptualization, and back for more experience.... These capabilities are developed through the combination of active engagement and reflection [to] impact student development [in] *a continuous learning cycle*.

—Janet Eyler[1]

Introduction

Reflection is much more than what is seen in a mirror's image. And reciprocity always matters. The giving and receiving, between the reflected and the reflection, grounded in Sacred exchange, are vital components to all forms of community capacity building, including those central to the mission of service learning in higher education. As John Dewey noted more than a century ago, "the spirit of service"—as students learn their lessons—becomes a part of the lessons themselves. And a reciprocity between learning and service helps socialize a more caring and critically aware citizenship and society. "High-quality service learning classes demonstrate reciprocity between the campus and the community, with each giving and receiving."[2] Chapter 2 showed how service learning is making vital contributions to both the learning process in higher education and to nurturing individual and community faith-health outcomes, even in a city, or, perhaps, especially in a city, marked by severe racial health disparities.[3] In CoCHY SLI, the undergraduate service-learning students turned in critical reflections of their experiences every two weeks throughout the quarter. Through these experiences, students were invited into a reciprocity with the African American faith community beyond the university's invisible walls—with the student colleagues on their service-learning volunteer teams, with the course curriculum inside and beyond the classroom, and with themselves toward a new understanding of their own possibilities through these course-guided risks.

The Community in Action sociology course was informed by Paulo Freire's vital observation regarding pedagogy: It can become "the practice of freedom... the means by which young women and men learn to participate in the transformation of their world."[4] This practice of freedom nurtures awareness and engagement. It nurtures a just citizenship of shared investments across differences and mutually beneficial outcomes. Reflection rests at the core of "best practices" for service learning to contribute to higher education achieving this freedom's practice.[5] Reflection is one form of journaling. It is a guided, topically oriented engagement with a larger theme or set of themes in a relatively free-form writing structure. Reflection nurtures an internalization of multiple reciprocities in the process (service learning, community-university, Sacred-secular, faith-health, race predominance differences, subgroup motive differences). It is a longer-term process than the service learning itself, especially in a set of projects like these—church-defined and church-designed—events, in terms of the participation of service learning volunteers.

Reflection demonstrates how pedagogy itself unfolds, that is, service learning is the model topic, yet far from the only topic chosen. This is at the core of the social sciences in general, and sociology in particular, and the analytic dialogue between one's personal background at the micro level, and structural dynamics beyond the self at the macro level. And for C. Wright Mills, one of the vital contributors to the discipline's history, all students of society should "know that [social] problems when adequately formulated, must include both troubles and issues, biography and history, and the range of their intricate relations. Within that range the sociological imagination has its chance to make a difference in the quality of human life in our time."[6] When working toward social justice and their degrees, students will encounter roadblocks, from apathy to more explicit barriers to success. This is all "part of the messiness of learning through praxis, and one of the most important learning outcomes is… their attempts. Through the[m], students develop engaged understanding and then link their personal experience to public issues."[7] Their reflections nurtured sanctuary, as a critical pedagogy of faith.

Reflection in a Critical Pedagogy of Faith

Journaling is an exploration toward insight. Required journaling is a curious mixture of engaged curiosity at a leisurely pace and completing (only) what is asked in pursuit of the desired "A" grade, a means of developing a new and uncertain understanding of one's self, as one also explores the undiscovered and rediscovered experiences that occurred just days or years prior to the reflection itself. The choice of one-third of the students in the class to not reflect at least once on their service-learning experience provides an uncertain insight. What is the lack of clarity regarding this requirement? Is it expressing resistance by acting against a course requirement they may or may not know how to respect? Is it absent-minded omission? Is it something else? I cannot be sure. For the 23 students who reflected on their service learning, the nuance of willingness and risk, of annoyance and discovery, was a helpful demonstration of what can work when students are willing to move around within themselves by engaging the three levels of reflection.[8]

As previously noted in Chapter 2, the six CoCHY SLI projects were, in effect, three pairs of topically themed symmetry. One pair of projects addressed "irreligious" taboo (responding to mental illness and preventing/surviving sexual assault). One pair prioritized nurturing late-adolescent abstinence.

And a third pair promoted whole health and a place for the science of health to be understood as an act of faith in enriching one's body as God's temple (a six-week, intergenerational walking program and a one-day health fair). Reflections from each of these three SLI workshop themes are analyzed later, each extending from historical foundations.

Nearly a century ago, the foundation for the CoCHY SLI project was established in terms that were as much practices and desired outcomes as they were constructs of pedagogy: active, experiential learning; civic responsibility; democratic purpose. These and other related terms were central to the perspectives of John Dewey and the "learning by doing in the contexts of our communities" paradigm he and others advocated. Consistent with W. E. B. Du Bois before him, and Carter G. Woodson and others after, Dewey wrote that a truly educated citizen is one who demonstrates civic responsibility with habits of thoughtful participation through good works for social change. "Democracy must begin at home and its home is the neighborly community."[9] Public education was created to educate citizens prepared to engage in the works of democracy. Graduating a well-informed and critically thinking population, prepared and able to be "servant-leaders" in the truest meanings, and most diverse and complete expressions of the phrase, was one among the primary purposes of higher education. The SLI project was grounded in these goals, with critical reflection as a valuable means to help weave these strands together.

A Willingness to Explore

Data were gathered from *The Community in Action*, a sociology service learning course taught by the author. The course was scheduled in synch with the CoCHY SLI projects. In the service learning course, students volunteered for each of the six SLI projects. And every two weeks, they handed in their student journals. The only parameters students were given was that their journals had to be at least two pages in length and could be on any topic of their choosing related to community, broadly defined (i.e., part location, part process, informed by a shared bond of affiliation, identity, or proximity). At least one of the four required journals had to address their service learning experience in some way.

The data were analyzed to identify emerging themes and subsequently explore those themes. All mentioned topics were identified, and focus was placed on identifying any themes that appeared to relate to the service experience and how that experience was connected to any aspect of student learning. Every effort was made to enhance analytic credibility and reduce any misinterpretation of the data. Due to privacy concerns, however, multiple coder triangulation could not be engaged; analytic triangulation was used.[10] The three approaches (i.e., conventional, directed, and summative) to qualitative content analysis were used, that is, the emergent specification of the conventional and deductive categorizing of the directed approach were used with the counting and comparisons of the summative approach. And where possible, other data moments of the course triangulated the journals. Taken together, these combined methods were used to explore the journal entries as critical reflections.[11] The goal was to enrich their understandings of a Sacred-secular reciprocity of learning and service. These included comments students made during class discussions, points of information stated when sharing students' journal entries in class, and peer evaluations for students' team members in which they commented on various journaling topics or the journaling process as a whole. From these content analyses themes emerged, along with the relative frequency and depth distinctions their student journals provided.

Learning Through Reflections of Service

For all but 3 of the 34 students, this course was the first time they had journaled in a structured way, within or beyond school. Despite, or perhaps because of, the newness of the activity, students responded to it with trepidation. This sometimes turned into annoyance, though generally, the activity was valued. The following was shared by one student in his second journal (i.e., fifth week of a ten-week quarter): "I am quite frustrated with class. Our journals are not specific enough.... I want to have an idea of what is going on before going into an unfamiliar environment.... The lack of communication is very frustrating" (John F.). How much guidance is "enough"? This moment of frustration has been referred to as part of "the shadow-side of reflection in service learning."[12] There is the basic "what do I need to know, and what do I need to do?" that John's critique suggests was less than he was comfortable with. Even though they were given that information, several students wanted more information to reduce their sense of the unknown.

Specific guidance regarding students' journaling was kept to a minimum by design. The goal was for students to operate in an environment that was, to a significant degree, guided by self-defined parameters of what, why, and how to complete any given journal. They needed to share on an aspect of community, and at least one of their journals had to address their service learning experience. The "cultural explanations… [with students] turning to me and saying, 'You didn't protect me from this!'"[13] is likely grounded in their understandable desires for "clarity" and to avoid uncomfortable moments. Yet those dissonant moments were a valuable part of the Sacred-secular reciprocity the service-learning experiences, and the course as a whole, were intended to engage. Student journaling themes are summarized in Table 1.

Table 1. Total Student Topic Mentions.

Service-Learning Projects	23
Community (e.g., Diversity, Inequality)	20
Homelessness	14
Pedagogy/Theoretical Connection/Other	13
Lima, Ohio (re: film, *Lost in Middle America*)	13
Music/Parties/Bars	12
Empathy	11
Economic Decline	8
Faith/Religion	8
Identity/Home	8
Sports	6

There were a minimum of 136 total topical mentions (i.e., 4 required student journals × 34 students). Three students did not submit all four journals, and approximately one-fourth of the time, students would have more than a single, topical focus in their submitted journals. Thus, a total of 225 topical mentions were generated. With 68% of students exploring their service-learning experience in some way, critical reflection as a service-learning process was done by most of the students in the class. And all but four students (88%) presented some form of either SLI or other explicit community-themed reflection, as these were the two largest topic groupings. Though homelessness was one of several social justice challenges associated with the urban arena we considered during the term, it resonated quite strongly and became the third most frequently mentioned topic. Perhaps most surprisingly, at a university that often defines itself through sports identity and outcomes, sports was the least frequently mentioned topic to reach the five-mentions threshold. And in a course that was anchored in the service-learning placement in one of six church-designed projects, faith/religion was among the least mentioned topics. Overall, a rich diversity of topics was considered in a variety of ways. Metaphor, comparison/contrast, demographic assessment, and urban conceptual application were among the reflective strategies students used to approach these diverse topics.

In addition to those listed in Table 1, other topics were discussed through three or fewer mentions, including biracial identity, the homelessness of a parent or other family member, the active alcoholism or other addiction of a parent, and the Pride Festival and how lesbian or gay identity informed personal challenges. The students' willingness to raise these ("noncourse") topics of concern speaks powerfully to the environment of support that was created and maintained during the course, regarding the journaling process, broad understandings of community's presence and absence, and the students' willingness to risk on paper to address topics of profound stigma, and in some cases, prior or ongoing trauma.

The journals appear to have helped nurture a collaboration that resonated with the students and bridged the differences between the primarily African American service-learning church leaderships and the predominantly White student body of the course. The journals helped nurture the sanctuary of an interdisciplinary imagination. They brought the two required textbooks to life by inviting students to consider the lived experiences of histories, health, and development models and other variations demonstrated through the specific SLI projects.

Willingness to Engage the Topical Taboo

Two of the SLI workshops addressed "taboo" topics, that is, topics that could be understood as shrouded in silence or otherwise masked in selective inattention. *Keepers of Sacred Youth* focused on the prevention of child sexual abuse and interventions for those who had experienced sexual assault at an earlier point in their life. Mental illness and the potential value of faith in nurturing mental health was the focus of *The Spirit of Body and Mind*. These two workshops, as Audre Lorde implored, turned silence into language and action by, in their cases, being willing to engage in the topical taboo. And student reflections appreciated the risk of the churches and church leaders willing to address them. Paul B., a *Keepers of Sacred Youth* volunteer, reflected as follows:

> On Saturday, May 30th, my team and I attended our event at [Sacred] Birth Ministries. Out of the seven group members, six were able to attend and one of the members' close friends came to assist. So our group had an excellent turnout.... A

teammate and I arrived early and we sat around waiting. Then we helped set up chairs for the upcoming presentations.... One outside speaker, Amy, arrived, and handed me a stack of papers and a pair of scissors. I cut out "spinning wheels" to create a kids' activity after the discussion.... The presentation included a video featuring [Felix the Cat] explaining the difference between "good" and "bad" touching. In between video segments, Amy addressed the issues each segment examined. It was well done due largely to the fact that children were involved with brainstorming ideas and situations instead of simply being told things by adults. After the video and the Q&A, the children were moved to another room to make the spinning wheels to represent reported child abuse cases.... *It was overwhelming, the number of those being abused.* Thirdly, we helped clean up, thanked our hosts, and left. I had a good time overall, and feel the event was a success.

The early arrival and assessment of group turnout and willingness to ask to be put to work was their starting point. Work was found for them in a way that directly enhanced the workshop curricula. Pedagogical assessments of the use of multiple media and participant engagements included the use of the spinning wheels student volunteers had prepared. And the act of empowerment for moving from silence to language and action was demonstrated in several ways. This included the respected anonymity of sexual assault survivors being able to give visibility to their victimization through the spinning wheel options, without having to publically stand before the church members and other workshop attendees. According to the spinning wheels, just less than one-third of workshop attendees (8 adults and 31 youth) were survivors of sexual assault. And almost half of those persons had experienced it in the last two years. This is comparable to the 28% lifetime prevalence of some form of sexual victimization in the United States nationally among teens 14 to 17 years of age.[14] The healing of the workshop included that moment of surprising visibility, the opportunity for those persons to know they were not alone and that both the workshop most specifically, and the church more generally, could now be understood by them and those close to them as a space of learned sanctuary, where an informed healing from sexual assault was taking place.

The structure and content of the *Spirit of Body and Soul* workshop on mental health did not allow for a comparable engagement with the taboo. Its curricula resources were not diverse, and those for gauging prevalence did not provide as full an appreciation of how widespread mental illness is. However, whatever it lacked, it made clear what mental illness is associated with, how those associations matter (e.g., nearly one-third of chronically homeless persons have a mental health condition, with upward of half having co-occurring substance use problems),[15] and how faith can be, and is, a resource in responding to this health challenge.

Nurturing an Abstinent Adolescence

As analyzed in Chapter 2, two SLI workshops addressed teenage sexuality using abstinence-only curricula. *Precious Patience* was a day-long workshop with follow-up sessions addressed in the youth outreach initiatives of the sponsoring churches. *Sacred Liberty* was a six-week curricula that ended with a ring ceremony. In it, participating youth were "marrying themselves to Christ." Jon B., who participated in *Precious Patience*, wrote the following:

> Held at a local elementary school, a local church came together to educate its young people about staying positive about abstinence in their lives and use their faith to fight any urges they might have. We had about 6 or 7 adults and about 20 children, ranging from 4th graders to juniors in high school. I thought this range in age might be a problem. But everything went off without any problems…. The day started out with a prayer led by the church's minister. [Then] the day's agenda was given to everyone. The group broke into two groups: younger kids (7th grade and younger) and older kids (8th grade and up). The speaker [for the older kids] was a woman from the county health department. She was very informed about sexually transferred diseases and she came prepared with a slideshow. The show included pictures of STD's effect on the human body and it was shocking. *I really thought this was an effective way of almost scaring straight the kids*. They were very grossed out and the speaker was able to get the point across that this happens to kids on a daily basis and she has to deal with this every day she works. The kids were totally affected by her speech and slideshow. Next, we headed across the hall and listened to the two ministers talk. Usually anything to do with religion, I tend to zone out. But *these men gave very moving and powerful speeches*…. about your body is your temple and why would you want to ruin [it] with sexual activity before marriage?… Then a speaker who had two early pregnancies and two STDs early in her teenage life [spoke]. Because she gave real life stories and shared her past, *I think the kids were really able to connect with her* and she did a great job…. Overall, *this was a great event*. I am so happy I signed up to go. This was better than I thought [it would be] and the organizers planned and executed it perfectly. The message of abstinence was really nailed in the children's minds. But only time will show the proof. This was a wonderful experience and I now plan on doing more events like this in the near future.

Like many service learners, Jon's reflection shows concern for age differences and other pedagogical details and provides insight into what and how these characteristics can shape information sharing, and for age-informed curricula to be a part of the health department presentation speaks to the care they give to this concern, as well. The "effectiveness" of the slide show discussing STI symptoms and other outcomes was the result of youth reactions to the disconcerting images. This "public health as scared straight" framing has a long history.

Reflective value was in Jon's caring attention to nonverbal reactions as valued data and his critique in recognizing the health department presenter's everyday nature of these outcomes. Here the dissonant reciprocity is between both normalizing and catastrophizing to make the link between sexual desire, presumably outside of heteronormative marriage, and painful consequences that are much clearer, stronger, and more influential in shaping youth's decisions and actions. To have these strengths be in a curriculum reciprocity with the young women who reflected on their personal-as-political lived experiences brought different understandings of these outcomes. Jon ends his reflection by sharing his interests in doing service learning and/or volunteering in the future. And, insightfully, he also raises doubt regarding the indicators of workshop "success" that matter most, stating that it is the long-term choices of the youth rather than those convenient short-term (primarily, adult) feel-good indicators that likely matter most.

Crystalizing Culture: Community, Wholeness, and "Healthcaring"

Two SLI projects were grounded in an intergenerational, whole health focus. *Generations of Wellness* was a collaborative, six-week initiative where four churches came together to focus on diet and physical movement partnerships among generations. A health care consult as the project began was recommended, and weekly, shared, walking goals were the primary activity, coupled with calorie counting, step counting, and congregational "competitions" for generating the most steps per congregational participant within each generation. *Ways of an Active Faith* was a single-church, one-day health fair. In it, a variety of health assessments were available (e.g., blood pressure screening, dietician consult, fire safety), along with brief wellness presentations, including the detrimental impact of teen drinking on brain functioning. These were coupled with "Fun Day" resources provided by a local youth science initiative, including "bounce house" inflatable play spaces and other toys and giveaways.

> I was not sure of the sense of community until I actually experienced it for myself. Participating in the *Ways of an Active Faith* project helped me understand and see

for myself just how people come together to help each other. Firemen, science professionals, and the church organization supported the children in safety and health care. (Kerri B.)

Kerri's reflection moved her from an earlier, conceptual class discussion about what is a sense of community (i.e., feelings-based perception of a cohesive bond shared among coresidents) and how it can inform and often improve the quality of life among those who share it. She was able to connect its lived meaning to the various service participants and the church leadership for their engagement in putting these various areas of health and well-being together using a life course approach and the value of a dialogue of health across generations. Another student, Susan G., was also a part of Kerri's service-learning team and provided a much more detailed and nuanced reflection of the same one-day workshop:

> Yesterday I participated in my group community project.... I was greeted by [Lady Bug], the program director. I offered to help unload the van to bring in supplies into the church.... I then helped fill bags with information pamphlets, and then went over the various activities with the representative from [youth science initiative], and what our jobs would be for the morning.... I was somewhat nervous about how I would explain the activities, and how others would react. It's not as though I haven't been in situations where I'm in the minority. But I did grow up in a predominantly white city. I don't want to seem as though this was a bad situation at all. Because it wasn't. It was just very different than what I'm used to.... I helped to explain the model of the brain, and the participants really started to get into it. *After learning what interested the kids, I could communicate my ideas to them.* It became much easier and fun!

As an active participant and servant-leader, Susan became comfortable communicating with the predominantly African American church leadership and youth and the predominantly White health service providers. She recognized and was willing to honestly acknowledge her growing sense of comfort as a process. Her recognition of racial difference between herself and the African American youth participants, though obvious, warranted being shared; it was an act of minor bravery in this current climate of all too often force-fed "color blind" responses to group differences. And following the lead of many other service learners across various projects, Susan made the pedagogical observation of meeting the youth attendees where they are to improve her communication of health information with them:

> [Then] the kids got into the bags we made and took out the noisemakers that were included. What happened next was a complete shock to the whole group. *All the*

kids started to pound on the table with bands, pencils, actual drumsticks, as well as with
the noisemakers. It was honestly quite impressive. They were busting out some intricate
beats…. Before we knew it, [Lady Bug] was up and dancing. And soon after, kids
followed. All of our team just sat there in awe of what was happening. *What a cultural*
experience! Never before had I participated in anything like this. They convinced me
and another group member to get up and dance, which was intimidating to say the
least. But I'm glad I got up and made a fool of myself because I had so much fun! At
noon the other half of the group showed up, and by that time things were starting to
wind down.

The spontaneous drumming, dancing, and spoken word enriched the relationship between movement and health outcomes. Beyond the formality of blood
pressure screenings and the science of the brain, the health value of a sense
of joy and willingness to share risk while sharing with others, the African
Ancestral Echoes demonstrated in the drumming rhythms, provided all workshop participants with the unique cultural experience of the music and moves
of joyful noise to which Susan calls attention. It is unclear the degree to which
the students were able to fully recognize that they were participating in a
Sacred act, the truest of dialogues between the Sacred and the secular in the
lived experience of service. Valuing the youth willing to share their beats,
while moving from the distance of intimidation to the caring act of Sacred
inclusion, made for the unique whole the event became.

The Susan G. quote leading this chapter ends by making an ethnographic
comparison between the elements of church engagement she saw during
the *Ways of an Active Faith* project day and her own church background.
Acknowledging the typical response to outsiders demonstrated in her church,
she recognized an apparent distinction, valuing that difference. And again, as
with other service learners, Susan expressed a desire for future involvement in
other community projects.

As one student noted, "Although the task of 'cleaning up' helped, and was
simple, I feel that I was not a part of the experience…. I left feeling that I had
not served the community to the best of my abilities…. Overall, the experience was not much of an experience." Other alienating student experiences
also occurred. The within-SLI group, segmented division of labor for all projects, was especially pronounced in this one. It led to highly inequitable service
and learning, both in terms of participation and takeaway(s). The "getting out
of something what one puts into it" truism was again demonstrated. With surprising honesty, this difference was pointed out by the "Part 2" group member
above. Across all events in which they participated, many students recognized

that the primary takeaways are seldom just the content of focus. These various movements beyond the predictable in them display the willingness to incorporate variations well beyond the boundaries of the more scripted or ritualistic actions; all the while these various service learnings placed value in the required ritual of critical reflection in the midst of their project-oriented expression of reciprocity between the Sacred and the secular. But as displayed in Table 1, the students were engaged with many more topics than their service learning experiences alone. While all emergent topics of the students aptly displayed the process, perhaps from among them, community is most relevant to nurturing sanctuary.

Place, Process, and More: Reflecting on Community

As defined in the course syllabus, this course was presented to and understood by students, as an exploration in the dynamic exchange between community as place and community as process. The course was also understood and engaged as a service learning course. Within it, reflection implied both an individual process (via the reflection journals) and a collective process (via having reflection be one portion of the optional, in-class sharing at the start of each of the four journal hand-in class periods, in small group project team meetings, in the project team class presentation, and in the written team paper). Though worth only 5% of a student's course grade, reflection was presented and understood by the students as an action of community—all the more when it was about a specific, community-themed topic. The required Flanagan and Langton and Kammerer texts explore community as a multidimensional, multilevel "arena," the metaphor Flanagan uses. The dimensions and levels of the arena, broadly defined, are what each of the open topic journals could be about, potentially including the one (or more) that was to address the students' SLI project directly. Finally, the *Community in Action* course was grounded in a "pedagogy of place."[16] The pedagogy-of-place theme was engaged by the students in the films they saw, where lessons of the lived experiences of community were presented with much diversity and uncertainty. Whether students were attempting to grow their sense of knowing home, considering the presence or absence of individual and group differences, engaging in a house party or community festival, or being open to a life circumstance different from their own with the distance poverty imposes, they sought to learn through their community service experiences, begin a formative critical awareness, or otherwise value the life lessons the course and its domains, community in action, provided.

Knowing Home

The maturation process of students was reflected in their course journal content beyond the SLI projects, including how they gave meaning to the term "home" as a space of familiar origin, a process of change and decline in a fast-moving world, or as an absence when want is most familiar. For instance, Ronald and Peter wrote the following, respectively:

> Growing up in [North Mullund], West Virginia, I didn't experience much of anything when it came to community…. Moving to a city with a huge population that covers [many] square miles has been a growing experience. [At college] I have met people from countries I didn't know existed. Moving to [the city] has been a bit overwhelming and I get homesick a lot…. Football is the one thing that reminds me of home. People in [the city] love their football as much as the folks back in [North Mullund]. (Ronald W.)

> There are many complicated dynamics which capture the essence of a city…. Having completed 3 years of college at 4 different institutions across the country, and finishing two consecutive years of AmeriCorps (Habitat for Humanity in [San Antonio] and CityYear in [Georgia]), I have had the pleasure of being exposed to many different communities and the races, cultures, ethnicities, religions, who make them what they are…. I am a cityphile, as I love the city and all the excesses and opportunities it presents. However, I also love rural areas…. It seems to me that the city needs the country to be important, successful, populated, etc., and vice versa. (Peter B.)

Ronald equates community with urban settings. Like a few other students in the course, for him, community is something different from the familiarity of knowing others, of much smaller numbers, and a small geographical scale. For him, to be in community is to have the experience of being the urban stranger. He suggests that his experience with community began (only) after his move from a small town in West Virginia to the much larger urban place in which he goes to college. He reflects longingly on a much smaller place that he misses, with only the passion for football they share as the characteristic of place that gives him a sense of the familiar. In contrast, like several other students, Peter wrote of home in a much broader sense, as a space of appreciation gained through travel and a place one has moved on from. To know home is to experience different places, while contributing in some way to one's own home, through the contributions made to the home of others. When the home rests in the urban setting, valuing a balance between the city and "the countryside" provides a greater appreciation of both. If reciprocity is vital to nurturing sanctuary, this rural-urban balance is helpful to knowing home.

Diversities Within, Comparisons Between

For many students, home was understood in terms of an absence some presence imposed, that is, coming to a greater understanding of what home was by reflecting on a place-related absence they experienced. For example, home as a place of greater diversity while documenting being melancholy and recognizing what a more diverse place provided.

Amy and Jacob, respectively, wrote the following:

> This past weekend I went to a concert at [Mason] University. I was excited about the concert but not so much about the place I was going. I could not get over the fact that everyone there looks the same. Visually, there was no diversity.... I just saw so many "intelligent" people there that aren't living in reality.... I grew up in a 97% white suburb of [Cincinnati]. However, my dad is a teacher and a coach at [Hawkins] High School where there is a high percentage of African Americans and Jewish people. I was lucky enough to have attended summer camps there and to be exposed to a more diverse culture.... *It seems that people will go where they are comfortable. Which is just fine. But it, in turn, looks like they are just avoiding the reality of our world.* (Amy H.)

> Growing up in [Dayton] Ohio I got the chance to experience a city with a variety of classes, races, and religions. There are numerous Catholic and Jewish private schools as well as public colleges and universities.... During my [elementary] school years, I got to see 5 schools in 5 years early on. In most of the schools I was in, there were no majority classes. [There was] an equal mix... an extreme example of a "melting pot" type town. In my neighborhood there is a housing development with million dollar homes, a [Section 8] housing and urban development complex, our public school, and numerous houses with 5+ acres on their property. In a survey taken from my high school, the population rated around 40% white, 40% black, and the rest a healthy mix of "other." (Jacob D.)

For Amy, to be at a concert in the largely White student environment of a nearby private university was to be with others who are in shared avoidance—even with her acknowledging the apparent contradiction of her suburban upbringing that was just as non-diverse as the nearly all-White college concert she attended. She acknowledges this with appreciation, and avoids indicting her childhood home, by also sharing two ways that diversity was a part of her formative upbringing through the diversities of the school where her father teaches and related summer camps she attended as a child. She suggests that, while forced-choice options are not ideal, to be comfortable with a high level of (just) Whiteness is to avoid "the reality of the world." This global view of a world beyond U.S. borders was quite rare, as only four (12%) made any mention of locations beyond the United States. And to use that global view to inform one's developmental home was rarer still. In contrast, Jacob writes of the many diversities that informed his early childhood. It was rare among students to include class differences as a continuum without immediately mentioning poverty or homelessness. Equally rare was Jacob's inclusion of multiple cultural components in a single journal entry including race, class, and religion. While intersectionality, the recognition of the relative and interdependent influences of multiple identities at once,[17] was mentioned in class, it was not a featured concept. Jacob was one of seven students (21% of the class) to mention it in one or more journals.

In the course, students were never asked to reflect on diversity. Their choice to do so was likely informed by the sites of the service learning, their professor being African American, and the tone of the textbooks and curriculum. There are many potentially difficult stories in the reflection process.[18] Some of these may include reflections on both presence and absence. For those willing to reflect on the diversity witnessed at their sites, service-learning students' immediate reaction was to compare their site experiences with home or with the university. The students of this service-learning course searched for meanings of omission within a social setting in their considerations of both present and absent diversities.

Theirs was a recognition that one's understandings of home change as one's awareness grows. Amy, Jake, and other students who addressed this theme recognized that their subjective experience of objective circumstances matters in helping them give greater meaning to the objective and its consequences, that multiple and varied motives lead people to gravitate to monoracial settings. And their doing so is often a result of unintentional acts of avoidance. And like Jacob and Amy, the truism of historian John Henrik Clarke, "History is a current event," remains resonant in this generation. For many, as they reflect on their past, they appreciate it for its differences, while also true to what one's sense of community nurtures, they place a renewed value on that past. Several students recognized that ethnoreligious differences often matter (most?). And the intersections of race, class, religion, and so forth, in some urban spaces, can be seen in polychromatic context(s) that inform local contexts in developmentally consequential ways. Throughout, though rife with inequalities of various kinds, many students placed value on education as a setting for developmental diversity in preparing for "the reality of our world" in their adulthood.

More Than (Just) a Place to Party

The party is among the seminal images of a college community. This was reflected in the meanings students gave to community as place and process. While many valued their service learning experiences, there was no topic of more passionate reflection than their pursuit of party spaces and the use of a sociological imagination to reflect on them. From the meanings of symbols and cues at a house party, to tourism and the pleasures of privilege when outside of U.S. borders, to a campus gathering, recognition of short- and longer-term change and the convenient post–Civil Rights Era embrace of the privilege of asserting color-blindness as a good thing, students gave diverse, communal meanings in their searches for a place to party.

> When I first arrived I noticed the style of music being played. They had Hip Hop music on very loud. This isn't my first choice, but I did like it this particular night because it set the mood of the party. Later that night a rock band was going to perform; my favorite style of music. When they began to perform, I noticed some people who were really excited… [while] some people drifted towards the back of the party. I thought it was pretty interesting how *music can bring together just so many different kinds of people*. I liked how the party incorporated different types of music throughout the night…. Another factor I noticed was all the diverse people that I socially hang out with. *I never really thought about skin color, race, or religion.* But I think it's so cool how I know and hang out with a community of so many different cultural backgrounds. The party was really easygoing and everyone was hanging out with everyone. (Correy M.)

> This past weekend was kind of fun. [But] the African American Heritage Festival… [and] the "Block Party" is not like it used to be. A few years ago people came to the Block Party and had fun and just met other people. Now there are not nearly as many people [and] there are more cops up and down [Highland] Street…. It's like the police just don't want anybody to have any fun at all…. I can understand policing the block party because recently there have been robberies, fights and even shootings…. *I believe the police should do what they have to do to keep people safe…. But I just don't believe they have to be so strict….* I'm scared to drive around in my own neighborhood because I know there's a good chance that the cops will harass me. (Aaron G.)

Correy recognized community as a space of cultural cues and the formal social controls that inform how those cues unfold. Similar to the other party-referring students, Correy observed people's reactions to the musical choices as a potential indicator of multiple things: like/dislike, openness to a genre that is not one's favorite as a virtue, multiple genres in a single setting as a good thing, with Hip Hop as the preferred genre to "set the mood," despite it not being his first choice. In effect, music was a means of nurturing shared respect across differences and was symbolic of his relationships and a (desired? and) diverse reciprocity among his social circle.

Then, like many, Correy associated this reciprocity between diversities with "never really [thinking] about skin color, race, or religion." Perhaps charitably, this is a point of perceptual progress on a societal path toward a truer equity of interaction and deconstructing privilege. If that is the case, it speaks to a somewhat troubling level of selective inattention or monocultural repetition consistent with Amy's reflection earlier. This lack of thought about difference as a valued understanding of one's self was repeated in various forms and seems to be a generic fallback. It appears to be understood as an ideal of perceptual and behavioral equity. However, with minimal effort, in much of their lived reality, the fact that structural inequities remain, from which these color-blind persons benefit without acknowledgment, makes this a perceptual "shell game." It appears to have become a primary expression of reifying, rather than deconstructing intersecting privileges of race, class, disability, and any other characteristic of "cultural other."[19] The curious case of valuing one's supposed color-blind assertion as a good thing itself demonstrates a set of privileges reflected in the conveniences of that perceptual omission of choice and is one among the many contradictions of a post-post–Civil Rights Era generation.

For Aaron and for two other African American men in class, one of whom appeared to be biracial, consistent with the intersection of life stage, race, and gender likelihoods, an African American Heritage Festival is understood both in terms of what it no longer is and what it cannot be, so long as the perceived value of (according to Aaron) overt and excessive police presence remains. This experience is more than what occurs in a single community festival. It carries over to Aaron's level of comfort driving in his own neighborhood. Whether searching for a party or knowing home, the "criminalblackman"[20] is a corrosive presence as the perpetual suspect for any not-yet-committed crime. To the detriment of sanctuary, he engages the imposition of formal social control at the expense of his personal well-being. Police and the association with added safety is, at best, a dissonant presence and places him at great risk for personal harm.

In Search of Empathy: Perceptions of Poverty and Privilege

For many students, community was understood through the lens of their emotional, perhaps even spiritual, sensibilities. They experienced community as a search of, and/or for, empathy, that is, an understanding "wherein one is with the individual in a nonjudgmental fashion."[21] More than any other category or topic of critical reflection, empathy was the most interdependent characteristic linked with others: empathy and poverty; empathy and privilege, informed by awareness of a greater access to resources that privilege affords; empathy and the desired awareness of an (in)equality with another.

> The urban experience I will discuss is a collection of memories and experiences from my many trips to Las Vegas, Nevada.... I love to gamble and am certainly addicted to poker.... We spent the days at the pool drinking, then moved to the poker rooms and continued to drink, until we moved on to the night clubs where we proceeded to drink more.... We never really changed our routine or actively tried to learn more about the city than the vices being thrown in our faces.... I still have a love for Vegas and still travel there about twice a year.... I [also] have conflictions of feelings when I am having a good time on a vacation while at the same time there are homeless people in the city I am enjoying, whose hardships are unimaginable. I question why I am there, and why do I deserve this over someone else.... We have talked about the love/hate of the city [in class], and I guess I would say I hate that people have to live like that. I don't profess to know any solution, but it still is sad to me nonetheless. (Tab G.)

> There is no denying the fact that poverty exists. *Everyday walking to and from class, anyone will see a homeless person.* That is simply a fact that coming to [large, state university] one must accept. *How one chooses to look at poverty, may also vary.* I would most likely state that I have a structuralist view when it comes to poverty. I think that poverty is simply built into society. Poverty has always been here, and I believe that it always will [be here].... Living in a [city] has raised exposure to the homeless and poverty stricken. Some look at the homeless as scum. As people ostracized by society. I think those who live in poverty, obviously did not choose to be there. I feel that humans *could be a little more compassionate with each other. Yet there are other times that I do not feel compassionate toward people living in poverty.* Sometimes I can look at the homeless on [Highland Street] and feel angry. It is the same characters. Everybody knows who the "Rappin' Bum" is. I wonder if he actually needs money to eat, and resorts to entertaining to live. Or does he scam college kids with his patented "Help is on the way" lyric. One time I saw a homeless man holding a sign that read "Need money for weed." What was I supposed to make of that? (Bart G.)

Tonight I went to see the movie *Crash* with one of my roommates. I'm still reeling from the intensity and pain that this film so beautifully portrayed.... It's set in L.A., and used frames of different people's lives to express the continued racism that our country still struggles with on a daily basis. I've never cried so hard or so long in a movie before in my life. I am unable to adequately express the emotions it provoked. Here is a quote from the movie that is full of impact and insight: "It's the sense of touch. Any real city you walk, you know. You brush past people. People bump into you. In L.A. nobody touches you. We are always behind this metal and glass.... It's the sense of touch. I think we miss that touch so much that we crash into each other so we can feel something." As human beings, we tend to look in other places besides ourselves to find the problem. We use blaming techniques and reasons to cast blame such as gender, race, culture, socioeconomic status, etc.; many times, these problems arise from our own broken families and homes, and instead of dealing with the pain where it has begun, we tend to look everywhere but the origination. *Crash* does a lovely job of portraying this need to find and cast blame. Unfortunately because America is such a diverse country, and founded on bonds and chains of injustice because of race, that tends to be one of the first places people look to begin pointing fingers. In one of my diversity classes last quarter, we discussed racial profiling, and how everyone is "guilty." It is so easy for us to glance at a person's skin color and stereotype them.... I can only pray that as I work in this very diverse—but incredibly racially segregated area—that my racist tendencies diminish and that I would always be able to look at a person for their character and appreciate their culture.... Oh, that God might free this country from its pride-filled racist tendencies—and that we might realize that we need each other in order to survive. (Aria J.)

For Bart, it was the apparent poverty of the busy street adjacent to the university he attends. For Aria, it was the experience of a movie and the desire to understand the act of blaming differently. And for Tab, it was an emergent empathy demonstrated in his return from yet another vacation visit to Las Vegas. For the students experiencing community as a search for empathy, most often, the destination they were seeking was, at best, unclear. And the steps toward it often included recognizing the distance class privilege affords them. Steps of their community search for empathy are also informed by the uncertain, often unspoken, but acknowledged "feedback" among individual choice, group context, and life chances of structural access. At times this included looking on one's privileges beyond middle class guilt, with an insight beyond pleasure alone. And regardless of one's station in life, they acknowledged and considered interaction rituals[22] that inform so much of one's life. From action patterns of a vacation, to cross-class exchanges on busy city streets, or media representations of others' attempts to make sense of their lives through "blaming others," everything has a ritual often done in ways that reinforce the experience of community, perhaps even of sanctuary, for themselves and others.

Critical reflection was an important resource in many students being able to give meaning to the question of (global) interaction ritual: "How does globalization impact my life?" Reflecting on his warehouse job, Mark F. wrote the following in his final student journal:

> I work at a warehouse that ships items for Gap, Old Navy, and Banana Republic. After seeing thousands of boxes every day, I got to wondering where did this box start and who all has had contact with it? All of the boxes come from overseas. Bangladesh. Lima, Peru. Indonesia. Vietnam. And numerous other places. *After seeing these names of less developed countries, it made a theme of this class very evident in mind: Globalization.* As we have talked about numerous times throughout this quarter, globalization is a process that impacts not only the individuals closest spatially to this phenomenon. The reason the contents inside the boxes were made in these less developed countries is because it is the most economically efficient way to turn a profit. The labor is a lot cheaper and companies [can] expand by producing more of the product at a cheaper rate. As we have talked about in class, there are many impacts of globalization on a community. It is very apparent that globalization affects me directly, and I am a part of the process each and every day I work.

Mark presents this insight without overt emotion. Using his sociological imagination with an objective acuity, he delivers it with the practical recognition-as-justification of a financial manager or business person. While he did not write "no judgment," a phrase used to divorce oneself from the appearance of negativity or condescension in one's shared observation, Mark keeps it from being personal, per se—even as he acknowledges his personal role as "part of the process each and every day" that he works. The "to be continued…" implication of his recognition is also not directly stated, although it was implied with his invoking the transnational, economic hierarchy of less developed countries, salary differences, and the effects of these differences. For Correy M. and a few other students, these global dynamics were directly linked with pedagogy:

> In my theatre class, we haven't talked about theatre as much as we have talked about social issues and how those issues relate to the city structure. Theatre recitation has turned into a big sociological forum the past couple of classes, because we have a substitute [teaching assistant, TA] and, being from a foreign country, he went about teaching the class differently. In our first class, he explained how he and other South Americans view the United States. *He explained how we, as a people, are obsessed with consumption* [of] many products [including] large quantities of food. He also explained

how our culture, even though the country contains many types of people, is completely based on assimilation. *We expect everyone that comes to our country to conform to the principles that we value*. I then commented on how these values and most of our social norms and popular culture come from cities, more specifically Los Angeles and New York City. These two cities are in essence "hubs" which provide society with its frameworks and tells them what to like…. We talked about how people see Latinos as lower than themselves. This is where our reading of *Los Vendidos* came into play. In the play, an American business woman saw others as machines and could not distinguish between the men and the machines. This reflects how Americans in general probably view many "foreigners" in our country: not as people. This is a large reason why problems erupt in cities, because of the tension building and when there is confrontation (which is bound to happen in a city, where many people live), riots or other injustices…. Lastly, we talked about how theatre and sports affect society. It was a big comparison. [The TA] wanted some feedback on why live theatre was declining while sports were thriving, as both were clearly city-based programs.

Correy demonstrates a thoughtful, rich, practical pedagogy reflecting on globalization in its many-layered forms: immigration represented in the South American graduate teaching associate; his use of a different pedagogical structure and process in the instruction (again, presented without judgment of "better or worse"); openness to an unflattering critique of the intense American focus on consumptions, along with the TA's critique of assimilation as an imposition of "complete" necessity, toward inclusion as a within-country person of respect; the process of urbanized diffusion of various cultural patterns and tempos that transcend nation-state borders; the insightful application of a play's parable of persons being machinery, and, perhaps more critically, how the mechanics of "othering" occur, there being value in the consideration of outcomes of othering, with one among them potentially being unrest as a reaction to injustice; and finally, the "opiate of the masses" dynamic, in the American obsession with sports, again, engaged by a foreigner, reflecting on America, on a campus whose institutional worth is so often grounded in sports. The TA's juxtaposition of "dying" live theatre performances even as U.S. sports and television seem to be ever-growing provides another element of everyday globalization in Correy's practical pedagogy.

In both more and less empathetic reflections, many students engaged their sociological imagination and sought greater meanings to their reflection. For Tab, it was the love/hate relationship with urban settings. For Bart, it was the structuralist/culturalist dialogue of understanding urban outcomes. Segregation from our class and racial profiling from a course in the prior quarter were a part of the conceptual dialogue most relevant for Aria. These engagements with course concepts often led to more substantive insights, which included Tab's recognition of interdependent cynicisms that inform point-of-contact interactions regarding homelessness, the "singing for one's supper" dynamic of street performance lending to the question of the relative level of "true" need, the attempted use of humor—or honesty—by a person holding a highway sign, suggesting that the requested money will likely be used to purchase marijuana, quite inconsistent with the dire life moment holding a sign along a highway exit would suggest one is in. For Tab, such solicitations disrupt a pathway toward empathy, fed by cultural conveniences of the "charity mill" process. Poverty is typically about structural repetitions and systemic marginalization that manifest in individual outcome, and, at times, an imposed alienation and learned helplessness, because shared power, reciprocities of capacity building, and the decisions and actions of systemic change are too seldom a part of these or any other interactions across class difference(s). The short-term solicitations of a "humorous" appeal reduced Tab's appreciation of the very structuralist sensibility that informed his original observation. This moment of uncertainty and intimate dissonance can contribute to students' understanding of community as a search for empathy.

Critical Reflections from the Community in Action

What "destination" is at the end of critical reflection? It is engaging in the challenges of learning through service; being willing to explore; learning with and beyond the taboo; experiencing relationships between religion and risk through the lens of adult church leaders, youth in Black Churches, and their desire for sustained youth abstinence through ritual and faith rewards; recognizing wellness as an exploration of activities across multiple life stage and diverse domains of health; and, even as the service-learning activities were taking place, continuing to grow and refine one's sociological imagination across various topics of community in action, all the while being willing to engage in the formation— and perhaps partial resolution—of multiple dissonances that arose as the secular learning side of their classroom was brought into regular dialogue with the Sacred side of their service sites, curricula, and other capacity building throughout the term and walking away with an appreciation of how a pedagogy of place can be nurtured by invoking risks associated with the flow of ideas on blank journal pages they were required to write. These were learning points along the pathway of critical reflection from the 34 students of this service-learning course.

In 1920, W. E. B. Du Bois "made the argument for the broadest public education, for the expansion of the canon of general culture to include the lives and works of the excluded and oppressed. The objective was 'to make all intelligent'"[23] by exposing them to diversities within and beyond the classroom. For Du Bois, higher education, in fact all education, should be grounded in "the life of the race," inviting those both within and outside of it to—together—engage in ritual, exchange, and various forms of both learning and service. *Community in Action* heeded the Du Boisian call. It required students to critically reflect before, during, and after their service-learning experience, which likely increased the depth of their engagement with, and the breadth of their lessons learned from, both their service-learning experiences and the course as a whole. Reflection is one of the four principles of most service-learning definitions (preparation, participation, reflection, and evaluation).[24] The value of critical reflection is bringing to life the intersection of self-monitored learning, the enriching of multiple dialogues extending from the active learning ideal of Dewey, Du Bois, and others. This furthers the process through which collaborations of multiple layers and participants can be maintained, all the while nurturing the sanctuary within each person and within the many challenges of effective pedagogy as one's sociological or interdisciplinary imagination was being refined.

Consistent with, and much more than, Table 1 alone, critical reflection as an out-of-class requirement in an urban sociology course taught using an interdisciplinary curriculum contributed to nurturing sanctuary. As individual and internal capacity building of insight, these critical reflections were partnered with collaborative and external capacity building to the benefit of all participants. In general, students thoughtfully responded to the assignment, as shown in the reflection quotes. Not surprisingly, there were very different experiences of the SLI process, as engagements with student volunteers, church leadership, and those in attendance differed from project to project. This range of experiences even occurred within the same project (e.g., *The Ways of an Active Faith* team split up into morning and afternoon "shifts" rather than participate as a single volunteer group).

Yet even after considering the project and reflective limitations, many successes were associated with the whole of the SLI project and with the critical reflections in particular. There was a 94% follow-through rate for all four required journals. Second, nearly 20% of all students were willing to explore their own experiences of profound trauma and/or stigma through the experiences of an alcoholic or addictive parent during childhood, the class decline and homelessness of a parent or other close family member, or other challenging experiences that were "off topic" but understood as an opportunity to privately share their concerns. Three students who already kept diaries prior to class simply copied and handed in pages from their diary writings. These examples speak to the environment of support and access for students sharing places of risk within and beyond themselves.

Third, most students submitted more than the minimum required amount of writing multiple times, suggesting that they were getting enough out of the activity to exceed what was required of them. A handful of students engaged in a dialogue with me, sharing their perceptions of what the course was and was not and how that informed their experience of it. Their risk of non-anonymous, within-term critique was a wonderful affirmation of the environment of support the class established and maintained. Fourth, on the four days when journals were due, when presented with an opportunity to share their writing, one-third of the students were willing to do so as spoken word in class. This allowed them to engage in a public privacy with their peers.

And finally, this critical reflection as a process and part of their service learning experience allowed forms of conscientization to occur. In the truest Freirerian sense, conscientization occurs only with "praxis in the context of communion… as cultural action for freedom [extending from] the denunciation of unjust structures. [It] takes place in a [person] among other[s] united by their action and by their reflection upon that action and upon the world."[25] Encouraging and sustaining student investment in "cultural action for freedom," in the few weeks of a quarter, is a process initiated in the course. From what was required of the students, the personal as political was demonstrated in some form by all of them and in meaningful measure by students across a broad spectrum of worldviews. From socially conservative, religious doctrine, to traditional liberalism, to minimally socialist sentiments, students were able to increasingly demonstrate an understanding of political dynamics well beyond electoral politics.

Many students understood themselves as political actors and shared diverse forms of praxis. Direct engagement with the community took place. Understandings of servant-leadership were demonstrated. Non-anonymous, midterm course critiques were shared. Surprising vulnerabilities were discussed. Tensions of public privacy were engaged. Critiquing privilege along multiple lines of difference was demonstrated. And toward nurturing sanctuary, new observations and insights were shared.

Service learning refers to "reciprocal learning in that students apply theoretical knowledge to 'real world' situations, and, at the same time, connect the service experience to the course content."[26] Service learning is reciprocal learning, both inside and outside of the classroom setting, both inside and outside of the service setting. These critical reflections made a vital contribution to, and demonstration of, how the most intimate reciprocity contributes to healing and the conjuring of Sacred spaces both outside of, and within, one's self. In Part 2 (Chapters 4 and 5), two vital tensions of Black faith are analyzed. The text moves from analyses of how students experienced the pedagogy of faith, to the views of parents and pastors on erotic and inter-generational tensions of faith. Chapter 4 explores what parents and pastors value as the most effective faith sexual socialization of youth being reared in African American churches and specifies best practices extending from them. Chapter 5 explores how Hip Hop and other cultural aspects result from, and inform, lines of communication among generations of Black faith. By triangulating multiple data sources, four intergenerational domains and an "analytic dialogue" among them emerges. Together, these chapters move beyond an atypical service-learning, faith-health initiative to instead consider typical reciprocities of religious participation. They nurture sanctuary by specifying and strengthening how beneficial dissonance informs contemporary Black faith.

PART 2

TENSIONS OF FAITH

· 4 ·

THE EROTIC IN THE FAITH SOCIALIZATION OF BLACK CHURCHES

There is such a disconnect between our faith and our daily life. And that is where religion comes in. So Black youth just learn how to be religious and not deal with all the issues they are going through. But I have that openness in my church. Very much so. Even in the way of discussing sexuality. And even though we once weren't allowed to [speak of sexuality in the church]. But the pastor realized we are living in a world where people have those [sexual] secrets that do need to be heard.

—Carlyle Hampton, Youth Pastor Cathedral Redeemer Church

Today, the prevailing culture in Black churches is still one of silence, repression, denial, miseducation…. When it comes to talking about sex in Black faith institutions, many of our churches are in real trouble, insecure and inarticulate in matters of human intimacy…. A frank new discussion about sexuality and the sacred including women and men, gay and straight, young and old, students and faculty, laity and clergy, is urgently needed.

—Alton B. Pollard III[1]

Introduction

This chapter analyzes how parents and pastors teach the relationship(s) between religion and the erotic in the socialization of African American teenagers. As Pastor Hampton observed, the faith engagements and ritual of religious affiliation are too often disconnected from one's sexual self and from other life aspects understood as taboo and responded to as necessary secrets unto one's faith life. This artificial separation of the whole self into compartments of the sexual and the Sacred is perhaps nowhere more clear than in the religious sexual socialization of adolescents. In the cultural context of the United States, in which Black bodies have been hypersexualized in multiple ways, Black Churches have served as spaces of solitude and refuge from many, if not most, of the abusive outcomes and their many marginalizations. As adolescence turns to young adulthood, how do youth come to new places of knowing their Sacred and sexual selves? In our current moment of cultural uncertainty, life risks within and beyond the sexual, and refining the socializing role that continues to be played for many by African American churches, the disconnect Hampton spoke of remains. This chapter explores how that disconnect is (and is not) being repaired. The prevailing culture in many churches continues to be informed by the silences and insecurities Pollard wrote of. Yet more than any other racial or ethnic group, African American Protestant parents are far more likely to report having a higher comfort level talking with their teenage children about sex-related topics, such as birth control and moral consequences.[2]

This chapter explores how African American parents and pastors currently teach relationships between faith and the erotic. Ten focus groups were held: three were of pastors from across the city, including those from 10 of the 14 primary churches of the CoCHY project, and seven church-specific focus groups were for parents of church-affiliated teenagers. To build community capacity by healing the disconnect between faith and daily life that Pastor Hampton spoke of, and by challenging the prevailing environments of silence and misinformation Pollard wrote of, four themes emerged from the pastors and parents: Erotic Messaging, Safe Relationship Building, Strategies for Sustained Youth Engagement, and Pathways of Uncertain Inclusion for those on the margins of church affiliation.

Erotic Messaging: Faith, Purpose, and Love

In 1978, essayist, freedom fighter, lesbian, mother, and poet laureate Audre Lorde delivered a speech titled, "Uses of the Erotic: The Erotic as Power." She shared the essay at the Fourth Berkshire Conference on the History of

Women at Mount Holyoke College and later published it in her excellent collection of essays, *Sister Outsider*.[3] The essay explores the many forms of power. In it, Lorde specifies the role of erotic connections within and between women in maximizing the potential for capacity building and improved and more just outcomes in women's lives, and as a result, in the lives of all persons. It valued an emotional, spiritual, and visceral honesty among and between women and others and stated that said honesty is vital to the realization of women's power. Lorde refused to validate any lack of connection between compartmentalized elements of the self. Her essay recognized the centrality of one's most passionate desires informing one's Calling. The essay intentionally ignored the religious. Instead, Lorde engaged the spiritual less in vesting faith in a "Higher Power," or God, and much more in a "Holiness" of women's shared power of fellowship with and across differences; this, in relation to passion-filled motive, informs my use of the term here. Parents and pastors have their own Calling, and they typically nurture a comparable faith-led desire in church youth. Erotic tensions shape the socialization of that Calling. Their faith investments in youth seem grounded in a selective inclusion of their own teenage past and in self-critiques used to refine their faith sense of themselves. Capacity-building strategies of action are used by parents and pastors to socialize teenagers on how ways of faith and "uses of the erotic"[4] come together.

Begin a Dialogue Early

Prior research suggests that, over a generation ago, in the early 1980s, urban African American teenage males viewed 16.1 years as being "the best age" for beginning sexual intercourse.[5] Since they felt that was the best age for having sex, talking to them about sex and sexuality should begin well before this occurs. Parents and pastors agreed. While what they viewed as "early enough" to begin an informed dialogue of youth sexuality varied a great deal, beginning the dialogue early was the emergent consensus. Alfred Preston, a 23-year-old church affiliate, recounted the following:

> The church and parents in the church, especially the Black Church, have been sweeping things under the rug. We don't talk about things because we are ashamed about certain things. And our parents didn't talk about 'em to us. So, we don't even know how to talk about it as kids. *My dad's sex talk with me? I was 17! I was 17! That's a little too late, dog* [group laughter].

Earlier in his comment, Alfred spoke of how uncomfortable his father was and how his father's discomfort coded to him the discomfort he was to feel in addressing erotic experiences in general and sexual experiences in particular. And for this awkward exchange to occur on the drive to his freshman college dormitory made the exchange all the more curious. This was magnified still further by the fact that Alfred had been raised around older cousins in a large, tight-knit family. So his older cousins had already "schooled him" on many of the challenges and other nuances of eroticism and sexual desire. Given the research of Pollard[6] and especially the reflections of a young man having just experienced his father-son sex talk just six years prior, there is a need for open and frank discussion of sexuality early on in adolescent faith socialization, as several parents and a few pastors suggested. Hampton, a 30-something youth pastor, observed the following:

> You could put me out of a job [as a youth pastor] and I'd be happy. Now we are trying to move in the area of where it is more prevention. Now that you are twelve? *Now we are going to talk about things when you are seven.* We are going to start introducing [the conversation then].

A difference of a generation did not change the sentiment. Robert Kay, a 60-something pastor, stated the following: "Children's sexuality starts long before they are teenagers."

The consensus recommendation that emerged was the need to begin talking to children about sex in elementary school and to do so with a focus on prevention—of sexual activity, of sexual assault victimization, of STIs and other adverse health outcomes, of any negative outcomes associated with initiating sex prematurely.

> I was just saying in a conversation today with a youth pastor, a Christian education director. How *a fourteen year old young man in the congregation "popped a cherry" on another fourteen year old.* The little girl happens to be the pastor's daughter. That is another person in a congregation who doesn't seem to get it that fourteen-year-olds don't need to have time alone if you have a pack of condoms on your bedside table.... In my congregation I have some young kids that I am doing premarital counseling [with]. A couple; *they experimented with each other sexually the first time after college.* That blew my mind in this day and age. I am having this one dimension [re: the 14-year-old], and yet over here, this [post-college sexual debut] is happening.

Here, Pastor Ronald Baltesante was explicit in what most often remained both unspoken and understood: There is an idealized sexual dialogue to occur.

The idealized age to begin was sometime in the college years, within the framework of committed, traditional, heteronormative courtship, and with the overt inclusion of parents, pastors, and other adults who seek the best interests of the young people. Short of the ideal, African American parents and pastors are prioritizing dialogues of prevention informed by empathy, beginning in early adolescence.

Nurture Empathy

When talking about the erotic and the sexual in a faith-grounded adolescence, how should the content be framed? "With empathy" was one of the most hopeful responses consistently emerging among African American parents and pastors. Talk with youth informed by an appreciation for one's own experiences of erotic maturation was another response. This was especially true among parents. Hattie Alton, in her early 50s and pastor of a mid-sized Baptist Church, suggested the following:

> I think that it [the success of faith-led sexual socialization] depends on how we teach forgiveness. How we teach Grace, mercy, discipline, and self-control. And *how we teach who we are as human beings in relationship to being created in the image of God. That is going to make a difference.* If you start by telling young people "[Sex is] going to be treated as sin, and anything you retrieve, you have to hide," youth will end up doing more [of what is forbidden]. Because they have to think [about hiding it].

Fostering secrecy is to be minimized and ideally entirely avoided. To do so, it is vital to nurture the sanctuary reflected in the interdependence among forgiveness, Grace, mercy, and self-control. Such nurturing is "becoming fascinated with and immersed in the other… [with] reflective concentration and reflexive awareness."[7] To empathize is to communicate with care, by remembering where one was as an element of listening with a caring heart, and it is central to the core of successful erotic socialization of African American teenagers. Marshall Moton, a 28-year-old father of a six-year-old, observed the following:

> One thing I would like to see more of is sexuality being [addressed by the] person at the head. We got to. *We don't embrace the culture of the youth.* Um, you can't tell them that the culture they grow up in and they like is bad and then expect to reach them. One thing that I actually learned from Elder [Stanley Godwin] is, with respect to youth, [our head pastor] doesn't condemn. He says, "Let me sit down and listen to, and try to embrace what attracts them so much. So I can show 'em the right way." We bash their clothes all the time ("All the time," [two women agree]). And how sexual

they are. We're down on them so much. We should do a better job of *embracing the culture in which they live*, so we can reach them a little bit more.

"Becoming fascinated with and immersed in" the lives of teenagers in the church, meeting them where they are, rather than where caring adults would like them to be, will embrace the culture of African American youth and bridge the two generations through dialogue. The too-often minimized sentiment that tolerance is not enough was intended to address the respectful inclusion of individual and group differences among women. Lorde suggested the following:

> The mere tolerance of difference... is the grossest reformism.... Difference must be not merely tolerated, but seen as *a fund of necessary polarities* [emphasis added] between which creativity can spark like a dialectic. Only then does the necessity for interdependency become unthreatening. Only within that interdependency... can the power to seek new ways of being in the world generate the courage and sustenance to act.[8]

While the more libratory and feminist/womanist implications of the sentiment would likely be challenged, if not rejected outright by many, African American church-affiliated parents and pastors shared a similar sentiment. Many recognized the essential value of youth differences as something other than a threat to an idealized "sanctity" of Sacred socialization. This can perhaps be most respectfully done when one looks to caring peers who, at a similar point in their lives, were sexually active, leading to teen pregnancy. They now look upon that as a part of their personal "necessary polarities," enriching their creativity in service of the Sacred.

> I gotta know where you're coming from. "What do you know, child about Bible stories?" Because everything in The Word is covered. It's how it is dialogued [with youth]. *So they can understand on that level where they are.* My husband always says, "Accept the child where they are, not where you think they should be." What is your level? We have to come to those levels, collectively. (Kate Jones; pastor, in her 40s)

> The majority of the mothers in the church have at least one child out of wedlock.... And a lot of them are now married with additional children and families.... And our children who are now teens have seen the struggle. The older child was the first born out of wedlock.... We try to have classes where we have just girls and just boys and allow them to share openly and say things they go through. And *because of that, I really do feel like the percentage [of sexually active teens] is really low.* I spend a lot of time talking with the children. And I know what they are in terms of their sexual experience. (Alice McGraw, in her 30s)

We have a generation we cannot hide these things from. If they don't learn it [in church], it's always good at home. But if it doesn't line up with the church youth leaders, youth are going to go out and find out what they can, and find it the way that they can. (Carol Osgood, a mother and youth leader, in her 40s)

Osgood acknowledged that with the current generation and an age of any information about virtually anything being only a few fingertip touches of technology away, with hypersexual images and popular media, using faith-informed blinders of any kind will do little more than alienate the youth from a disingenuous church environment. Thus, empathy is understood and valued more, both for and within the adults in the interaction, as well as in terms of what is fostered within the youths themselves.

In one of the most elaborate analyses on this theme in recent research, two subscales and structural equation modeling were used to show that "religious practices [combined with] interaction with others in a context of supportive and trusting relationships... increases moral orientation toward altruism [and] empathy."[9] For many teenagers, faith-engaged interactions with adults are a valuable resource in how empathy begets empathic urban youth. It allows for the emergence of some of the most Sacred elements of reciprocity across generations in addressing a complicated topic and life stage. The memory of symmetrical circumstances bridges the generational divide. Parents and pastors are moving from a starting point that seems to be coming earlier in children's' development, informed by adult remembrance of how it was to be their age. Tensions remain as both parties strive to navigate the uncertainties of youthful discovery in the faith-informed erotic socialization of African American teens.

Dissonance in Religious Erotic Socialization

A sense of spiritual unrest is likely as old as questions of faith and the Sacred, preceding institutional religion, since they are grounded in a dialogue of dichotomies: good and evil, Heaven and Hell, sinner and Saint, and so on. The balance between thinking and believing, while not a convenient dichotomy, is another among the many possible tensions faith can engage. For those who lead a religious life, such people "feel that the real function of religion is not to make us think, to enrich our knowledge... but rather, it is to make us act, to aid us to live."[10] Balancing relationships between old stories and new wisdom is a part of this tension. "Biblical accounts favor

monogamous marital sexuality as a gold standard of sorts. But the matter is
more complicated than it might first seem."[11] Those complications include
more than particular definitions of a behavioral ideal. Tensions in living this
"real function" are often most apparent in a cognitive or spiritual dissonance
regarding behaviors of passion in the development of the young.

In 1956, Leon Festinger and his colleagues explored perceptions, values,
and behaviors associated with the "Seekers." Their leader's predictions of the
destruction of much of the United States by flood did not occur, and these
disconfirmations of prophecy led to multiple date revisions. Yet most staunch
followers remained, which led the researchers to suggest a theory of cognitive
dissonance:[12]

> When people with strongly held beliefs are confronted by evidence clearly at odds with
> their beliefs, they will seek to resolve the discomfort caused by the discrepancy by con-
> vincing others to support their views rather than abandoning their commitments… [by]
> reestablishing cognitive consonance without sacrificing their religious convictions."[13]

Even without considering the impact of faith affiliation and its consequences
of thought, motive, and action, "For African American youth, issues of race
and gender identity are especially important, as these may interact to create
unique experiences of stress and dissonance."[14] Various other forms of dissonance remain in the religiously anchored socialization of African American
teens, some of which resonate among many parents and pastors. For Miller
Masterson, a 24-year-old youth leader in his nondenominational church, this
dissonance is grounded in intergenerational role modeling and a consistent
hypocrisy he feels youth see in the behavior of older adults:

> [They] get away with it [sexual behavior inconsistent with that congregation's faith
> pedagogy]. Older persons and other persons can be untrue to faith. They can choose
> that disrespectful kind of way. But I still accept people. People go over the line. They
> feel they can get away with something. [As] young people experience changes in their
> lives, puberty-related, they get certain standards or rules to follow. And they say, "I
> can't do this. I can't live this life. I'm all messed up. So, why even try?" And a lot of
> them know they have done bad things. So they go out [and] try a lot of stuff, because
> [they think] "I am young and I am going to go do these things anyway."

For Masterson, youths are keen observers in their search for giving a lived
faith meaning, and this observation intensifies during the adolescent years
out of which they just recently matured. Inconsistencies of older persons are
among the decisions and actions "untrue to faith" that magnify a sense of

non-belief in youth. This is made still worse when one acts as if one is getting away with something, even as church-affiliated others easily see beyond efforts to keep up appearances of faith adherence different from their everyday lives. For Pastor Orinda Brinkley, reducing a dissonance of the Spirit is about the truths of the pointed finger, that is, the need for a willingness to look at one's self and one's own contradictions as one gives meaning to the apparent contradictions of others. Consistent with the engaged empathy discussed earlier, for Brinkley, the presence of dissonance is especially true when it comes to remembering one's own youthful past. To reject youth seeking to nurture religious affiliation, or anyone else doing so, is an act of dissonant faith:

> I think the church needs to always have the "umbrella" [of ethical values] that probably gets sinners. Christ died for us so that you don't screw up, and then decide that because you did, that you are no longer welcome in the church. *Because we got some Holy folk in the church that ain't never done nothing wrong.* (Brinkley)

For Brinkley, to define someone as being no longer welcome within the church is an institutional act of spiritual dissonance. To act against the meanings of the crucifixion and resurrection of the Savior is to act against the foundations of one's faith. For Brinkley, this is the tension, or dissonance: being unwilling to access an empathy central to a possible faith. For Youth Pastor Marjorie Sorenson, a mother in her mid-30s, an intergenerational dissonance rests in parents requiring their children to participate in church when they themselves do not attend:

> A lot of times you have children in the church who come to church and their parents don't. We drive it harder among those kids because we know that their parents aren't active. But because the youth who still come [despite their parents' absence] want something so bad that they're so faithful. We know that we have to try harder."

One among the most overt instigators of a spiritual dissonance is the question for which too many youth are then scolded if they garner enough sense of self to ask: "If this churchgoing is such a good thing, why do I have to go when you don't go?" For these youth, a dissonance may become stronger with each required week in which that generational difference is demonstrated. In the socialization of African American teenagers, spiritual dissonance takes many forms. These include experiencing religious socialization as a "game" of hiding contradictions as one looks upon older persons "getting away with" inconsistent behavior and parents and adult youth leaders in church not being transparent and willing to prioritize their own choices and life outcomes of the past, instead engaging in a different form of faith hiding. Many youth are being socialized with "Do as I say, not as I do" parenting. That inconsistency bleeds into other decisions and actions beyond the erotic. One pastor remembered the following about his own experience of late adolescence: "I saw the church and then I saw everything else I do as two separate worlds. And I didn't know how to connect them. So I didn't know how to talk about sex [from] a Christian perspective until I got much older." Connecting separated worlds. A part of being more effective in the faith socialization of youth in the future is valuing the erotic footsteps the past can provide.

Erotic Footsteps: The Now and Then of Valuing History

History plays a vital role in specifying the means, strategies, and structures of change in a then-past that can be used for today. As the late historian John Henrik Clarke said, "History is a current event." Parents and pastors valued these ideas through multiple references to, and utilities of, history in the erotic faith socialization of 21st-century African American teens. When asked why she valued her affiliation with her small, tight-knit, Baptist congregation, Heather Marsdon, a 25-year-old mother of a 6-year-old and a 4-year-old, invoked the relevance of personal history:

> I value the fact that in this church we have a lot of love. And I feel like family, and [get that level of] support. I been here since I was young, young, young, so with my daughters being here and the history that I have and my family has here. That's what I value.

For Marsdon, her history as faith and faith as history literally create a current and ongoing event of her own youth socialization that continues for her both as a person in her 20s and as a young mother. Just as she was raised in the church, she has remained and is now raising her own children in that same church. If the personal is political, the historical is personal, as well. Perhaps history becomes most personal when grounded in the arc of one's own maturations in living a Sacred life. Herstory within that congregation can be valued because the present moment of feeling like family and knowing the love associated with it is not new. That personal longevity shapes what the congregation was, is, and is becoming.

For Vance Wilson, in his mid-30s and a father of two teens, his personal history as a teen father informs how other young men likely view him. Again conjuring empathy, he reflects on the age-appropriate assumptions the young men of that church may make and is uncomfortable with the decisions and actions to which an incomplete history may lead them:

> A lot of the problems with the youth is, a lot of them know [parts of] my history. Being a single parent. Having two kids out of wedlock. I was a father and I had these two kids by the time I was 22. They don't see the struggles I went through; in and out of court trying to get visitation [then] custody. They don't see that. Only thing they see is the finished product. And they think, "Well, if he did it, then I can go that route and still finish where he's at." Not necessarily, yunno. There's a lot of people that don't make it through. And *the struggle is what they don't see.* All they see is the finished product in the end.

While all knowledge of history is incomplete, some consequences of the unknown are more of a problem of erotic socialization than others. Wilson explained how he tries to use the less well-known elements of his journey as the iceberg metaphor, with a far greater mass resting in the unseen. For him, it is a presentation of do as I say, not as I do, as the consequences often bury lesser men. For Youth Pastor Hampton, historically, to a great extent, it was the contributions of many strong women that have been central to the faith-informed erotic socialization of African American adolescents:

> When you look back to the old days, before they had all these programs and stuff, it was grandmas and aunts and those kind of people that stepped in and handled a lot of stuff. [Many nods of yes, and "Mm, hm" in agreement]. *There's a great heritage in churches* getting the bad rap. A lot of times we have been there to help. You can tell with how they respond. Did they really listen, or do they just think, "I got it"? And some people who think they got it, [won't] get it until something [bad] happens. We've got an excellent teacher. *Where the history of dating comes from.* [The senior pastor] does an excellent job backing it up. We spent six months talking about dating. Not just saying, you shouldn't do it and then go on home.

The implications of these fathers is less about programs being inadequate and more a lament desirous of a "simpler time" in which the informal social ties of faith were enough and the less personal and more formal contemporary process is perhaps part of the problem. And, regardless of whatever "change in effectiveness" conclusions one might draw, the heritage itself is to be honored to a greater degree than what is currently taking place. The pastoral leadership valuing details of dating history provides an opportunity for both adults and youth to gain a new appreciation of the layered elements of the erotic. Like history, enriching an appreciation for its erotic relevance across the life course takes time.

Overall, a consensus emerged suggesting that history—more in the process, interactions, and demonstrated concerns—needed to play a more central role. The paradox of being guided by a text that was written millennia ago, while simultaneously not placing enough value on the far more recent institutional, familial, and personal histories within the congregation, was not stated directly. Advocacy emerged for sharing with youth historical rationales behind church rules, to provide an ethical and religious grounding of contemporary practice. Stanley Garson, a father of three in his late 30s, raising his two teens, noted the following:

> A lot of times we say something is wrong because we're not familiar with it. I like to wear the do-rag for my hair. A person [in church] condemned me for that. I asked them why, and they couldn't tell me. She just told me I was wrong. Why was I wrong? I'm not in a gang. I'm not holding up a bank. I got a job. I'm an elder at a church. What am I doing wrong?…. Yeah, stereotype. All I did was wear a do-rag to lay my hair down because that is what my barber told me…. And this person had a fit when I came in the door. "You can't do that!" It really turns the youth off. Now, there are certain things I don't agree with. The sagging of the pants. You know, I just don't [agree with that].

When is a do-rag more than a piece of clothing? When are appearances given more importance than they may deserve? And when is the absence of a faith-grounded rationale about what is (in)appropriate a necessary part of the meanings of these "rules" of an engaged faith? Garson's comments prompted the following exchange:

M1:   But there's logic to that.
F1:   There is history behind it. You should tell kids why they shouldn't wear saggy pants.
F2:   You can't just tell them not to wear saggy pants, you got to tell them *why* they shouldn't wear saggy pants.
F1:   People in this church know the history behind that.
F2:   In our forefather's day, they couldn't afford no belt.
F3:   … didn't want the slaves to run….
F1:   When my son was real little, we would be in the mall, and we sat and watched people. And I said "Look at that now. Let's see how many steps he is going to walk before he's gonna pull his pants up." We counted 'em. We might get to three. So I'm putting that in his head. I don't know if he ever wore them saggy or not, but I know he knew about the history then. Now he's seventeen.

Appearance politics and the history behind the erotics of clothing falling off of one's body, a do-rag defined as inappropriate for the church setting without a clear historically grounded reason why, and the mixture of historical rationales and different eras of the African American experience being invoked—all of this is being exemplified by a historical life lesson between a father and son from the early childhood of a now 17-year-old young man. Most popular writing about sagging pants traces its history to the rise of mass incarceration and the no-belt style of prison pants permeating community settings as the 1990s began. Historical rationales were then created, perhaps to mask the much more recent, homoerotically charged influences that are most often associated with sagging pants. Even here, the exchange illustrates the value these parents placed on the role of history in the presentation of style and the symbolic behavior and appearance codes within and beyond the church walls. Within and beyond the erotics of style, from the rather superficial to the far more consequential, history is a current event. Whether understanding church as a location of one's own intergenerational rearing and then of one's children, or needing to make hidden history more visible to help reduce the likelihood of teen fatherhood, or providing a religious history of dating, or discussing the longstanding contributions of women church elders, or determining the history behind "appropriate" attire inside and beyond the church walls, the past plays a vital role in the present. Beyond empathy and dissonance that is spiritual, erotic footsteps matter and—however unevenly—continue shaping the faith-informed erotic socialization of African American teenagers.

"Safe" Relationship Building in Contemporary Black Faith

However erotic messages are presented, they can mean little without some degree of clarity regarding their desired outcomes. Amidst the challenges of dissonance and empathy, of recent youth discoveries, or historical structures and strategies, African American parents and pastors do have a sense of what the parameters and outcomes of a possible safety can be and are. We know that "formal (e.g., Sunday school) and informal networks (e.g., friendship circle) tend to foster trust and feelings of mutual obligation among individuals."[15] In this mixture of formal and informal, what is a safe relationship? For African Americans and others, "churches are spaces where norms of trust and reciprocity are reinforced."[16] For parents and pastors, how does trust nurture the sanctuary of safe relationships among African American teens? Pastor Carla James suggested the following for teenagers:

The safe relationship is in a church. *It starts with the trust factor.* Am I safe to talk to you that you won't criticize me or get us [put out]? *"Am I safe with you to talk?"* That's where the relationships and the fellowships begin [as they] build the relationship of trust when they feel safe. That's a safe haven [when] you've got a youth that feels safe because you built that relationship with them. "I'm able to talk freely. I'm not judged by what I say. I know the church on the whole is a safe place."…. We have to target everything that's affecting the church. There may be some issues with homosexuality. There may be some issues with handling money.

For Pastor Ronald Baltesante, a safe relationship is one

built of honesty and trust. Dependable and understanding the values that I believe that our God requires within a relationship…. But sometime we make the Bible sound like it is the book of damnation, rather than making it a book of comfort like every other book they read. I guess what I am saying is, you got to make that book, can I say "Okay, with it, I have an understanding of compassion. Let me read what's in there. This is a good book. Can I make that Bible be the same book without losing the truth of what it is all about?" [much agreement from others] And we have not learned to present it in such a fashion. Uh, just what I said when I called a safe relationship at least amongst uh, male and female or any others who's been honest, truthful. Folks are not taking advantage of a little bit of trust in guidelines with God.

In safe relationships, the norms of trust and reciprocity are vital. They are as true in speaking of the formative nature of youth sexuality as they are when speaking about handling money. Like many other pastors, Baltesante emphasized the process of coming to a greater appreciation of the Bible as a grounding in caring, rather than as a text of scolding for what one is not doing. Similarly, for Carla James, being able to take this into consideration and communicate beyond the fear of saying something that (at the extreme) gets someone expelled from a church are among the measures of creating— and sustaining—a "safe haven." For many, this possible trust is the respect for boundaries, and flexibility is essential. A "one-size-fits-all" set of rules was consistently viewed as inappropriate for nurturing the sanctuary of safe relationship building. Osgood, a mother and youth leader in her 40s, stated the following:

[Churches] have to do a lot of definitions when you say a "safe relationship." Because *when I came to the church, the type of life I lived, I didn't need to hug, touch, kiss, or look.* You know what I mean? Being in touch means that you're in touch with me as an individual. It's a one on one…. So a safe relationship for some people is no hugging. No kissing. No going over to nobody's apartment. Somebody else's safe relationship might be defined from within the parameters of the church.

This describes boundaries of a compassionate distance to avoid even the implication of violating personal space. Like others, Osgood recognized that the level of touch one sees in the church defines a prioritized range for public displays of affection. These are among the factors that assist in refining the definition of safety. This can be combined with Baltesante's biblical base and the lessons of intimacy that anchor the representations of relationship building as central sources of shaping the foundations for the building of safe relationships:

> I was watching Creflo Dollar the other day [a prominent African American minister in Atlanta, Georgia]. Got one of the fashionable big churches. And he's dealing with the same problem we talking about at this table. He said *"We no longer having sex in the parlor. We got sex between the pews."* The church cannot fail to take information that we get and share it. You can't just tell people what's going to happen.... I have a friend who is a pastor and a medical doctor at [a nearby research hospital]. He came into one of our joint College of Bishops [from] different denominations [with] slides to show us the ramifications of sex and smoking. It was graphic.

As Osgood explained, one's personal history is consequential in these representations. For her, definitions were vital for appreciating a growing sense of intimacy as faith and trust in touch over time. Without these allowances for a gradual emergence of trust and clarity, risks and expressions of the unsafe will needlessly and avoidably increase:

> You have to let the young people know what their values should be. A lot of children are exposed to so many things. So much peer pressure and so many worldly [things], movies and TV and all that. You have to be right there with that child. *Constantly re-instilling spiritual values in them so they know what a safe relationship is.*

As the exchange of ideas in these pastors' focus groups continued, the dynamics of safe relationship building in rather traditional terms became a recitation—of a televangelist, in effect, "scolding" his megachurch congregation, concerning sexual hypocrisy within the church in the absence of a *moral* safety in relationship building, the literal and vocational merging of faith and medicine as a return to nurturing fear for having violated the sexual safety of the virginal ideal. Here, referenced through an art-of-science slide show of disease outcomes, science and faith were understood and presented as symmetrical and mutually reinforcing. The building of safe relationships must, in this pastor's view, be informed by the negative outcomes of disease one risks with the unsafe. And a different pastor emphasizes repetition in an effort to

minimize the risks of digressing into faith hypocrisies, returning to the basics
of traditional repetition as vital for the peer pressure and worldly things that
too often lead to *unsafe* relationship building among youth and others. Yet the
single most frequently valued action mentioned by parents, but also raised by
pastors, was encouraging, and being comfortable with, youths in groups. John
Garmon, a parent of a 14-year-old, shared this exchange with his son:

> He said, "I was talking to some girls, I ain't gonna' lie to you. But," he say, "Yunno,
> I ain't get the numbers like I thought." *Well, at least you all was in groups.* And that's
> what he talking 'bout: "Yeah, we was in groups. Talking." (Father says) "Will it hap-
> pen again? I mean yeah, yeah, alright. Well then who's your supervisor, man?" (group
> laughter). (Son says), "Oh they there, they there." I say, "Yeah."

The "supervisor" question is at once understood through the quality of a safe
father-son relationship and an appreciation of the son's presumably heteronormative actions. It provides a moment of levity, even during a light but
serious exchange when one's son has disobeyed his father's request. The supervisor can also likely be understood at once as both the veiled and symbolic
reference to the Lord and expectation for adhering to Christian doctrine in
secular settings. Relationship safety, goes the reminder, rests in the presence of
living a life of the Lord. The supervisor and the related humor of recounting
extend from a shared appreciation of the challenges of contemporary faith
parenting: the work metaphor understood as reinforcing the need of the son
to reflect a "who you are when no one is watching" truism of high character,
guided by keeping a parental supervisor in mind.

For other parents, like Alicia McGregor in the youth ministry at Grace
Cathedral Church, the safest relationship building is exemplified in chaperoned activities with small groups of church youth:

> A lot of times, the town hall meetings are the tip of the iceberg. *And then we have
> 'em in smaller settings. And we take them out.* And a lot of times there may be ten or
> twelve of 'em out. And you'll get the opportunity to spend some time with one or two
> of them. And they will express things to you and it is an opportunity to talk to them.

Predictably, beyond the comfort assigned to group activities and chaperoned
events in small group settings, there was very little willingness of parents
and pastors to acknowledge faith-grounded, formative erotic expression of
church-affiliated youth. As reflected by Renatta Farmsley, a parent of two
teenagers, "It's definitely not promoted [i.e., formative intimacies among
youth]. Now *they do group activities.* But I think they're trying to say, 'You

have plenty of time to go there.'" And for Mattie Scott, a parent at a different church, "In our church, we have girls in um, and boys that go together in our church. *But I think that we are so upfront in our church that our kids know what we stand for* [i.e., idealized chastity before marriage]."

What Works? A Dialogue of Formality and Popular Culture

For African American youth faith leaders, a goal that was consistently sup-ported across the project was maintaining youth activities to foster within the young passionate commitment to a Biblical faith walk reflected in their atti-tudes, intentions, and behaviors. Four themes emerged from among the many strategies of action parents and pastors felt were working well: events and pro-grams, "a bridge too far?" (i.e., challenging the limits of religious curriculum), peer role modeling, and between generations (i.e., structured interventions of intergenerational exchange). Summary and analysis of these themes follows.

Events and Programs

Along a continuum of formal-informal, there are five program types that were most frequently supported. The first of these was a "Lockdown." In the same Baptist congregation that has a "junior church" (i.e., a space for young people to define the whole of a service of, by, and for their age group), Jackie Bates, mother of a 13-year-old girl, described the event:

> On [April 19th], we are having what you call a "Lockdown." For, what's the ages? Twelve to seventeen or whatever. *They're going to stay [at the church] all night. And we're going to have activities.* This is co-ed. Boys and girls. We're going to be watching movies, playing games, whatever. And they're going to have adults supervising all night. I'm one of them. And they're going to sleep here all night.

This type of program can merge the secular and the Sacred, with various activ-ities under the watchful eyes of adults. To give structure and adult supervision to the lessons of intimacy from follow-up questions, the lockdown allowed them to hold hands with one another as they sat watching the movie. The organizing adults valued the younger kids being able to see the older, near-peer young people express a formative intimacy in this way. A second program type was health fairs. Similar to the structure and content of the two whole health-wellness service learning projects (see Chapter 2), these events valued faith as fun with safe intimacies and nurtured a protection of one's body as a temple unto one's God and faith.

> We're having *a youth and children's health fair* this Saturday. [We'll be] dealing with some topics [like] STDs. Slides are going to be shown. Dealing with their physical, their body nature, substance abuse, the things that take place in adolescence. Getting involved with drugs. The things that happen to their bodies when they have gotten involved with drugs…. Having this type of program allows them to then get in session. Open up. (Teresa Walters, youth pastor)

Walters describes the goal of the health fair being most consistent with making a life course wellness to nurture one's body and faith being among the most valued expressions of sustaining youth affiliation. From participant observation at a Sunday service at the church, similar to many churches, perhaps as many as one-third of the adults in the congregation were overweight, many substantially so. The health fair extended from this recognition of the value of enriching one's health as long-term life choices. From the lockdown congregational "slumber party" to the health fair, events that work also occurred in other mergings of the Sacred and the secular, including an intergenerational panel. They were held at the churches and structured so that an equity of power in both structure and content characterized these programs. Youth Pastor Kate Jones said the following:

> One of the programs we have, and I started it last year, I call it ["Holler and Be Heard!"]. It is a parent-teen panel. I've done it at different churches. I have the teens write out the questions. No bars hold. There's five parents, five teens. And I open up like an hour talk show. I have a youth co-host and I tell them, "This is what the youths are talking about. In order to hear what they're saying. I'd [holler and be heard]." The youth come in and say "How you doing?" They'd say, "Holla." And I'd say ["Holla and Be Heard!"] [waves hand to illustrate gesture]." It kind of came out of that. What youths can identify with, and parents can identify [also]. We kind of use this program to talk about the issues. And the *main questions I've gotten across to the board* at [three] different churches. "Can we talk about sex?" and "Can we talk about condoms?" And… we open the floor and sometimes we only get to about two questions. The other general question is peer pressure. So we use that as an opportunity to dialogue. And everybody gets [heard]. And nobody talks back to anybody. And then we bring in the word of God. And it's working.

Another strategy parents and pastors valued was gender-specific "Sacred Circles" or rap groups. Vance Casey, a 30-something pastor at a large church,

worked with the youth pastor of another church to share resources and improve consistency and turnout:

> One of the things we do that Brother [Newton] here and I are involved in, is one of the
> groups that we have [together]. Our young groups of junior enrollment. *We have our*
> *bi-weekly meeting. It is rich. It is flat honest.* During our meetings, we have a circle like
> the old rap group. It really does allow the [young men] to establish confidentiality and
> trust. Basically, I always start out by saying, "Well, how many went out and got kids
> this week?" Everyone looks around and they see that mindset. I use that reaction to
> provoke them. And from that, they know right then and there, "Okay, now we gonna
> talk. Because he's already on this particular subject of sex." This twice-monthly open
> dialogue where, to the best of the collective effort of the organizers, confidentiality is
> maintained, allows these young men to enrich a sense of fellowship within their own
> congregations by nurturing shared sanctuary that bridges the two churches. Humor
> does not mask uncertainty, or minimize fear. Instead, it is a resource for taking the
> topics and one another as seriously as the moment and subject matters demand, while
> also sustaining a space of shared joy and caring. Balancing the more and less formal
> dynamics with the elaboration of less formal follow-ups between the Sacred Circles."

Casey continued:

> The second thing I do is, Sunday through Saturday, we have hands-on with them. *We*
> *make telephone calls throughout the week.* We visit them in their homes with their par-
> ents. As youth leaders, we are hands-on…. I put the fear [of God] into them. "Don't you
> ever let me catch you! I don't even have to catch you being or doing out in the street."
> [Without] fear, they're not going to listen because they're hard-headed. And the major
> thing, you cannot convince a child on how to walk if *you're not walking it yourself.*

Casey affirmed the centrality of empathy again through the need for the adult
youth leaders to demonstrate in their own lives the things they advocate in
the Sacred Circles. From the Sacred as shared slumber, to the merging of science and faith at the health fair, to an intergenerational talk show format with
anonymous questions, to expressions of a Sacred Circle, parents and pastors
specified alternative strategies for challenging silence, repression, and misinformation as "the prevailing culture in Black churches."[17] With each new
strategy of action, they are nurturing a cultural change that works.

Where Is the Bridge Too Far?

When specifying what worked, adult youth leaders recognized that a spiritual
dissonance of boundary testing characterized uncertainties both within and

beyond these events and programs. These tensions of boundary testing took several forms. One was their recognition that perhaps too often, they value discussions of morality with their teens over any other form of engaging the erotic.[18] Thus, youth pastors and others often do not follow up on any behavioral considerations beyond the moral edict and its biblical anchor. "Thou shalt not" appears to often be the only parental guidance. There is little if any willingness to explore nuance, meaning, or other aspects of the erotic as a dialogue of faith. Youth Pastor Charlotte Rowlings stated the following:

> It's true: a lot of parents don't instruct. What role can the church play? What can you do? How much do you *go into the boundaries of people's homes* as far as these issues go? 'Cause it's a pretty touchy subject. In my church, we just came from our annual conference that we have every year in [large Southern city]. We have seminars all week long. And one of the issues I wanted to discuss was sexually transmitted diseases. And you would not believe how many resisted. I had to go to our board of Bishops to get approval on this topic. And they said, "You know, that's fine." But *I had a lot of opposition from the parents.* 'Cause they wanted to know, "Why do we need to talk about this in the church?" So where I struggle, and my husband, too. We struggle working with issues of sexuality, and it's traditionally not a topic that we talk about in the church. I mean we talk about it one-on-one with our own kids. Some parents do. But most parents say, "Just don't bring home a baby." "Just don't get a disease." "Just don't bring any reproach upon our household." Without sitting down and having these critical conversations with them. What I'm finding out is *parents really don't know how sexually involved their youth and young adults are.* They're thinking just regular [vaginal] intercourse. Whereas, these youth—as young as 9th grade—[are] involved in heavy sexual activity. Our challenge right after the conference was how to describe to a big group how you feel. After you have your meetings do you sit down and have one-on-one conversations with every young person who's dating? How do you handle that?

Parental willingness, congregational willingness, and the formal approval of the ministerial body of their faith—for Rowlings, all of these were a bridge too far. They were boundaries that had to be crossed in new ways. And all the while, 13- and 14-year-old children within her church are engaging in anal sex and other sexual behaviors beyond the "convenient" violation of the idealized heteronormative missionary position. And hers was not an especially fundamentalist denomination, as religion is a good indicator of attitudes toward sex but not of sexual behavior.[19] Where is the bridge too far? It is likely quite close to home. When caring and empathy have been established, the personal and intergenerational can be important in furthering a more informed erotics of faith. For Pastor Phillip Curvelle, the personal and the formal are vitally important:

I think it's a matter of talking to your child or the young person you're working with and *finding out where they are*. For example, my niece… she's 18 now. And she's respected what I've done [for] her. Her mother told me that she had a little boyfriend. And she said, "Well I want [Uncle Phillip] to meet him." So I met this boy's mother and father. And we all sat down in the office of the church and we were all pretty clear, that the dad was aggressive [i.e., protective] and I was too. Because, the dad was like, "This is my son." And I said, "This is my niece. So let's talk." And I said, "You know, she is the Christian girl. Now, she is not going to have sex until she gets married. Dating is not a problem. But let's talk about boundaries. You know. What are you gonna do? What do you think would be permissible?" And then we all talked about that. I think *a lot of times, the parents don't be real*. They just hope that she doesn't do that. "Well, let's keep it real. How far should his hands go?" And I made it clear. Because I was 17 too once. God knows what I did. I look back now. I was so bad, the way I did. I look back, I was really, really stupid.…

And I don't tell her what she should and should not do. Certain things like kissing, holding her hand. You know. Certain things. "How far should he go? Your hands don't touch my niece's legs. My niece's breast. You don't do any of that." To be honest with you, personally, don't tell nobody I said this. Put it on pause (jokingly, referring to the tape recorder): I don't care about the kissing [but] I wasn't gonna tell her that. Because I just thought, it wasn't going to do no good.

It is important to discuss explicit boundaries, formalize the next steps so the serious nature of what is being discussed is all the more apparent to all involved, conjure empathy of one's self at a similar life stage. And, as a male, it is important to remember the meanings of gender privilege and power inequalities and how they matter in formative sexuality. As best one can, recognize the challenges of agency and that what choices the two youth actually make is up to them. Anchored in biblical considerations of the dangers of making "provisions of the flesh,"[20] Curvelle demonstrated clear behavioral boundaries and what the biblical and interpersonal consequences would likely be to their violation, all while recollecting his own personal history of faith-informed rules he did and did not follow, stating that he did not "tell her what she should and should not do," even as he is telling all involved the shoulds and should nots of their formative intimacies. In short, there are approval-seeking complications in clarifying what boundaries can and cannot be crossed. Whether more religious and doctrinal, or interpersonal and empathetic, what works is a willingness to risk boundary clarity thoughtfully. Parents and pastors increasingly value places of shared (dis)comfort, knowing that the limits of comfort for some must be pushed if a framework for what works is to be collaborative and effective.

Peer Role Modeling

Another practice of faith socialization that most frequently emerged among parents and pastors' values was encouraging evangelical servant-leadership toward peers of the church-affiliated teenagers. Less overt was practicing one's faith in everyday interactions and reinforcing faith foundations by doing so. Pastor Carla James suggested the following:

> I said, "If you know somebody's doing something wrong. You know they drinking. You know they smoking. Don't hang out with that person. And then he gonna' tell you if he gets to high school and he say, 'Hey man, ride with me over here.' You know the guy got a gun. What are you going to get in his car for?" I said, "There's just some things you got to use your common sense. Say, 'Brother, naw. I get with you a little later.' Everybody in the school done told you that guy's carrying something. Everybody telling you about sex and stuff. You see them things. As parents we don't get to see that. You get to see that kid all the time—act like that." I said, "*You're the best example for that kid* in the whole wide world. We're not. So you be the best focus out there."

For Renatta Farmsley, a mother in a different church than that of Pastor James, the sentiment of youth faith in everyday leadership is similar:

> I think it's their foundation. What they get at home, and what their environment is. That is encouraged here [in her church]. If you see your brother that is your friend going this way, and when we're trying to teach you that you should be going that way, *help them out. Pull them up.* Say something to them. We emphasize that here. And I think it does roll out with them when they're in school or in other settings.

In another church, this intent was more explicit, as in this exchange between three mothers:

> M1:   I think that means something to our kids, that if they bring an unsafe child or person in here…
>
> M2:   They know they're in fellowship. They're bringing people in here.
>
> M3:   You know, my daughter told me about a little girl in her school that is an atheist. And she was saying, "I try to teach her every day." She snuck her Bible to school one day so she could talk to her. And I hear her on the phone with her a lot, trying to teach her about God. And she said, "You know Mom, when she's ready, I want to bring her to church." And I said, "We'll go get her."

To live their faith, in the spirit of Genesis 4:9, teens are to be their "brother's keeper": Share their faith, behave with caution and care, reach out to "unsafe" others and atheists, breaking school rules if need be to share the Word. To bring others to church is to live a knowing Gospel. This works in building safe relationships, with and beyond their peers.

Between Generations

A common thread in "what works" is nurturing the ways adults and youth interact. This is explored in detail in Chapter 5. While some intergenerational exchanges are overtly youth-centered and more egalitarian (e.g., Holla and Be Heard!), others are more traditional and hierarchical. Among the latter was Pastor Kate Jones's challenging denial of a mother regarding the sexual activities of her daughter:

> We had to get her, her pastor, and her parents and sit down and have this difficult meeting with *this mother who was in denial that her daughter was sexually active*. She wasn't having [vaginal] sexual intercourse, but she was involved in other sexual behavior. And it wasn't even with a young boy in the church, but someone just in her neighborhood. She told me, "because he knows I'm a church girl and he said this way I wouldn't get pregnant. I would stay a virgin."

In a single conversation, Pastor Jones helped move a mother from seeing her daughter as a virginal ideal to acknowledging that she is sexually active and that her sexual activity included oral and/or anal sex. This is surprisingly prevalent among many religiously oriented young women; they have been led to, and perhaps want to, believe that by not engaging in vaginal sex they can remain a "virgin."[21] This is often associated with these religious young women and men having both riskier and unprotected sex. This causes spiritual and behavioral dissonance because preparation of informed intention that a condom represents makes extramarital sex that much more sinful. In this meeting, framed as "youth-as-the-immoral-problem" across generations, the pastor mediated a moment of what was heard as bad news. A similar framing and approach was being adapted in a churchwide, town hall framework, with strategies for youth church and teen groups in secular settings discussed earlier. Alicia McGregor of Grace Cathedral Church said the following:

> I think one thing that really was refreshing to me was the town hall meetings we had in conjunction with them [youth-centered teachings from their pastor]. Because they [the town hall meetings] *forced parents and adults to answer these questions*. By hearing the questions asked and the topics brought up by the youth…. My daughter's not that

old. But I know it would have created a dialogue if she was that old. If we hadn't had [it] before, we would have had to have the discussion then. And it would have forced us to live in a certain way to honor what [pastor] was talking about. So, not only was the information covered, but *it had to blow open the door for discussions at home* (murmurs of agreement from others). And that was invaluable.

Soon after, the following exchange occurred:

Father 1:   When we discussed sex and dating, some youths were asking questions [about] what the grown folks would be doin'. Yunno', as a married couple.

Mother 1:   (interrupts) Right! Yunno', "Is oral sex 'sex'?"

Fa1:   (interrupts) "Is oral sex fine? Is, is being, is fingering wrong?"

Mo1:   Yeah.

Fa1:   And I. I don't think it's wrong. And, yunno', people are like, "C'mon now."

Mo1:   And "Is masturbation okay? Since y'all don't want us to ask that…."

Fa2:   Sex, right.

Fa1:   So… yeah. Some of the questions they were going through. Phew! (pause) Adolescents be doing different things.

Parental concern nurtured a willingness to risk, from hidden and hush-hush to visible and valued within and beyond the teens, with leadership from the pulpit allowing, and in fact encouraging, still more explicit follow-up dialogue to occur, all within the walls of the church. One mother, Diamond Rucker, noted the following regarding her church:

[In] our junior church, we have teen sessions and we will start out with a certain passage or lesson. A topic. And we open discussion. And we have a rule that *what is said in class, stays in class*. I substitute for the teen class. This allows them to open up to a lot of other things. By having those kinds of settings in the church, it helps at least to let them talk about it. We give guidance. We don't let them go everywhere. I mean *we stick to what the Bible says*. And we tell them about the three types of love. And we tell them that, *ideally, the one—eros love—is reserved for marriage*.

Though no other focus group was as explicit as the sexual acts mentioned in the focus group discussed here, two of the six other church-specific parent focus groups suggested that a similar dialogue was beginning in their congregations. Though more veiled and cautious, this process of change was helpful to parents and teenagers. A junior church existed in four of the seven congregations in which focus groups took place. In each case, they were guided by a small, rotating group of dedicated adults. It allowed for a still greater expression of youth honesty developed of, by, and for a faith fellowship of their peers.

Pathways of Inclusion

Who is (un)welcome in contemporary African American churches? Who is marginal, seen, and tolerated, and why? For multiple analytic and "good taste" reasons, parents and pastors were not asked these and related questions directly. However, their responses to other questions addressed how access and inclusion inform the erotic socialization of church-affiliated teens. Douglas noted the following:

> While the Black Church community is arguably no more homophobic than the wider Church community or heterosexist society of which it is a part, casual observations do suggest that it is perhaps more unyielding and impassioned than other communities when expressing its anti-gay and anti-lesbian sentiments…. How is it that a Church community so committed to the politics of racial justice can be so intransigent when it comes to the politics of sexual justice?[22]

Douglas concluded that this uncertain terrain is made still more complicated because the Black Church community response to same-sex desire and identity is informed by the general African American responses to the hypersexualization of the Black body and the intensely racially charged outcomes that have taken place as a result (e.g., lynchings). Whatever the context and motive, consistent with much prior research, in the CoCHY and CoCHY SLI projects, uneven inclusion of same-sex love and gender-bending in African American organized religion continues and impacts the erotic socialization of faith-affiliated teenagers.

Same-Sex Attraction in Contemporary Black Faith

For pastors and parents of church-affiliated teenagers, the presence of lesbians and gay men in the youths' lives could perhaps best be characterized as a troubled inclusion. Lesbian and gay teenagers were referenced as persons who help teenagers clarify sexual acts and/or discourage the minimization of issues of gender and sexual identity and as seekers of pastoral input for navigating a socially constructed dissonance between their faith and their sexuality. As one mother recounted, "Youth today know that oral sex is sex. Because I hear my daughters talk about it. They know full-fledged that it is sex. [From] the gay guys in their schools, they know it's sex even between males and males." Here, gay male teenagers are clarifiers of female teens' understanding of oral sex as a sexual act. Gay male schoolmates were presented by this mother and pastor virtually

without judgment or condescension. There was almost a sense of relief, as if she
appreciated the clarity and honesty of self inferred from her daughter's clarity
and friendship with her gay male friends. And, at the very least, these young
men reduce the convenience of dismissing anything other than heterosexual
"missionary position" sex as non-sex. For a mother (first quote) and a pastor
(second quote), homosexuality was one among the "issues" to be addressed:

> It was in the [school] environment I had him in where he was accused of everything be-
> cause he was a Christian. Now they were liberal. [In their schools], "Jesus can stay over
> here. But we'll chase the voodooist, the Satanist, the gothics, um, the homosexuals.
> And they can do whatever they want to do in this environment." And my son was not
> mature enough when he went there for the music. It was called the [Wellford] School.

> I'm sure that you've got a particular youth that feels safe because you built that rela-
> tionship with them. When you start to build those things that's when somebody feels
> safe. That's a safe haven. [Teen feels] "I'm able to talk freely. I'm not judged by what
> I say." The church on the whole is a safe place? No. Are there pockets of safety? Yes,
> when it comes to small groups. Because we have to target everything that's affecting
> the church. [In] this area there may be some issues with homosexuality. [In] this area
> there may be some issues with handling money. You know, everybody's got their issues
> in their lives and that's why I talk about programs.

The mother called her son's maturity into question in navigating the "lib-
eral" school environment that seemed welcoming to many student identities, with homosexuality being one among them. For the pastor quoted here,
programs are the means to address issues, using small groups to make the
church as a whole a safe haven. Homosexuality was an "issue" presumably to
be resolved in faith's favor, with an inference of the need for the lesbian or
gay person to change, though the specific means of responding to same-sex
desire as an issue was not explicitly defined. Later, in the same pastor's focus
group, a co-facilitator asked the following: "Are there any other questions
you would like us to ask that we didn't ask already? In response, the following
exchange took place:

Pastor 1:	I still want to know how you guys are dealing with homosexuality.
Pa2:	Laughter
Pa1:	Now that's…. (pause) I don't mean to. That's becoming a prob-lem. Big time.
Pa2:	It's an issue. Hmph.
Co-facilitator:	It gets back to sexuality as a *continuum*.
Pa1:	Exactly, and I need to know…. (pause) I need some help, y'all.

The first pastor (Pa1) was interested in hearing strategies of actions valued by others. He navigated the somewhat dismissive laughter of another pastor (Pa2) to directly solicit additional information. This then led a co-facilitator to more directly ask, "Anyone want to share briefly how their congregation deals with homosexuality?" The phrase "dealing with" may problematize the issue. Or, perhaps the phrase simply anticipates the likely sentiment among the pastors. A long pause of uncertain looks and unsettled fidgets took place. The first response beyond the pause was a pastor reciting a collective edict of condemnation: "Those that are part of the [governing body of his faith]. We made a public statement against homosexuality and same sex marriage. That preaches against it. Period! Against the promotion of it. You can't stop the government if it starts promoting it." Legalizing same-sex unions in the eyes of the state was understood by this pastor as the "promotion" of homosexuality, that is, not an action of civil or human rights but promoting an act worthy of condemnation. In this pastor's worldview, "government promotion" led its condemnation to be prioritized as an action of the religious governing body to which this pastor belonged. Consistent with prioritized condemnation, an appeal to "go back to the Word" suggests the reinforcement of Leviticus 18:22 and the handful of other most frequently cited Bible references to same-sex desire. Pastors consistently valued one-on-one, interpersonal responses within their church, yet defined it as a problem warranting interceding ministry, that is, intervention to prevent sin and move toward the nurturing of a soul-saving faith outcome. And most often, same-sex desire, recognized as taboo within most churches, would remain silent, hidden, left as an insidious presence that challenges the quality of faith within the congregation. When asked how to deal with that silence, one pastor said the following:

> After a lot of times when it gets to a certain level, it's obvious. But, but uh, the way that process is very…. You got to treat it very tenderly. With patience. You can't treat this person as if he. You can't treat them the same. You've got to take each and every case as an individual because they're on different levels, different avenues. In homes, like the Bishop says so, it takes time, patience, trust and prayer.

Problems are treated. Illnesses are treated. And in this treatment, tenderness and patience were suggested as vital resources of pastoral care. Same-sex desire was recognized as a malleable relationship between identity and behavior.

> Pa1:   The church needs to define what a homosexual relationship is. Because everybody who have a relationship with somebody of the same sex is not homosexual.
>
> Pa2:   That's right. They got homophobia now. (A lot of unintelligible talking)
>
> Pa1:   Same-sex relationships. If I took a little drink, does that make me an alcoholic?

Defining the "threshold" and/or makeup of homosexual persons and relationships was linked to homophobia. The same pastor who shared dismissive laughter in the previous exchange said "homophobia" with a tone of condescension. Same-sex desire, when acted on, by inference, only a few times, was linked to the excessive use of alcohol, a potentially addictive substance, of both pleasure and abuse. Here, the inference is that engaging in "a little" same-sex behavior would not make one lesbian or gay. Yet to act on same-sex desire is to raise the question of "abusing" sex, even as one may not claim "lesbian" or "gay" as one's identity. A progressive recognition of an important separation between behavior and identity was also linked to the metaphor of engaging in "abusive" behavior, like being an alcoholic.

This exchange was followed by a brief discussion of an (at that time) recently published *New York Times Magazine* article, "Double Lives on the Down Low."[23] The article explored the social networks, behaviors, and related identities of African American men in major cities including Cleveland, Atlanta, and New York City. To be "down low" was to keep one's homoerotic desire and sexual behavior veiled and largely unseen, as one maintained an otherwise heteronormative identity and life. The pastors who were aware of and had read the article distinguished between sexual behavior and sexual identity. They shared the inference that, just as the behavior can be understood in terms of continua of engagement, affiliation, and identity, there is also a continuum of responses by pastors. None of the pastors said anything approaching "radical inclusion,"[24] where some pastors—even in mainline, centrist churches and denominations—are moving beyond tolerance and openly recognizing and including lesbians, gay men, and genderqueer persons. Beyond uncertainties of tolerance and patience, there was no clear consideration of how the church might be a force for change. For many, including Hattie Mae Howard, who led a small Baptist Church, the mixture of problematizing and showing compassion was clear:

> Howard: I have got some dealing with homosexual relationships. So when you say romance, which one are you referring to? Because I think

> that is really challenging to be able to deal with romantic rela-
> tionships in a Christian context when you have *all of these different
> competing sexualities* to deal with. I have the late bloomers [female
> and male virgins in their early 20s] and their relationship. I have
> one that is very young. 13 or 14. And I have one who is involved
> in a homosexual relationship, and they're both 15 or 16. I just
> found out about the homosexual [couple] maybe a month ago. So
> to give them a safe environment. Um, your question was again?

Co-facilitator: Um, are the youth in your congregation actually engaging in
                   moral kinds of romantic relationships?

Howard: Okay. Then, yes. Yes. All types of romantic relationships.

The co-facilitator "coded," and likely imposed on, the potential flexibility Howard was beginning to express. They (mis)used the word "moral" among a group of pastors, when one among them had volunteered homosexual ro-mance as one form of romance "to give them a safe environment." Across all three pastors' focus groups and[25] participating pastors, this was perhaps the closest any pastor came to respectful inclusion of same-sex desire as a part of their sexual socialization of African American church-affiliated teenagers. Nowhere was there an acknowledgment of the church potentially being a part of a problem of disingenuous identities and veiled or otherwise "double" lives. Nowhere was there a presence in the dialogue of responses to same-sex desire being a problem of heteronormative stricture and institutional myopia. Possibilities for any of these types of extended nuances were also minimized, given the timing of the question being raised near the end of what had already been long focus groups. (Even) in a project exploring faith and the sexual socialization of African Americans across generations, the consideration of same-sex attraction was itself marginalized. The emergence of same-sex de-sire, behavior, and identity in a majority of the focus groups speaks to its sa-lience and unsettled presence in contemporary African American churches.

Evangelical Empathy: Being Compelled by Faith

Perhaps the most unique testimony across all data collections of the CoCHY project occurred when a focus group father recounted his recent experience of being "compelled" by faith. After having been both stern and negative in responding to a gender-bending stranger, after hearing what he felt was the voice of God, the Father, he followed up with that same individual he had previously rejected. To appreciate his testimony and its relationship to faith in the erotic socialization of African American youth, one must understand what preceded it. The focus group topic had turned to safe relationship building and different ways that can occur in one's faith walk. Rochelle Farmer, a mother in her early 30s, had just suggested that one's faith

> should be reflected in everything we do. From the time we get up until the time we go to bed. Because what's in us is going to come out. If you don't have nothing, no substance, there is nothing to come out. But if God is our center, when we wake up, we are thinking about Him. Then all through the day it should reflect Him. Whether we are talking, driving, working, whatever. If Christ is on the inside, then it should reflect on the outside. Can I get an AMEN? (Enthusiastic "Amen!" responses followed.)

This brief testimony nurtured an evangelical energy among all the parents in the group. It led Jacqueline Donnell to speak of different settings in which she had engaged with others "in the household of faith":

> I have spoken to a lot of people on the phone who I've never met. Just in conversation, you feel that connection. You know when you are talking to a Christian. You walk into a room and there is something. Of course we are supposed to be Christian people, and [when] we are, people know. Total strangers will come up to you. And you will also know the people that you are supposed to go up to and say something to, or in some way minister to. Because you can reach someone that someone else cannot. And you can plant a seed. And someone else may have to water that seed and make it grow. Because I have read that we have to do good to all men, especially those in the household of faith.

Anchored in a garden metaphor to acknowledge the uncertainties of "yield" and growth in the process of a living faith, to engage with others is a duty, even or especially when they are total strangers or in some ways different from those with whom one might most comfortably share their faith. All this was guided by the suggestion that to make a Christian connection with others is to appreciate the ways in which their developmental process is being informed by how parents express, and by doing so, model for them an evangelical empathy to nurture the household of faith. January Donner, a mother of two teens, then said the following:

> When we exhibit love, whether it is a smile or meeting someone's need, or whether it is caring for a child that has no father. You know, that is how we show Christ. That is how the spirit comes alive in us. His spirit comes alive in us. It is an action thing, you know.

Guided by empathy and compassion, this is consistent with a willingness to nurture. Then a father of a 17-year-old son said the following:

I think about the word "compelled." Being compelled. It is a natural compelling to do what we do. To be like Christ. You don't really think about it. You just do it. I mean, some of us think about it. I myself, I thought about what I did after I did it. Most of the times, I think later. If I think [too] long about doing it, it won't get done. I mean there is some things that you plan on doing. But if you're, for example, if you are going to help someone who looks raggedy. Or, I guess. I don't even. I'm getting off the subject. But um, we are warned about the strangers that you meet and deal with. Then one Sunday on the way to church, there was this real broke down looking cross-dresser. *He looked like a real beat up Diana Ross with a dirty wig on* [scattered, tentative laughter followed]. And so I had my family. And I was on my way to church. And he comes out of [a drug store] down the street. And he said, "Do you have a couple dollars?" And I wanted to be authoritative and strong. So I said, with all my might, "NO!" Like, "Get AWAY from me!" I've got my family in the car. And as I drove to [church], it was the voice of God said, "That's my child." You know. And so, on the way to church, I never spoke a word to my wife. But as I sat through the service, I thought about that guy's face. But when I went back to [a local arts district and gay-identified neighborhood] on a Monday, I saw him walking down the street with his wigs and stuff. Draggin' around. And I said, "Here it is God. What do I do?" And when I went to work, I was talking to one of the kids I work with and the guy [cross-dresser] shows up. And I said to the boy's mother as I was giving her her son's check because he hadn't come to work. They have a food pantry where I work at, and they were going to get food. And I said to her, "Well, there's this guy." And I explained what [had] happened. And she said she knew him. She went to school with him. He's schizophrenic and it happened in his later years. And *when he came back, I gave him a couple dollars. And [now] we got a relationship. A friendship. Or an experience.* But it wasn't something I could think about. It was just something that. He's very disturbing. But it turned out that he has schizophrenia. He thought I was the pastor of the church. But I am a screen printer and I work there at an old broken building that is not a church anymore, it is a youth center. And so, *we became friends.* And it turns out that he is a self-medicating type schizophrenic, who buys crack from—Or, is served "flavor." They call it flavor in the streets. The people who sell drugs. He self-medicates on street medicine rather than on medicine he gets from the psychiatric hospital. And *he is beginning to start wearing his regular clothes.* But I am saying that in retrospect. Many times when he came to me, I couldn't stomach him. But, *there is a compelling [urge] to do things that we wouldn't normally do.* And that comes from being in a congregation where we have allowed the word "relationship" to be more than, I don't know. That comes from being in this particular place where I get the right kind of water and soil and growing, in a way that allows me to be compelled or strengthened to do some things. And we don't often testify to those kinds of acts. But I think that a lot of us can speak of a lot of things we do, that we wouldn't [otherwise] do. It's being transformed and compelled as well.

Perhaps this father was emboldened by a tone of inconvenient outreach that had immediately preceded his comments. His actions demonstrated evangelical empathy, that is, exchange among concept or theory, motive, and action, while challenging one's sense of resistance or repulsion. Outreach is typically easier when others are conveniently safe objects of charity and/or who look, think, and interact like oneself. Bridging the distances of a challenging person—and doing so apparently informed by sharing a sense of the Sacred and by charity—makes evangelical empathy more complicated, perhaps even substantially so.

Through his recounting of these experiences, he tied the various other shares together by describing not just a single incident or encounter, rather sharing it as a layered set of exchanges with multiple—non-family, non-church—persons, within and beyond his work environment. He described the complications he encountered both within himself and in considering the personal histories that inform how he is modeling being compelled by faith. For him to share this in an environment with high expectation for heteronormative attitudes, motives, and behaviors was brave and exemplified the "personal as political" in expressions of nonsexual erotic faith. This father's example led to a discussion of "prodigal son" experiences of moving away from faith or at least from religious participation. We considered what churches can do, both to reduce the likelihood of them occurring, and, when they occur, nurture re-affiliation through evangelical empathy, be it erotic or otherwise. This led to Shirley Bestwood, saying the following, with the father then interrupting her:

Bestwood:	I think it is just about being real, you know. If you make a mistake, I think a lot of mine [church-alienating experiences] have been wanting to teach me a lesson so that even if you erred, they can still see the love of Christ in you. Because you go back and you say, "I'm sorry." So I think in that way *God still used me because [I was] humble enough* to go back and say "Look, I was wrong. I didn't say that right." So they can still see this is the way you do it, if you do go back and say—
Father:	Sorry to interrupt. I told that guy, "You know, when I first saw you," *I told him exactly what I felt.* And he accepted it. And it turns out he was raised in a church. And his mother died. And he said he never had a friend while he was in church. And [now] we get together. We pray with each other. And he can pray. A devout prayer, literally. At this point in his life, he is more in a [drug] user mode, and he doesn't want to pray in front of me. He said he gets on the bus and people say, "What the blank are you doing in my seat? Get the blank away from me!" And that is the real world, you know?

Faith as empathy across differences is one among the means of refining the pathways of inclusion for church-affiliated parents of African American teenagers. As Donner suggested earlier, love is an action thing. Those that might appear to be the most challenging persons because of their complications may also prove to be among the most rewarding.

In the vein of evangelical empathy toward the erotic and faith socialization of church-affiliated teenagers, in addition to the topics considered earlier, African American parents and pastors also considered the relationships between faith and other themes, including shame and self-esteem, authority and faith adherence, teen pregnancy, and the enabling of Black men. Length and primacy prevent a fuller consideration of these and other emergent themes. As discussed earlier, throughout the focus groups, participants often intentionally merged safe relationship building with the church setting as a safe space. A reciprocity of these things was valued in nurturing sanctuary in the contemporary faith lives of African Americans across generations.

Conclusion: "Uses of the Erotic" in Developmental Black Faith

What is the place for the erotic in the developmental faith of church-affiliated African American teenagers? This chapter has demonstrated how this answer is being lived in 21st-century African American faith. Previous research "laid the groundwork for healthier notions of the sexual self within the context of Black religious experience and thought."[25] By focusing on the presence and uses of the erotic in the faith pedagogy of African American parents and pastors, this chapter nurtured that groundwork.

Erotic messaging is playing an increasingly valued role in the religious socialization of African American teenagers. A very strong consensus emerged that advocated for a very early beginning of the erotic socialization of teens, perhaps as early as elementary school. But perhaps the most heartening elements to emerge from the focus groups are the priority they placed on empathy as a point of reference in engaging with youth; spiritual dissonance that takes many forms, with critiques of adult faith hypocrisies being among the most useful for successful youth socialization; and history—personal, familial, institutional—as a vital resource in the dialogue among the erotic, the sexual, and the institutionally religious.

Safe relationship building in faith-informed settings has historically been an uncertain terrain. Trust was understood as being at its core. For parents and pastors, this process begins with the opportunity for youth to share honestly and in ways where they know they are being heard without condescension and judgment and without any shame or alienation resulting from these faith-anchored, intergenerational exchanges. They valued the recognition that personal history always matters and informs the limits of what is appropriate when bridging social distances and the talk, or other engagements, that may occur in these spaces of faith. In the very same focus groups in which parents of teenagers recall how they behaved as teens, often acting against the rules and boundaries that were agreed on, these same parents (still) placed great value on the safety of group activities, even when not being chaperoned by an adult. And perhaps most hopefully, focus group participants seem increasingly willing to be explicit in the language they are using and in bridging the Sacred and secular of a faith pedagogy toward a more whole erotic understanding of self. Though one might critique the pace of change, to the benefit of the teenagers and others, progress is being made.

That progress, however, is ripe with uncertain inclusions. While the ideal of behavior and identity remains intensely heteronormative, spaces for moving beyond moralizing and judgment are apparently slowly being created. A compelling evangelical empathy looked different from the typical outreach of charity as a tempered inclusion. If one were to reach out to a man wearing women's clothes and a woman's wig, could this person's progress in faith include a continued cross-dressing gender identity? While the answer to this question is beyond the scope of this chapter and book, for the erotic pedagogy of faith among African American parents and pastors to place value on inconvenient inclusion at all is something more than faint progress. And all the while, outcomes these persons of faith are striving to prevent continue to be at the forefront of their faith practices. As Audre Lorde suggested, the mere tolerance of differences is not enough. Thus, interaction rituals of traditional faith socialization of African American teens are not enough. In fact, like tolerance alone, said rituals may actually be abusive. Many of these parents and pastors are both redefining and developing new pathways for the present and next generation of Black Churches.

The near-complete absence of considering the possibility for a healthy sexually active teenage Christianity other than adhering to the virginal ideal is both understandable and troubling. When African American teenagers have viewed 16 as the ideal age for sexual debut for over a generation, there is great worth in refining how faith socialization can inform sexual patterns in relation to this age of sexual onset. When so many religious parents have no idea how sexually involved their children are, the space of sexual taboo that

Pollard wrote of, as cited at the beginning of this chapter, remains. Yet, as their testimonies and remarks show, parents and pastors are making progress toward bridging any "disconnect" among faith, sexuality, and the rest of teens' lives. This apparent movement toward greater visibility of erotic exchanges is quality progress. Informed by the contributions of this chapter, may the pace and breadth of progress in enriching these connections continue to grow.

· 5 ·

STRENGTHENING THE BRIDGE
BETWEEN US

Intergenerational Capacity Building
in Contemporary Black Faith

We present church as somehow holding, stifling, keeping youth from really experiencing life. When a child's been hearing that for 14 years, they think that there's
just some great, "golden apple" outside of the church walls. "And I've got to go get
it!" And that unfortunately becomes dangerous…. Youth don't care about Tupac
[Shakur] or Biggie [Smalls]. They care about who's successful…. And when we present Christianity as not being able to be successful, then that brings the challenge.
—Youth Pastor Carlyle Hampton
Cathedral Redeemer Church

Critical analysis can help us explore individual and communal hypocrisy, betrayal,
and miseducation… requir[ing] of others that which we [do] not do ourselves….
Change requires disruption…. Empowerment helps the Hip Hop generation come to
know and love their authentic selves…. We need to listen to one another and learn
to communicate so that we can *engage in intergenerational dialogue*.
—Cheryl Kirk-Duggan and Marlon Hall[1]

Introduction

How do Black Churches bridge generations? Pastor Hampton uses Hip Hop
icons to suggest what he feels youth find appealing beyond the church walls.
Kirk-Duggan and Hall use Hip Hop as a generational label to emphasize how

vital forms of dialogue are in order for intergenerational empowerment to occur. True for any culture and institution within it, generations are never silos—distinct, stand-alone entities, with no movement between them. Because of the fluidity of time and the actions of many in any given period, there is interdependence between generations. Institutionally, this generational interdependence is at the core of capacity building. Capacity building is "maximizing the local area assets of individuals, families, organizations, and others, [that] can then be brought together to share in and collectively nurture an improved quality of life within" that institution or local area.[2] Consistent with recent research,[3] this chapter explores capacity-building patterns of faith in the reciprocities among generations. It analyzes how youth and others are bridging Hip Hop and other tensions of age and era toward the enrichment of 21st-century African American faith. Bringing up the "next generation" of faith, is not new. In 1903, "according to W. E. B. Du Bois, most historic Black congregations provided programs specifically geared toward the young."[4] Research since has found similar, more detailed figures consistent with that of Du Bois.[5]

To provide 21st-century explanatory richness to these earlier analyses of the intergenerational context of religious socialization, the CoCHY project, and especially the CoCHY SLI, were entirely devoted to exploring the details of how these youth engagements are unfolding in contemporary Black Churches. The analyses of this chapter are a product of the project's five qualitative platforms being triangulated (see Chapter 1). Doing so allowed this chapter to explore the faith engagements and resource sharing across generations, extending from the collaboration of church youth, church leaders, health service providers, and academics to further community capacity-building outcomes and the living faith within and beyond contemporary African American Churches.

How are these patterns of generational interdependence currently unfolding? This chapter answers this and related questions to build on the answers provided in the pedagogies of faith analyses of Chapter 2. It moves beyond answers provided in the erotics of faith "What Works?" section of Chapter 4. In doing so, it analyzes the resources and patterns of exchange among teenagers, their parents, and their pastors at the everyday core of contemporary Black faith. From an analytic dialogue across the qualitative data platforms of the CoCHY project, four domains emerged, which characterize these intergenerational relationships: Spiritual Dissonance in Intergenerational Faith, Enriching a Living Faith, Intergenerational Dynamics of Hip Hop, and Pathways Toward a Faith Future. Each domain is explored in detail.

Spiritual Dissonance in Intergenerational Faith

Tensions are fundamental to faith. The afterlife dichotomy of Heaven/Hell is consistent with others. Holy/unholy. Saint/sinner. And other either/or's are also central to idealizations of many faiths. I raise them here because of the ways in which dissonance in various forms was expressed within and among generations of faith throughout this project. As discussed in Chapter 4 regarding the erotic socialization of African American teenagers by church-affiliated parents and pastors, the presence of spiritual unrest is not at all new. Some sense of uncertainty is likely as old as questions of faith and the Sacred preceding institutional religion, since they are grounded in a dialogue of dichotomies mentioned earlier. "For African American youth, issues of race and gender identity are especially important, as these may interact to create unique experiences of stress and dissonance."[6] Various forms of dissonance remain in the religiously anchored socialization of African American teens.

Cognitive dissonance is a social psychology innovation that is understood and experienced in the life of the mind.[7] It is an extension of the "double consciousness" concept of W. E. B. Du Bois more than a half century earlier. Du Bois's concept recognized the lived experience of life tensions among African Americans. "One ever feels his twoness—an American, a Negro; two souls, two thoughts, two unreconciled strivings; two warring ideals in one dark body, whose dogged strength alone keeps it from being torn asunder."[8] Recognizing potential limitations of dichotomous boundaries, Cynthia Dillard is among those exploring ways to move beyond double consciousness through a dual self in dialogue "in search of a place called home."[9] Giving meanings to its spiritual expression is one part of this effort.

Spiritual dissonance is the faith-centered expression of this duality. Whether expressed institutionally as the dialectical model of the Black Church, the experience of religious agitation and disconfirmation, challenges of religious recruitment in faith-oriented organization building, or another aspect,[10] spiritual dissonance informs the intergenerational lives of African Americans. It can take a variety of forms, including (a) life stage and testing one's relationships to authority, (b) navigating challenges of the religious marketplace, and (c) mediating through both-and expressions of continuums of faith, where dichotomies are recognized as potentially underdeveloping faith frames and instead where the contributions of these tensions to a living faith can be expressed in healthy ways.

First, perhaps the most consistent expression of this faith-informed identity across generations was giving meaning to the "Prodigal Son" as a life stage. DeShawn, a 17-year-old who regularly attends church services, is an active leader in his church's youth ministry and values himself as a faith-affirming role model among his peers. He stated the following:

> There's a high school senior group where all of us seniors come together. Pastor [Forthright] gives us extra tips on college. What we might experience there, and how not to change our beliefs. A lot of kids don't continue to go to church when they go to college and [don't] keep their relationship with God as strong as they once did. We talk about that.

For DeShawn, as for an increasing share of teens socialized within the church, the transition from high school to college is often associated with change in one's religious beliefs and/or behaviors.[11] He later noted, "I know there's a men's ministry that a lot of our youth go to." Thus, for DeShawn and other teens, gender-specific and age-group-specific gatherings have a value-added impact, reducing the likelihood of (even short-term) non-church affiliation during this life stage transition. Other adults looked back and reflected on how they experienced this life stage. Jermaine F. was a teen father and now as a 25-year-old has an 8-year-old he is raising in a large, nondenominational church:

> I left and came back. I was raised in a Pentecostal Church. Mine was a home type of thing. Your family goes to church and when you get home [you see them] breaking away from the church. I was seeing it as pointing the finger and saw the church as being judgmental toward me.... I think I was about 16 or 17. You know, how your parents tell you, "I did this and that." And they are telling you pretty much not to do it. But you're like, "Just let me go through it!" You understand what they are saying, and you know it ain't right. But you want to experience it for yourself. "We used to kick it [i.e., party, etc.]. And now we don't kick it no more." Now dad, you shutting down my kickin' it just because you quit? I wanted to do it too. So *it made me rebel* even though I knew in my heart I was wrong.

For Janette Lane, a mid-30s mother of a 14-year-old, consistent with the understanding of DeShawn, it was the college experience that fostered her "rebellious stage":

> That's when that happened for me. I did the same thing he did. But mine was when I went away to college. Then I came back and I wanted to go to church when I wanted to go.... When I came home from college I felt that needs to be my choice. For so many years you go to church because that's what Mom and Dad want you to do. And

you are not able to really focus in on what can I get out of this… and *you go through that rebellious stage*. Some of us go through it early. Others late. Some are right on point. The good news is when you become a young adult and begin to experience real life, the first person I called on was Jesus. And I knew exactly what to do and how to do it when I was in need. That's when our own individual relationship with God happens.

DeShawn and Jeannette emphasized the life stage of rebellion. For Jermaine it was a pattern of behavior of life beyond the church setting and socialization, because he "still wanted to go through the same things that 'regular' teenagers go through. Just because I'm in church that shouldn't shut down my experience of growing up, bumping my head and doing whatever."

The "rebellious stage" Jeannette Lane refers to is expressed in and through teenagers' testing boundaries. This is comparable to the prodigal son, though it was less about departure from the church and more about asserting one's presence and desire for independence within it. For example, there was a moment where a teenager's immature disruptions negatively influenced a Sunday's youth ministry, and her youth pastor responded as follows:

> So, I say [to the teenager] after church, "Go get your parents. Either you get them or I'm gonna get them. And you don't want me to go get them." So the parents come into my office. It was three young men, and one young lady. There weren't enough chairs, so the parents were standing. And I started. And this young lady says, "Now, look, Pastor"—"And I said, 'No. You've talked enough during service. I don't really need to hear from you now.'" She starts going off, and I just said, "Get out. Get out of my office. Now. Don't look at your mom. This is my office. Get out." You think I'm scared of them? Get out. When I'm at your house, I'll look at the parents and say "What are you going to do?" I've done that on occasion. If I'm outside the walls of my church, and a child is acting stupid, I will look at the parents and give them a chance to do something. At that moment I wanted her to feel it [i.e., authority of youth church leadership]. So, her parents stayed there and I proceeded to handle things. But *that affirmation comes from my senior pastor*. So, if a parent says, "Well, forget him. I'm going to see Pastor [Collins]!" then they'll run into a wall there. Because he's gonna say, "Well, you have to go back to Pastor [Hampton]." So, affirmation becomes a very important issue when dealing with youth from the position of authority.

Pastor Hampton felt comfortable responding to the youth's rebellious disruption of service—in fellowship with other teens as well—extending from the affirmation of his senior pastor. His comfort level then allows the youths—and their parents—to come to an understanding. Behavioral expectations mediate their life stage dissonance and affirm their character development as maturing persons of faith. Role clarity is mixed with a clear reaffirmation of behavioral expectations of the teens and the consequences for violating them. Pastor Hampton challenges the teen's use of a nonverbal appeal to her mother to distract from the life lesson he seeks to share with all involved. His goal was having all the youths, primarily, and the parents as well, experience emotional and spiritual consequences of her actions within the church walls, including contrasting his office in comparison to the home of the young girl's parents. By doing so, he reinforced a spatial association of church setting with moral and behavioral authority. He increased youth investment in church-appropriate behavior within and beyond the church walls. Whether responding to being in places youth should not be during church services, eating in places where food is not allowed, or, after service, addressing disruptions of youth-centered services, youth leadership is nurturing sanctuary by engaging their intergenerational authority.

In addition to the Prodigal Son life stage and related tensions of religious authority, a second means of spiritual dissonance across generations moved from the micro, individual level to more macro, institutional questions of competition, the health of churches, and more broadly, of organized religion. Pastors linked the Prodigal Son process beyond the life stage of youth maturation. They questioned how the choices people make to leave the church, whatever their age, are impacting the church as an institution. While "religious marketplace" was never used, "competition" was used, and individual-level spiritual dissonance was seen as impacting the church as a whole. Pastor John Washington said the following:

> I tend to be real about the church as it is in America. America is a competitive country. Therefore the nature is for us to be competitive. So our young people are faced with competitions every day. So if you are talking about decline, let's be honest. Churches are a business. We are trying to turn the bad into the good. And the bad is trying to get the good to be like them. We are trying to teach young people, even the older people, a different way of life than what they are doing. And if we are to succeed, they have got to be constantly bombarded. They are confronted every day with issues and ideas about what is going to work. If I have an hour and a half with you on Sunday morning, there is another two and a half hours [elsewhere] that is competing. So it is about getting them in and keeping them in. It's competitive.

This recognition of nested contexts and how they are interdependent with one another recognized church declines as one of those potential outcomes because, in this pastor's view, churches can decline and close their doors permanently. The "business model" is then understood within a dichotomy of behavior change. Here, success is a product of uneven competition because on time alone, there is no comparison between on-site time and the rest of a person's life beyond church settings. And if the battle is to be joined, multiple domains of its ubiquity must be engaged on a regular basis. To do so, one pastor engaged his own personal competition and intergenerational life experience of the personal-as-political:

> Is the church really in touch with now? I came out of a single-parent home. My father left me. The only thing I remember of him, and I'm [in my 60s now]. The most vivid image I've got of him is at two years old standing at the back of the house watching him walk up the street and never seeing him again for [over 30] years. Then, my *step*father was an alcoholic. He always used to beat my mother and throw her up against the wall. So my thing is, what do I have to compete with? All I knew was men walking out. Okay, now if you are going to teach me that there is a better life, and show me some evidence of what this better life is all about—rather than me trying to find it through blind faith—then you ask yourself the question, is the church really in touch with everyone who is there?

He linked current concerns regarding family breakdown to his own experiences of "broken family," abandonment as a survivor of abuse within his childhood, and the meanings of men. When this pastor focus group finding of church as "business" and "competition" was presented at the follow-up sessions, parents and pastors became annoyed, perhaps even offended. In the spiritual dissonance of churches, for Pastor Franklin and others, the use of the business or market model is part of the problem and is leading churches to their decline:

> That's the difference between being a businessman and a shepherd. As a businessman, I don't mind at all [i.e., five people leaving, if seven persons "replace" them in the pews]. But if I'm a shepherd, then I'll leave the 99 and go and get the one. And so, the question is, *what are we doing to keep the one from leaving?* Too often we blame the sheep for leaving. Because if I was a teen, and if I was involved in certain places, I'd leave, too. And I know I'm not supposed to say that. But since we're in a room of mature ministers, I can say that. And so we need to ask ourselves why is the one leaving. And you know what the easy answer is? Not because they just want to go out partying and drinking and having sex. It's not always because they don't have a mother or father, or good home training—that's not it, either. It's not always because they hate God, they hate the church, and they're just disrespectful. That's not always the reason, I think. Sometimes your questions just don't get answered.

As the "church as business" finding was discussed in the follow-up session, an annoyed look was shared between two parents in the room. In addition to the nonverbal testament, at a whisper level they stated under their breath the hope that it was not their pastor who would say such a thing. Then Pastor Franklin's likening his duty to that of a shepherd was strongly supported by the other parents and pastors in attendance, not even as metaphor but as a statement of fact.

To Pastor Franklin and the desired sentiment shared by others, the market model was counter to the shepherd model and vested faith in an arithmetic of alienation and an economic illusion. Later, Pastor Franklin reflected on the symbolisms and substance of success and the role of churches in these definitions:

> *Sometimes you look at success and salvation as two separate entities.* So if I have to become one or the other, and that's the mentality that's been driven in my head, then [speaking as a lapsed teenager], "I at least want to experience some success before I come back to salvation".... It looks like, that somehow outside of your realm of faith and family, you have to find this "thing" that you're looking for. And once you've gotten it, then you come back. Every individual wants to be successful. It's in our DNA. But presenting it like they need to go have fun and then come back to church is a mistake. A gang leader wants to be successful. So he exerts his authority over other people. So how do we get our youth to understand and to maintain their moral values? By teaching them "You can maintain your moral values, your character within the confines of the Christian faith, AND you can still be successful. You're gonna get your degree. You're gonna marry your fly honey. And you're gonna have some fly kids. AND you're gonna love God." There ain't a young person alive that won't grab hold of that.

Following from this perhaps a question could be raised regarding the accuracy rather than the efficacy of such a dissonant call and response among church-affiliated adults or where a both/and dialogue between these models may exist. Clearly, business elements inform how churches engage desired affiliates, just as all businesses strive to appeal to consumers. In the contemporary pattern of agglomerative economics, with larger corporations, be they in media or food, technology or automobiles, there are fewer and fewer, larger and larger entities as the landscapes of market competition across industries get redefined. And, though large churches are not new, the birth of the phrase "megachurch" and the uncertainties of storefronts and smaller churches in many urban settings suggest that the business comment, at least as metaphor, may be more accurate than some were comfortable acknowledging.

In addition to the rebellious stage, Prodigal Son symbolisms, disruptions in church settings to challenge religious authority, or tensions related to the use of the business model, perhaps the most intimate form of spiritual dissonance that emerged was inconsistencies between the professed religious values and church behaviors, and parental modeling of a living faith beyond religious settings. Faith is understood and biblically defined as "the substance of things hoped for, the evidence of things not seen,"[12] and the modeling of this substance and evidence by parents is an important aspect of intergenerational exchange. Donyelle, a 23-year-old who recently aged out of his teens, observed the following:

> From a young son's perspective, when we look at our parents' lifestyles, they don't reflect what they're sending kids to church to get. Our belief system, our faith is shaken. Pastor talks about move out on faith, right? But our parents cry about bills every week. Live paycheck to paycheck. Their lifestyle does not reflect the faith they are trying to instill in us. Then we're supposed to be religious or spiritual? And they talk about having a spiritual relationship with God. But our parents, supposedly bringing us up in the ways of The Bible, don't exemplify the relationship they're trying to instill in us…. So, parents try to be honest. [But] they're so scared because you don't want [kids] to get involved in certain things. (A woman says, "Uh-hm.") And *when you open up honest dialogue, it puts perspective to religion youth get on Sunday morning.* And they sayin', "Oh, so now I know why it's wrong." As opposed to some mythical creature that [a woman giggles] you're telling 'em, whose name is God. Whose son they never seen, died on a cross. And you're sayin' that, "As long as you follow him, everything will be alright." Well, the same God you say you serve. Things don't seem to be alright for you. [A lot of agreement from others, "Uh-hum," and "There ya go!"]. So you want me to follow *that* God?! That's my thing.

Donyelle presents multiple tensions, or a spiritual dissonance. One is simply the parents' willingness to risk honesty. How much of what kinds of honesty are too much or the wrong kind? This is the question parents constantly ask and answer. The words-actions relationship of parentally invested faith is profoundly important, as meanings from it are being inferred by the child. There is dissonance within the parent and consequent dissonance in the forms of raised questions on the part of the child. Thus, Donyelle suggests that parents are the socializers of an intergenerational spiritual dissonance informing youths' faith development.

Donyelle went on to suggest that, as a result, the probability of other youth risk behaviors may in fact increase, while he also critiques what he understands as an incomplete or bounded effect of Sunday morning religious service. This sentiment was echoed by many pastors and parents, including Alicia Everton, a mother and lay church youth leader:

> Youth have a bunch of phonies raising them. They [i.e., "phony" parents] come to church. They shout. Speak in tongues. What have you. Then they go home. And not only are they cussing around the children, and doing all kinds of inconsistent things, but when they think the kids are sleeping at night, they're sneaking around with Tom, Dick and Harry. And the children know what the real deal is. So they start to develop this *hate* for the very person who is their mother, or their father. And then they look around and think we're supposed to be the true Christians. *So they start to look around and say, well who are the true people?* Because if mama is not true, or father is not true, sometimes they can't figure out who else really is true. So then they begin to judge everyone in the church as phonies.

Consistent with Donyelle, Everton recognizes and respects youth's ability to observe and give meaning to espoused values, behavior within and beyond church walls, and recognize the contradictions within those parental patterns. She also calls attention to the questions said contradictions raised within the youth and the "major blow" to youth that results from these dynamics. Donyelle goes on to suggest probable outcomes of this religious and spiritual dissonance: "Then we go out and we get pregnant, or join gangs because we are trying to gather the relationship that we're not getting from the experience that we're supposed to be getting on Sunday morning." Everton also addressed potential consequences among the young people in ways that were consistent with Donyelle:

> The children were resentful and so bitter. And I believe it's because they have a bunch of phonies that are raising them…. So when the child comes to church and you're working with them in one area, *they get angry at the parents* because they say, "That's not what you said at home. You said it was ok for me to do this. But you get here in front of the pastor and you're a whole different person." [Lots of agreement from the others.] So, *is the parent really happy in their faith? What do they really believe?*

Parental spiritual dissonance likely manifests as bitterness, anger, and resentment in the child. And within this generation of heightened awareness and the heightened willingness of youth to voice their experiences, they may become brazen enough to call it out in faith settings. Everton also raises the implication of what is perhaps a "faith feedback loop" in which this reaction of youth, instead of being freeing to those of either generation, magnifies dissonance within both parent and child, in turn leading the parent to be still more unhappy in her or his faith. Here, happiness in one's faith is a parental resource useful in moving the child from (mere) ritual adherence to the "practical living" of faith engagement and the joy that results.

Consistent with Chapter 4, a both-and dialogue approach might again be more accurate. This dialogue can be especially helpful similar to other mediators of spiritual dissonance in its relationship with and beyond faith-informed erotic and sexual socializations. Yes, contradictions of church-state separation and lavish lifestyle hypocrisies of many faith leaders harken to corporate CEOs making 400 and more times what the average worker of their corporation makes. And yes, churches do engage the dialectic model in their priestly and prophetic functions,[13] assisting in the giving of greater meanings to human life and beneficially exploring the transcendent elements of the Holy, the Sacred, and other "big" ideas. As others have suggested, as leaders of a business with a spiritual conscience, "Dealing with people in terms of shepherding [them]… looks toward healing in a holistic sense… we who have been called to be brothers of and joint heirs with Christ are to be undershepherds one to another. We are members one of another in the body of Christ."[14] Here, the metaphor of shepherd has both symbolic and material utilities, especially in the African American church tradition regarding eras and societal transformations in both recent and distant history. Yes, true to the sentiments of pastors, parents, and young adults in dialogue with one another across different data events, perhaps the African American church is both a business and a space for a shepherd's home, gathering and guiding others to nurture sanctuary in that same home of their own: yes, valuing the departing few and the constant many; yes, both-and.

While reflecting on the building of safe relationships among African American teenagers, church-involved and otherwise, Pastor Baltesante suggested that safe relationships are those grounded in sustaining one's faith: "The Bible is a book of damnation and a book of comfort. [And] with it, readers have an understanding of compassion…. Everybody who leaves the church don't leave God." Authority and rebellion, damnation and comfort, businessman and shepherd, leaving the church without leaving God—These are among the many expressions of spiritual dissonance, a fruitful dialogue among differences rather than a win-lose tension of any kind. It is these dialogues of faith taking place in and beyond contemporary African American churches across generations, dialogues toward healing pathways between generations.

Enriching a Living Faith

Among the more valued themes that emerged from intergenerational exchanges was the often complicated process of enriching a living faith. Building on previous comments of 23-year-old Donyelle, young people process their faith in many ways, including how they observe their parents and other adults engaging their faith. What many value is creating and sustaining an environment in which young people can acknowledge what they do and do not know in an environment of shared respect. From my in-depth interviews of teenagers, two different expressions of this were demonstrated by Aaron (17 years old) and Marquis (16 years old):

TPS: Do you feel like you know what you want to know about God and your faith?

Aaron: Right now I don't have a clear direction of what I need to learn. Whatever I can learn is fine with me.

TPS: Do you think church is inspiring?

Marquis: I think so, a lot. Pastor [Washington] always teaches us life lessons. It's kinda weird, cuz whatever you're going through he speaks on, just at the right time.

TPS: Are you learning what you want to know about God and religion at your church?

Marquis: Yeah, that's basically what I was saying.

Aaron has been reared in an environment of faith support strong enough to allow him to acknowledge to me, a near stranger, what he did not know and what he was in the process of growing to know better. He acknowledged that his place in the development of his faith is not where he wants it to be. And, importantly, he presented this observation without judgment or any suggestion of being irresponsible or flawed and showed that he is open to learning a variety of things that can nurture his faith walk. Marquis also did so, stating in a very matter-of-fact fashion the value he places on the accessibility of both his youth and senior pastors. He acknowledged an appreciation for gaining different kinds of support and growth in his faith from both of them. This was partnered with high-quality lines of communication for Marquis to feel a sense of serendipitous timing of the youth ministry sermons. For both Aaron and Marquis, consistent with other religiously engaged youths of the CoCHY project, salient, accessible life lessons consistently emerged as clear and valued youth ministry content and as a means of their enrichment of a living faith.

What emerged from respondents was that faith tension, or spiritual dissonance within the child, may take many developmental forms and is informed
by their intergenerational engagements. Following from Chapter 4, talks of
sexual maturation among generations are their own paradox of faith. Cynthia
Ellis, a single mother, recounted that the open lines of communication she
nurtures with her teenage son has limits and is also informed by faith. The
quality of communication between parent and child led to her son's willingness to state these limits directly to her:

> He said, "Mom, I will talk to you about anything. But sex, I won't." But having pastor
> talk with him [is valuable]. Pastor knows his boundaries, and still is asking questions
> anyway…. I think just saying, "Even if you have things you don't feel comfortable
> sharing with me, you can always go to your pastor, and I'm ok with that," helps the
> pastor, and helps build *a continuity of relationship with everybody involved*.

For Ellis's son, his intergenerational communication is predictably marked by
gender and role boundaries that intersect. Though her son is unwilling to talk
about sex with her, their family communication with their pastor allows her
son to seek him out as a resource for dealing with sexuality that is not just about
the more typically religious and moral realm of sexuality. Dating, intimacy, and
safer sexual expression were all implied as options for dialogue between the
pastor and the young man. The sex discussions were beyond abstinence alone,
demonstrating a beneficial balance between the Sacred and the secular in
these intergenerational exchanges. And because of the shared respect between
herself and her pastor, Ellis appreciated the pastoral access in the rearing of her
son. This extends from a gendered communication "division of labor" in his
faith-informed decision making with which all three parties are comfortable.

In addition to gendered and role divisions of faith labor, intergenerational
faith exchanges are also demonstrated in the balance between the private
and public faith of church-affiliated teenagers. As shown in Damon's experiences here, this includes private prayer, perhaps the most intimate of faith
expressions:

TPS:	Let's talk about how you live your faith outside of the church. Do you pray?
D:	Yes, sir.
TPS:	What are some of the things you pray about?
D:	Just anything, really. But the one thing that Pastor [Caldwell] says is that, "Everybody makes it seem like praying is such a big ordeal." All praying is, you speak, God listens. God speaks, you listen. You just basically rap to him. Like, "God, I'm going through this, and I need help with this…." You

> don't need to get down on your knees. Although it's good to show respect. But I mean, if you're in your car, just start praying right there.
>
> TPS: Have you ever had a prayer answered? And, if so, what's a moment either in your recent past or something that's really vivid that speaks to you, as an answer to prayer?
>
> D: Yes, I have. It seems like me and God haven't been on the same page with me and [basketball]. I thought where I wanted to go was where God wanted me to go. But instead he wanted me at [Eastern] State.

For 17-year-old Damon, who went on to be a Division I college athlete, prayer is a regular part of his enriching faith. Regarding time, place, and structure, the pastor had made it clear that flexibility has value and that tradition need not be a reason to prevent him or anyone from praying. Even in the midst of a life outcome that was inconsistent with what he would have desired, true to his spiritual dissonance, there was never any hint of that life circumstance leading him to doubt his faith. Instead, the opposite occurred, as Damon was led by prayer to a new appreciation of his next steps for college and the growth of his athletic career. Articulating at 17 a relationship to faith-as-prayer and an unexpected life outcome beyond what many adults could articulate, Damon summed up his prayerful experience:

> And I kept praying, "Show me where You want me to go." And my mom and dad said they started feeling like this is where God wanted me to be. I was frustrated for a while since it wasn't what I wanted at first. But in the end, what you might want isn't always what God wants for you.

In slight contrast, Damon respected and appreciated the church decision to fast as a fellowship toward the help of paying for a new building and church move. His spiritual dissonance was one of sacrifice between what was reasonable for him as an athlete and what was workable for him in fellowship and faith being at odds. Yet his faith was enriched with, and through, this tension:

> TPS: Are there other religious practices that you participate in besides reading the Bible, prayer, and attending services?
>
> D: I try to fast, but I have a little difficulty with that, since I need to get nutrition in my body as an athlete. But fasting's important.
>
> TPS: When have you made efforts to fast?
>
> D: We've fasted as a church before. We purchased new land recently and the whole church tried to fast so we could get the money as a down payment for the land. We're like in phase 2 or phase 3 now. But I'll be in college by the time all of that happens.

Damon struggled to participate in the fast. Trying to fast, the meanings of fasting and fundraising, the phase they are actually in—These are quality details for him to be aware of, to appreciate, and to view this collective effort as part of his religious practice beyond the Bible, church setting, and private prayer. Damon participated knowing that the intended outcome is something he would not be in the city to see. Thus, he was engaging in a faith action for a promise others will share in more directly than he will. These are his actions of enriched faith informed by intergenerational exchange.

Black Faith's Beat Box: Intergenerational Dynamics of Hip Hop

Likely, more often than need be, Christianity and Hip Hop are often framed in terms of a tension existing between them, where opposition narratives soon follow. Yet, for a growing number of scholars, "the ultimate goal is to develop a theoretically sound pedagogy that meets youth in Hip Hop culture just as Paul tried to encounter the Corinthians in cultural forms familiar to them, mov[ing] beyond the prevailing comfort zone of [many] Black churches."[15] What follows are examples that emerged from among the intergenerational exchanges of the reciprocity between Hip Hop and contemporary Black faith.

First, sometimes Hip Hop is as simple as the appearance politics which clothes provide. When 16-year-old Dwayne responded to being asked what he likes about his church, he identified being able to wear comfortable Hip Hop attire to church without condescension or judgment from members:

> I really like that I can be myself. I can wear this to church [i.e., casual, Hip Hop "gear" he wore to our interview] and it's no big deal at all. There's no looking down on you. Maybe there are people looking down on me and I don't know it. But I talk to the head pastor and *he talks to me just like he talks to anybody else*. My youth pastor is like my spiritual father. If I put on a suit, they'll say I look nice, and if I'm wearing what I have on now, they'll say, "I like your shoes." You don't have to dress up to be there because it's not about that. It's about praising the Lord.

One among the things Dwayne likes best is not having to wear one's "Sunday-go-to-meetin'" clothing as an expectation for worship at his small, nondenominational church. His measure of not being looked down on includes the consistent line of communication between him and his senior pastor, regardless of how he is dressed. Points of praise are shared with him regardless of whether he wears a suit or baggy jeans, a shirt manufactured under the name of a Hip Hop clothing mogul, and athletic footwear. A "come as you are" willingness by most, if not all, of the church enriches his living faith and allows him to more comfortably value the "spiritual father" label for his youth pastor. While he acknowledges that others within the congregation may have judgments they do not share, being okay in the pastor's eyes allows the tempo and focus of the congregation to be welcoming and respectful to his Hip Hop sensibilities.

As noted in the "Erotic Footsteps" discussion of Chapter 4, in a larger and more traditional Baptist Church, Stanley Garson had an experience quite different from Dwayne's. Garson was scolded by an elder for entering the church wearing a do-rag:

> A lot of the Hip Hop performers. They're not young. They're 37, 38 years old now. Yunno what I'm sayin'? They impacting my youth *and* the youth today. People say that's the age gap. Naw. Not really.... A lot of times, we say something is wrong because we're not familiar with it. For example, I wore a do-rag for my hair to church. A person condemned me for that. I asked them, and they couldn't tell me why. She just told me I was wrong. Why was I wrong? I'm not in a gang. I'm not holding up a bank. I got a job. I'm an elder at a church. What am I doing wrong?.... Yeah, stereotype.

For Garson, the age gap of Hip Hop is challenged by the very age of many of the popular performers in it and the fact that many among the most popular are now intergenerational in their influence, having influenced him when he was in his adolescence and now influencing his young teen children as a father in his late 30s. For him, the do-rag response of the elder was a product of limited familiarity, and that familiarity was informed by a stereotype of a criminal or gang member. He infers that the absence of reasoning makes it up to the elder to adapt and be inclusive within the church setting rather than viewing it as an act against appropriate faith. Yet later, Garson considers an intergenerational Hip Hop tension of his own. He states outright that he does not approve of sagging pants in church, primarily for historical and erotic reasons (i.e., a history grounded in chattel slavery and male-male sexual exchange in prisons). Thus, within the intergenerational expressions of contemporary Black faith, the "line drawing process" regarding the personal politics of appearance in Hip Hop are very much in flux.

The second major emergence of Hip Hop across generations in contemporary Black Churches is its presence as a style of service delivery, narrative presentation, and other respectful inclusions within full and youth church services. Consistent with the *What Works?* section of Chapter 4, at five of the seven churches at which parents-of-teens focus groups were held, some mention of Hip Hop's respectful inclusion was made. These include the following remarks:

Mother:	That's the name. It's [Feast of Faith] Youth Church. Just like we have our senior church, our youth also have a totally separate church with their own trustees, deacons, and a little more Hip Hop in their service. Pastor [Martin] is their pastor.
Father:	We do "New Generation," our "youth church" for 7th to 12th-grade kids. It's the same as the adult-side service, except it's done on a youth culture level [including] the flavor of the music style, which would relate to the youth culture.
Youth pastor:	We have parties [for youth] at our church. The thing that cracks me up the most is that a lot of the kids stand around and they don't know what to do. They're confused. I got some of the hottest Christian Hip Hop playing. It's better than most of the stuff on the radio. But *they don't know what to do* because they've been conditioned. "I'm in church. I'm not supposed to be able to dance, etc...." And I walk in and say, "You're confused, aren't you? You don't know what to do. Part of that's my fault, as a leader in the church, and *it's the church's fault. We have not told you.*"
Youth pastor:	It's been either-or, and not the "both-and." So they're confused. Some of my youth are getting it, and are realizing they don't have to live in a bottle.

"Hip Hop… has the potential to exercise a prophetic gifting—speaking directly to society just what needs to be said. There is indeed room for that in the church [and] is beginning to show influence in the faith."[16] From the "flavor" of music and recognition of age-appropriate engagement of a new generation, to the direct merging of traditional structure, leadership, and format in the feasting of a Hip Hop faith, to the uncertainties experienced by youth when bridging what they experience as a dissonance of culture and context, that potential Charles Howard and others[17] write of is unfolding right now in Black Churches. Perhaps most vitally, Youth Pastor Hampton acknowledges that churches have directly caused confusion among youth that could have been avoided when they invite, in fact, encourage, a merging of the secularly anchored Hip Hop with youth's faith at a church-hosted party. The formal socializing—or perhaps even the presence and value of the dissonance itself within it—emerged as one part of the next step to enhance the use-value and contributions of an effective church. Another youth pastor's bottle reference uses the symbolic extreme of an entrapment in a small, enclosed space. Yet the ability to see outside one's restrictive boundaries remains. Both this youth pastor and Pastor Hampton imply that many within churches of multiple generations possess a longing for greater access to the world beyond the boundary, a world of "prophetic gifting" or a beneficial cohesion of Sacred and secular reciprocity that is at once behavioral, processual, and stylistic. Across generations, living their faith beyond the bottle continues to progress.

Beyond do-rags, Hip Hop clothing in general, and the personal politics of appearance regarding what is worn in church, nearly all of the youth and several adults expressed an appreciation for bringing their faith and Hip Hop together in and beyond the styles of church service. At 17, Edgar enjoys engaging the reciprocity between Hip Hop and his faith:

> TPS: Besides reading the Word and prayer, what other religious practices do you do?
> E: I listen to a lot of Christian rap. There's a guy named [Delmar] at my church, he has a pretty good group and is trying to get his label out. The name is [Gangs of Grace]. They just take the beats from non-Christian artists and use them for the Lord. It's like good music. I like the beat, and now I can at least listen to the words.

Implicit in Edgar's appreciation of how he experiences this artistry is an unspoken comparison of what he does not have to do. Because of his access to Christian rap, he does not have to reject significant words used or foul language. He does not have to surrender good music that is true to his preferred style. He does not have to ignore the entrepreneurial creativity of a peer who is seeking to extend a market that is within and beyond his own church. He can celebrate the sampling musical process that was a part of the very foundations of Hip Hop itself, while being as true to his faith as any spiritual or hymn he might also listen to.

Finally, beyond clothing, worship style, and music, other symbolisms matter and inform each of these previously noted elements of Hip Hop. While likely being both resonant and profoundly incomplete, symbols can be useful, even and especially when they engage an intentional dissonance. The dissonance rests in the choice of artists to use language that may run counter to the very theme of the song itself. They might also engage in sentiments that have nothing to do with the apparent faith that is being represented. Thus a cross is worn and becomes a Hip Hop trope bridging the Sacred with otherwise secular jewelry. Unclear is the degree to which this is being done primarily, or even partially, as an affirmation in an abiding faith engagement and consciousness. Oftentimes, when one is still very much in the primary age group of a Hip Hop cultural resonance, such a symbol may take some (presumably, temporary) distance from religious engagement(s) and/or negative outcome of diverting from faith adherence so that youth can value the cross differently in their broader utilities of faith. One 23-year-old noted the following:

> Regarding symbolism, I would definitely agree. I think that although here it [i.e., thoughtfully engaged symbolism of visible, Hip Hop stars] would be a great asset only because church youth could probably relate a little bit better.... For teens, the fad is to wear a cross. Because R. Kelly has a cross on a chain [Group agrees, "Mhmm, Right! Right."]. Or Kanye West's song: *Jesus Walks*. So as long as you can say *Jesus Walks*, it is okay to curse in the same sentence because he curses in that song. So, as long as you have the basic tenets of faith and you remember a little about what your grandmother told you when she made you go to church when you was real little, then you are religious. [A long, drawn out, "Uhhhhhh-hmmmm...," from a woman]. So, I think it is symbolism.... [Others: "Yeah!" and "Teach, child," and "That's right" and other chimes of agreement from other group members]. So, because youth don't know who they are yet, it's trying to get them to identify with something they themselves can't even use yet.... [Youth] believe, "If I follow certain practices and I don't mess up too bad, I'm gonna go to Heaven." And that's as far as a 13 year old can go.

Even when the Hip Hop example is itself one of a dissonant faith, youth are engaged in ways that allow the faith lesson to not be entirely soiled—perhaps enhanced—and that because of this process of engaged faith contradiction, Hip Hop stars are a valuable asset coming from the mouth and persona of a valued public figure. This young man recognizes that developmental stages matter, and simplistic clarities of youth, even when grounded in superficial symbolisms, are not all bad. They may in fact be the foundation many adults have access to in being religious, but to be spiritual is further along the developmental continuum of growth and renewal in one's faith walk. This engaged faith walk is where the dictates themselves resonate in ways that demonstrate a strength of belief—in one's actions outside of church walls—that is, in the sense of who one is when no one is watching and that even when religion is being characterized as a historical entity grounded in childhood memories of one's grandmother, via Hip Hop or otherwise, being "truly" religious demands much more beyond superficial, symbolic engagements and implicit ritual.

Additional Pathways Toward a Faith Future

What are the nurturing pathways of intergenerational faith exchange? Chapter 2 provided part of the answer in its analyses of the pedagogies of contemporary African American faith and the priorities of youth-faith-health resources among participating churches of the CoCHY SLI project (see Chapter 2, Table 1). In its analyses of erotic socialization of contemporary faith, Chapter 4 explored strategies of action parents and pastors valued most, including the events, programs, and other capacity-building resources most beneficial to church-affiliated Black teenagers. In this chapter, the previous sections on faith, spiritual dissonance, and Hip Hop provided additional examples of the structures and strategies that contribute to the faith dialogue among generations. What follows are five additional pathways that emerged as making beneficial contributions to nurturing sanctuary in contemporary African American faith. Perhaps the seminal foundation regarding these pathways is one of perspective in the relationships between doctrine and shared respect, between rule and relationship(s). Similar to the sentiment that consistently emerged from the pastor focus groups and a majority of the parent focus groups, Carlyle Hampton, a youth pastor at Cathedral Redeemer Church, suggested that for these pathways of faith to flourish, a healthy balance must characterize youth inreach, outreach, and programming:

> That's the balance you're hearing. My sister [in faith] here has spoken so much about relationship and being available. *Rule without relationship brings rebellion.* When you have rules, you also have to have relationship. That's the balance. So I know that a lot of what you're hearing now is rules. But that's very important. Because if you don't have an environment that is set, if youth don't have structure, then that environment will be chaotic.... That's why kids get in gangs. Structure. In the gang, you late for a meeting, you get a beat-down. You don't bring it [i.e., one's share of expected sales], you get a beat-down. Or you don't do it, and you gotta do push-ups. And y'know what? Kids love that. They love structure. So, *within the rules or structure, if you couple that with relationship,* then you will have a well-balanced family and a well-balanced youth ministry. That's how God has to be presented. Because a lot of times there are a bunch of rules presented when it comes to faith, but not relationship. So you rebel.

Like other aspects of intergenerational dissonance explored earlier, rebellion may actually be beneficial in the life stage maturation of faith among persons moving from adolescence to young adulthood. Pastor Hampton's larger point is the need for churches and a "well-balanced youth ministry" within them to have those rules and both material and symbolic structures to be reinforced through the building of quality relationships with the teens: including the Hip Hop parties at church described earlier, including the assertion of caring authority, and including words of praise for the clothing youths are wearing, whether Hip Hop gear or a freshly pressed suit. Rules *with* a caring relationship allow other pathways to flourish.

Second, in the aforementioned quote, Pastor Hampton emphasized being available. Perhaps this is a given, but because of the diversity of leadership styles that inform many churches, there is worth in emphasizing the fundamental of access. As 16-year-old Durrell stated when I asked if he feels church is a good place for help, problems, or family concerns, "Yeah. And if it's not, *I can schedule a meeting with my youth pastor* and talk about that kind of stuff." Whatever help he needs, he can gain different kinds of support and growth in his faith. One mother, Antonia Keller, suggested the following:

> It's very important for the youth to feel like they have an open-door policy as it pertains to the pastor. They can talk to him/her in confidence, and feel like they'll be… treated like a human being, instead of just a kid who doesn't know anything. Their feelings, concerns, opinions matter; and they'll be able to get advice, or at least a listening ear without judgment."

It is important for youth to have their confidentiality protected, as they protect the confidentiality of others, share in respect across generations as persons who "know something," and not feel that what they say will be negatively judged in condescension:

> That's something I really appreciate about our leader. That the message is always going out from our senior pastor. In the midst of an error or mistake, he says to the youth *"Don't you run away. If you gotta run, run to my house."* When you build that type of relationship with the young people, they trust him enough to speak with him.

The pathway, the recognition of its openness, and the character of information sharing within it, were among the most vital intergenerational pathways of faith among parents and pastors. When that pathway exists, as stated earlier, parents like Laurie Johnson appreciate it.

Third, consistent with the special events and programs the SLI projects analyzed in Chapter 2 and the regular youth programs that parents and pastors discussed in Chapter 4, the structure of youth fellowship is important to this relationship building. Among the structural elements of greatest importance are the size and scale of gatherings in which intergenerational exchanges take place. Anthony, a 15-year-old who attends a very large church, noted that there are "lots of small groups in the church, not just one time with everyone. I like that, even though the clique type stuff still happens. But, it's not too bad. People call me a 'nerd' sometimes and other stuff. But I have good friends here, and the youth pastor's nice." Consistent with Anthony's experiences, a youth pastor emphasized his use of small groups:

> On Wednesdays we do discipleship, which to me is key. That's the opportunity we have to really teach and train in the faith.... On Sundays I have over 200 kids, so I can't disciple them on Sundays. *In discipleship we can break into small groups.* And that's where they get an opportunity not only to hear, but also to speak out and ask questions, and get answers for their questions. But we do sermonize, preach, and give the Word. Discipleship gives you these opportunities, and present[s] the Word of God in a way they can walk it out and live it out.... Those small-group ministries are an opportunity for more of a personal touch.

While Anthony values the benefits of joining with small numbers of persons from his youth's experience, the pastor grounded Anthony's experiences in research findings about motives for leaving church. This small group approach allows for a peer-to-peer "co-counseling" model of *engaging with* scripture over and above being talked to and encourages a much more interactive faith curriculum and a more detailed examinations of a living faith. This structural intimacy gave rise to a fourth expression of intergenerational faith exchange: diversity and depth. Similar to the former teen mother who presented in the *Precious Patience* SLI project (see Chapter 2), Brianna, a 16-year-old in a small Baptist church, shared the following:

> Sometimes when it's just us kids, the youth leaders bring in some kinda, I don't know. Like, wayward folks, and that type. They are believers and all. But their life got complicated in some kinda ways. What the streets do to people sometimes. Like, we had some former crackheads and alcoholics and stuff come in and talk to us. They all come back to the Word. But sometimes they go way out to get back to faith.

The "way out" Brianna spoke of is where more complicated life experiences can be effectively explored in a small group structure. Leona Franklin, a youth leader and mother of two teenagers, observed the following:

> Sometimes in youth Bible study, I'll bring in people. Prostitutes. Girls who have been on crack. Women who have been beaten down by their husbands. Our children listen to them. And when they leave church, the children have a better understanding of how faith can matter in very different lives.

Bringing secular outsiders in and valuing their strengths and resilience, their expertise in "fallen" faith, and their return to a knowing faith life enhances youth's understanding of risks and relevance faith. Teenagers like Brianna can value their own faith more by seeing it through the life experiences of others.

The "inreach" of bringing secular outsiders into youth services is a valuable means of intergenerational faith socialization of contemporary African American churches. *Outreach* is a fifth pathway. The primary venue and most enthusiastically presented example for outreach of adults to teenagers is in their school settings. Not surprisingly, while parents and lay youth leaders enthusiastically recounted examples of school interactions, few youth expressed appreciation for this means of intergenerational faith. Victoria Smith, a mother and lay youth church leader, recounted the following:

> We not only work within the church, but we also go out on their territory in the schools. And the teachers know us. We meet their school friends, etc. Whenever they have a part that's going on in school, normally the youth department supports youth in any of their activities. We give a report to our bishop and elders' class on Sunday mornings and then we'll do follow-ups and have meetings with the parents, and find out what other areas they might need help with. *The principals love to see that the church is that concerned about the young people.* That they would come out into another part of their life and be involved. When we go, we talk to their teachers. We introduce ourselves, leave our church card, and tell them we are their youth pastors. And if they can't contact the parents, we're the ones they can contact and we'll come in concerning any issues. We drop anything and go be there. Being a youth pastor from [Grace Granted Community Church], they call me "warden" because I'm the one that will drop in unexpectedly. You just never know when I'm coming to your school. I try to visit at least four schools during the week. They allow me to go in the classrooms, and observe. "You don't want to mess with her, cuz you never know when she's coming." The teachers really do love it. I get a lot of calls—if there's an issue, or if a youth comes in very withdrawn, *they'll call us* and ask what's going on with them. Normally, I'll ask what time is their lunch break, and if I can't go, I'll call one of the assistants to be there for lunch. It's a lot of work, but it's really been successful. *Now the youth are actually calling me.* So I'm able to minister to them, and if they can't get a hold of me, they have eight other numbers they can call before they make a decision.

These are ways the "department" term and metaphor are exemplified: relationships at multiple schools, across multiple levels of leadership (principals, teachers, counseling staff), with multiple visits each week. And, even as "the warden" label and prison metaphor are caringly used by the youths themselves, the rule and relationship balance has been established and maintained, such that youths call her or one of her eight (!) assistants before making a critical decision. This outreach provides an engaging exploration of church-state separation (or, perhaps more accurately, collaboration). Similar to the SLI projects, these lines of information sharing enrich a longstanding historically grounded reciprocity between the Sacred and the secular. They are demonstrating a living faith for youth through the relationship between academic performance and church participation. They recognize that this relationship can be engaged in the school setting, as well.

Paradoxically, in the aftermath of the focus group follow-up meeting in which this and a similar statement was made, multiple parents also attending were teachers or other school staff members. They too were church-affiliated parents raising their children in church settings. And they expressed concern about these initiatives. One went so far as to formally ask persons from a church to remain off school premises. In contrast, in parent focus groups at two other churches, parents expressed their concerns regarding teachers or other school staff who had responded negatively to their children's choice to bring a Bible to school, after having been asked not to do so. So, this outreach is indeed a resource "triangulation" among family, faith, and school institutions. They are also in a dissonant dialogue. There still remain multiple tensions and uncertainties regarding both the appropriateness and manner of engagements between church affiliates and school personnel.

And finally, a participatory, capacity-building research project can play a valuable role in the intergenerational pathways of contemporary African American faith. As demonstrated in the previous chapters and the examples presented earlier, many youth, parents, and pastors, both more and less formally, valued CoCHY and its SLI project as faith-enriching resources. One example among them is that the dialogue between the Sacred and the secular through a research-prioritized pathway can sometimes be a better means of initiating valued outcomes, over and above outreach from one church to another or in schools. Harkening back to the questions regarding competition and the related market model, two pastors suggested the following:

> Sometimes it is hard, because you get into the "Who's in charge?", "Whose name is gonna be on it?" exchanges. So something like CoCHY is almost like *an organization that's apart from all of that* saying, "Look, we've done some studies and we found out that if you guys do your job, then your kids will have a better life." That's how I presented it to the parents. They were like, "Hmm. CoCHY spent some money. And if we do our jobs [as parents], then our kids will have better lives." Parents get that. They go, "Wow. Then your job is to help me do my job. I'm with that."

I think it's great. Everyone here, although we are one in Christ, God has given each of us something [different] to accomplish. So one of the things you get into is the agenda. We all have it. Being able to fellowship we can lay down for a greater agenda. One thing CoCHY does is, like any para-church organization, its strength is getting a bunch of churches together. *No one can compete with the other.* We're still human. I've stretched my hands out and I've gotten a chance to meet folks I didn't know.

CoCHY works as collaborator and mediator, and because the collaborative agenda was research driven, toward improved faith-health outcomes, the "buy-in" could unfold gradually, while respecting the different leadership styles and structures across a diverse group of churches. These pastors willingly acknowledged the presence of a competitive landscape. The realities of the religious marketplace and developing sustainable means to both navigate within it and enrich a far greater collaborative spirit than currently exists were valued. That independence turned into interdependence by having a project from the respected local, state university nurture an environment of shared mission, despite its uneven history with the local African American community. Though not without inconsistencies and incomplete collaborative outcomes, concerns about getting the credit were substantially reduced. One youth pastor observed the following:

How you help the community is, first of all, to *invest in it.* That's one of the biggest issues of youth ministry in the urban church. I can name pastors on my hands at predominantly Black or urban churches that are full-time youth pastors. Or even part-time. So the issue is investment. Yet our youth themselves spend thousands of dollars a year. Surveys say now that the average teen between 13 and 17 will spend $1,000 of their own money per year. That's insane! When I was 15, ain't no way I could accumulate that much money, no matter how much grass I was cutting. But nowadays kids have a different economic ideology. And so the idea becomes one of investment. I was impressed that you guys [the CoCHY project] invested. All you're gonna do is help me keep my job. So when I present this to our elders, I'm asking for a raise. [Laughter.] Data shows that if you invest in me, and I invest in your kids, then our community and the church will get a long-term return on that investment.

Conclusion

Reciprocity, the Sacred exchange of valued resources, among generations in all core institutions, is fundamental to the mere survival, never mind the possible flourishing, of any society. At this uncertain time in African American history, in this increasingly disparate, globalized, and technologically driven

world, this truth is especially important. In his detailed and prescient exploration of a practical theology for contemporary Black churches, Dale P.
Andrews[18] suggested the following:

> Critical emphasis in the pastoral care of black churches is its corporate nature....
> Community ethos is an important resource for pastoral care, while the community
> itself [also] functions as a critical care provider.... Spiritual values place pastoral care in
> the context of mutual care. The reciprocal character of care reflects African values that
> place an individual's life in relation to the environment, community, and cosmology.

This book as a whole, and this chapter especially, have analyzed various
engagements of that practical theology. The "context of mutual care" was
perhaps most clearly reflected in, and demonstrated by, a community-based,
participatory, SLI that was part of a larger research project. The CoCHY project and especially the SLI were a means with which these churches enhanced
their capacity-building contributions. By providing lessons toward enriching
a living faith, they are enriching a community ethos. Their patterns of interaction empower each generation, and interactions among them, to further
religious institutions and the community as a whole.

Yes, the endemic cultural influence of competition and market structures
well beyond metaphor alone influence these faith dynamics in uncertain
ways. Yes, including religious outreach in schools, many pathways of intergenerational faith are themselves dissonant, often acting against the very use-
value of the practical theology Andrews, this book, and other similar research
are exploring. And yes, all of these dynamics are unfolding in a period of
increased secularization and increased fundamentalisms. Recognizing the limitations of either/or dichotomies, many both/and models of intergenerational
faith engagement are flourishing. They are exemplifying success from being
within the church, as well as providing structures for faith-informed rebellion
within the context of intergenerational dialogue. They are interacting with
parents in ways that challenge how their parenting may be planting the seeds
of faith alienations of their youth. And yes, though not without its staunch
critics and resistance, progressive Hip Hop as a generationally transcendent,
youth-centered resource is expressing itself in what appears to be an increasingly valued way. As demonstrated in the previous analyses, the presence of
spiritual dissonance, in all its expressions within and among faith generations,
is essential to any faith future, African American and otherwise. Each of these
domains of intergenerational faith is being expressed through pathways built
from a vital reciprocity between rules and relationships.

For Pastor Ronald Baltesante, safe relationships are those "built of honesty and trust. Dependable and understanding the values that I believe our God requires…. [We] got to make the Bible, so youth can say '[I'm] okay with it. I have an understanding of compassion.'" Consistent with Pastor Baltesante, Eddie is a 16-year-old who attends church (only) when he has to, in a family where religion is a gendered affiliation. His mother and grandmother are staunch believers in the Word, while his father and uncles couldn't care less. When I interviewed Eddie I asked him, "What's a lesson about God you value that you've learned in church youth services?" He said, "I think trust, really. You just always have to believe that there is a God and that He's always going to be there for you. I don't know why I always come back to that. But I just think it's all about trust."

This chapter discussed trust, reciprocity, dissonance, and dialogue. It analyzed how Pastor Baltesante's compassion and Eddie's youthful and profound insight emerge from intergenerational resource exchanges at the core of church affiliation and, ideally, faith itself. Yet too much parental and pastoral malleability and/or too many repetitions of rules outside of the balance of caring relationships appear to be as bad as too little. And beyond competition are collaborations, nurturing trust through Sacred-secular symmetries of fellowship, research, service, and bonds of a common destiny. Caringly, these collaborative bonds can be shared without judgment, without condemnation: "Girls who used to be on crack" are blessed to be in recovery today, and former sex workers can play a role in the proactive faith socialization of youth. A Prodigal Son life stage is quite common and can itself feed one's faith. Hip Hop has a valued role beyond fad in enriching ways all generations engage the Sacred. As the sentiments of this chapter's respondents demonstrate, each of these can, and are, being marked by the balance of rules and relationship.

To further intergenerational pathways of faith, these are among the both/and faith curriculum and sensibility of success and an important means of not needlessly complicating 16-year-old Eddie's vital insight of trust. Toward its realization, shifts in programming and presentation may need to be preceded by a shift in Christian consciousness, toward a new definition of success and its multiple dimensions and diversities, toward growing faith missions in more inclusive and multidimensional expressions, with and beyond learning saturated with service, toward engaging both Sacred and secular resources that can most effectively and engagingly nurture sanctuary, now and into the future.

CONCLUSION

· 6 ·

COMMUNITY CAPACITY BUILDING
TOWARD NURTURING SANCTUARY

Faith is a house with many rooms. There's plenty of room for doubt on every floor.…
Doubt is useful. It keeps faith a living thing.

—Yann Martel[1]

Each generation must discover its mission, fulfill it or betray it in relative opacity…
[including] a certain communion of the faithful with Sacred things.

—Frantz Fanon[2]

Introduction

Much of the existing research on African American religious involvement tends to focus on religious affiliation being one or more of the following: (a) a valued set of practices and interactions of institutional engagement; (b) a buffer or mediator between personal, familial, environmental, or other pathology; (c) a Pan-African process of return to faith roots of cultural legacy and reclamation; and/or (d) a vital political institution of collective uplift, within and across many historical moments and into today.[3] To contribute to the first two of these research strands through a unique "three-legged stool" of collaboration, *Nurturing Sanctuary* analyzed the contributions of a group of churches that worked with health department staff and university researchers to improve the means through which the churches enrich their faith-health, capacity-building missions. Capacity building is "maximizing local area assets of individuals, families, organizations, and others, [so they] can be brought together to collectively nurture an improved quality of life."[4] Community capacity building is the "nurturing" of nurturing sanctuary. Sanctuary is a specific room in a place of faith. It is movement to a place of refuge from the tensions of nation-state transitions. And, perhaps endemic to all its uses, sanctuary is the enrichment of Sacred sites, be it in a spiritual or physical location. Sanctuary, "places of communication with the spirits, portals where people enter the Sacred,"[5] invokes the Sacred in attitude, perception, behavior, and location. How pedagogy and tensions, both erotic and generational, are nurturing sanctuary by building community capacity in African American churches is the contribution of this book.

The first quote that opens this chapter values the vital reciprocity between faith and doubt. The remark is made by a fictional character, Pi Patel, in the novel and film, *Life of Pi*. In it, Mr. Patel has survived a harrowing journey at sea of intense isolation and surprising collaboration. He has lived to tell his story, years later. Pi's life is understood as a metaphor for any and all persons who seek to, in reality, grow within and beyond profoundly challenging circumstances. In the second quote leading this chapter, Dr. Fanon's is a very real analysis of the past and present of colonialism on the African continent and its reciprocities in the minds and spirits of the colonized and the colonizer. Fanon's book is a doubtful critique or perhaps a near rejection of the utilities of faith in the progress of persons of African ancestry toward liberation. These two quotes can perhaps best be understood as multidimensional and reciprocal. Like the preceding chapters of this book, these two quotes are a dialogue. There are many rooms in the house of faith. This book has explored these rooms, including those where exchanges among generations engage with Sacred things. As these analyses of pedagogy and tensions have demonstrated, community capacity building and faith can be expressed in many ways. Community capacity building encompasses multiple levels of both Sacred and secular assets, the persons, social networks, sentiments, and skill sets that make the process of improving local quality of life possible. As this book demonstrates, "Faith is a project in building community capacity."[6] *Nurturing Sanctuary* has demonstrated how African American churches are building capacity in the 21st-century religious marketplace. Taking the diversity of religious affiliation styles and patterns into consideration, this research has provided a unique focus on various complexities in African American faith and how resources from within and outside of churches are assisting in their resolution. This capacity building across subgroups and data platforms, longitudinally generated from a diverse group of congregations, is a rare combination. *Nurturing Sanctuary* has extended this research by (a) evaluating tensions and challenges facing African American churches; (b) illustrating capacity-building components, patterns, and outcomes in and through them; (c) demonstrating the use-value and impact of spiritual and secular resource collaborations that are addressing and contributing to the reduction of health disparities; and (d) highlighting emergent faith-health best practices for the present and future of African American faith. By doing so, *Nurturing Sanctuary* enriches the longstanding legacy and current dialogues of religious research regarding spirituality, contemporary religious tensions, and the future of African American faith. In this final chapter, the book's contributions are briefly summarized and best practices associated with each theme are specified. And finally, a few of the most relevant next research steps toward refining a P.E.G. (Pedagogy, Erotics, Generations) approach to faith are presented.

Enriching a Pedagogy of Faith

When most effectively engaged, pedagogy is inherently reciprocal. An exchange of information occurs between persons, to the mutual benefit of all involved. While reciprocity can be biblically understood as "reaping what one sows,"[7] it is the expressions of shared norms of Sacred exchange, the expression of "harmony bonds governed by the search for fairness, rhythm, equity."[8] These were the foundations that informed the SLI workshops of the CoCHY project. Chapter 2 analyzed the six SLI projects that demonstrated both the challenges and triumphs of creating—and sustaining—a project of community-engaged pedagogy guided by the interests and leadership of predominantly African American churches.

Among the main conclusions extending from this chapter are how uneven, yet still effective, the meanings and mechanisms of collaboration are when the mixed motives of diverse churches come together. Some congregations are eager to violate the market model of resource competition. They look forward to the opportunity to enrich win-win shared outcomes by instead embracing the structure, content, and leadership reciprocities of collaboration toward shared benefit. For all participating churches, but especially for the three SLI projects that did so, the formative foundations were laid for new models of shared capacity building and the potential for collaborative best faith practices into the future. Second, while faith and health are among the most fundamental reciprocities that exist, they are also marked by dissonance and risk, some of which is acknowledged, while others are less so. Only two of the six funded SLI projects were willing to address two among the more challenging relationships between faith and health experienced by youth, that is, mental health and surviving sexual assault. The most valued faith-health promotion topic in the open SLI grant solicitation was abstinence. Yes, the sexuality of youth is indeed important. One might ask how and how well the moralizing motive of the church tradition serves the health disparities and more holistic health challenges that exist in African American communities. *Nurturing Sanctuary* analyzed the many ways in which contributions to the reciprocity between faith and health are being enriched, with and beyond morality alone.

And while very much a variable, success can be achieved when the secular priorities of research-driven, community-engaged health pedagogy fruitfully dialogue with the faith foundations and intended outcomes of churches. Despite the challenges of establishing and sustaining the mobilization of youth leadership in youth-centered curricula and programming, each SLI program created multiple expressions of success, to the direct benefit of youth within and beyond the participating churches. A pedagogy of faith (always) matters because the contents, strategies, and patterns of information exchange are vital cultural components to establishing and maintaining sanctuary. Within the SLI and beyond it, the workshops succeeded in enriching and sharing in that sanctuary.

In Chapter 3, grounded in the process of critical reflection, nuances of multiple faith-health reciprocities were shared in the critical reflections of service-learning student journals. Analyzing their experiences within and beyond the classroom, they were a course requirement for all students of *The Community in Action* sociology course for the term in which the SLI workshops took place. Students were required to write on any community-themed topic of their choice. Regarding human interactions with and through Sacred sites, "Reciprocity occurs in the physical closeness and the benefits derived at these locations. Some of these sites are perceived as portals for the mind to access a different level of consciousness and gain information and greater understanding from which well-being can be promoted."[9] Critical reflection often invokes similar kinds of changes as an engagement with oneself and the recognition that the Sacred can manifest through one's willingness to dialogue with tensions, between one's values and behavior, one's knowledge and actions inconsistent with that knowledge, one's assumptions regarding larger societal outcomes and how individual choices inform them, and between the conveniences of joy and the inconveniences of pain, both of which may simultaneously extend from a single choice.

As expected, no students explicitly reported experiencing a "different level of consciousness." Still, as Chapter 3 showed, it appears that many, if not most students experienced marked changes demonstrated by the places they were willing to go within themselves, to complete their student journals. Table 1 of Chapter 3 summarizes the frequency of the topics students explored, and their service-learning experiences were the most frequently considered topic. Perhaps nurturing new places within themselves as Sacred—and dissonance one may find there—students reflected on the challenges of not fitting into settings and identities. This included sexual and nonsexual expectations and the challenging and sometimes life-threatening circumstances in which they found themselves as a result. These service-learning students reflected on the homelessness of parents and other family members and the emotional and spiritual challenges of interacting with community expectation when one's parent is the local vagabond of their small hometown. Mental illness and substance use/abuse connected more and less directly to struggles maintaining housing were also a part of these reflections. Regarding the faith-health reciprocity of parent-child role inconsistencies, what can intergenerational respect mean when the primary resource across generations with one's parent is the person the student had to "parent" through various behaviors and years of active addiction? A pattern emerged where the students who were the most willing to risk going to the most challenging places seemed to grow the most. They did so through new understandings of themselves, their loved one(s), and of the course, the theme of community, both in its larger, societal sense, and in the small, intimate social circle expressions as well.

Through students' critical reflections of the SLI workshops, many came to a new understanding of societal inequalities, how community as place and process and exchanges between them matter to life chances and consequences associated with them. These pedagogy outcomes were perhaps reflected most completely in the willingness of students to do more than simply recite middle class convenience narratives of guilt and charity and the benevolent other. Instead they engaged with relationships between life chances and their relationships with family background, local area context, and individual choices. Though the most comprehensive or holistic expressions were rare, they were present in most. Students recognized and took responsibility for participating in many things in the world that warrant change and acknowledged that as citizens, they are agents of change and do engage (in) them, with *The Community in Action* course being one of the many means through which these warranted changes are occurring.

Tensions of Faith: Navigating the Erotic and the Intergenerational

In her vital 1984 essay, "The Uses of the Erotic: The Erotic as Power," though Audre Lorde never uses the word "faith," for her, erotic elements are an essential reciprocity with faith:

> The erotic is a measure between the beginnings of our sense of self and the chaos of our strongest feelings. It is an internal sense of satisfaction [and] once we know the extent to which we are capable of feeling that sense of satisfaction and completion, we can then observe which of our various life endeavors bring us closer to that fullness.[10]

It is impossible to support the view that all sex is Sacred. And it is entirely accurate to say that the erotic is far more than sex alone, that one's understanding of passion and self is central to an engaged faith. "The chaos of our strongest feelings" are fundamental to faith. Thus, erotics matter to faith because, as Audre Lorde wrote, an understanding of one's passionate, purpose-driven self is central to the core of one's identity, engaging the whole of who we are and who we are becoming, informed by the presence and absence of faith. Part 2 of *Nurturing Sanctuary* placed Lorde's sentiment in a dialogue with African American religious leadership. Most broadly, Chapter 4 focused on what parents and pastors feel is working in addressing passion-centered attitudes, motives, and behaviors among teenagers currently being socialized in predominantly African American churches. Perhaps more narrowly defined, Chapter 4 is an analysis of the meanings, possibilities, and socializations associated with Sacred and unsacred sex. They emerged from the focus groups with parents of churchgoing teenagers and those with pastors of churches with teens in them.

Chapter 4 began with these parents and pastors specifying the erotic messaging they value in the current, Christian socialization of African American youth. This included when to begin (very early), how to begin (with empathy, and the memory of oneself as a teen), tensions in the primary paradox of idealizing a chaste sexuality during the very life stage in which hormonal intensities and hypersexual socializations are seemingly most everpresent (e.g., valuing youth discovery of sexual excitement), and how history can and should matter (often used in ways that stigmatize aspects of Hip Hop style). Throughout, there was a strong, though most often implicit, recognition of the challenges of these themes across the life course, in the desire to be "true" to one's faith, without being hypocritical. Parents, pastors, and young, nonparent, focus group participants emphasized many strategies of action that are both large scale with many moving parts and partnerships (e.g., the CoCHY project itself), and on a smaller scale, with deep historical roots (e.g., nurturing environments where peer-to-peer role modeling among youth can flourish).

But perhaps the most challenging elements of the entire chapter were the uncertainties of who can be welcome in places of faith and how a "sense of belonging" can be acted on. Same-sex desire in and of itself is predictably viewed as something to be "treated," corrected, and solved. And, by inference, an identity (e.g., self-defining as a Black Christian lesbian) is predictably understood as troubling and disruptive. These words were not used, but their meanings were expressed through the raised questions of one pastor focus group ("What is anybody doing about homosexuality, y'all?"), to the handwringing and body language shifts that occurred during the parent focus group in which a father of a teenage son recounted multiple experiences of evangelizing to a cross-dressing, gender-bending male he saw one day on his way to church. Like all such pathways of inclusion in broadening faith-informed uses of the erotic, these means of contemporary faith socialization are incomplete. The definition and diversities in building safe relationships appear to be receiving increasing attention among these faith leaders. Given the "line drawing" of appropriate and less so being fundamental to organized religious engagement, how this might change in the future—with so many in leadership positions apparently desiring it to remain unchanged—is uncertain.

Chapter 5 examined the pathways and challenges of intergenerational faith communication among contemporary African American Christian parents, pastors, and teenagers. What exchanges are taking place among generations of African American faith that nurture sanctuary? From the focus groups, in-depth interviews, and service-learning initiative workshops, to answer to this question, four analytic domains emerged (Expressions of Spiritual Dissonance, Enriching a Living Faith, The Presence and Praxis of Hip Hop, and Pathways Toward a Faith Future). The chapter analyzed how each of them both reinforce and challenge intergenerational relationships in contemporary African American faith. The presence of relevant reciprocities is Chapter 5's first conclusion: youths and adults, tradition and innovation, cause and outcome, life-stage faith alienations simultaneously partnered with public and private ritualized faith participations, and the size and salience, and sustained institutional strengths, of religion in an era of secularization, megachurches, and the contemporary religious marketplace. These are among the relevant reciprocities and dialogues of spiritual dissonance. Intergenerational relationships are a part of, vital to, and inform, each of them. These generational exchanges are a "cause," in that they instigate change in the churches themselves, in the parents, pastors, and teenagers, and in the health outcomes they experienced. And they are an outcome; that is, from the structures and strategies of action used within these houses of worship, relationships among generations emerge and change over time in many ways.

In these four domains, complexities of living Black faith were demonstrated, and the absolute necessities of enriching caring, authentic, and sustainable lines of communication among generations were perhaps most prominent. This is consistent with research that has demonstrated ways in which communication among generations within and beyond religious settings enriches shorter-term health outcomes of youth, in addition to increasing the likelihood of long-term faith affiliation.[11] Chapter 4 demonstrated the "how" of these improved outcomes and tensions that challenge them. Availability, the reciprocity between rules and mentoring relationships, and enriching a balance between the inreach of enriching experience of youth while at church and the outreach of engaging elements of faith with youth beyond church walls were among the key aspects within and beyond these emergent domains. From these and more, a pedagogy of faith, and tensions of faith, both erotic and generational, are the focus and contribution of the chapters summarized earlier. Each of these themes gave rise to best practices briefly considered here.

Best Practices Within and Toward Faith Futures

This book was written guided by the general view that (a) faith and health are positively related to one another, (b) religious involvement can be a beneficial means of engaging faith in ways that enrich the faith-health relationship within and among generations, and (c) community-university collaborations can nurture helpful resources that otherwise might not have come together. The faith-health relationship has been demonstrated with much research over many years and is perhaps best demonstrated in comprehensive research reviews.[12] After detailed meta-analyses of a wide diversity of research, the authors conclude the following: "Most studies have shown that religious involvement and spirituality are associated with better health outcomes, including greater longevity, coping skills, and health-related quality of life."[13] Because African Americans across the life course report being highly religious,[14] the beneficial faith-health connection among African Americans is especially valuable to understand better.

Following from Martel, I have explored faith as a house of many rooms, and details of the rooms matter. Thus, the local context surrounding them likely does as well. How that context informs the findings of the preceding chapters may not have been accounted for as completely as one might desire. These concerns may be perceived as all the more relevant for research extending from a purposive sample of churches that sustained their participation in a faith collaboration across nearly four years. And while individual church affiliates were compensated for their project participation, the churches did so while receiving virtually no congregational compensation. Perhaps any "best practice" suggestions may be too general and too limited to be helpful. Having acknowledged these challenges, what follows is a brief, theme-specific presentation of emergent best practices from the pedagogy and tensions of faith of the CoCHY project.

Best Practices in a Pedagogy of Faith

Given Chapter 2's description and analysis of a set of service-learning workshops, interdisciplinary service learning is itself a best practice. Church-initiated and prioritized foci of the projects and their mechanisms and means of learning through service are essential. These are made stronger when coupled with a patient and broad-based outreach for participation, across multiple levels of leadership, through diverse communication channels, and within an environment of support for sustained collaboration. Encouraging congregational risks of stigma and prioritizing innovation within the proposed workshop themes are vital, given that too often, traditional institutions led by traditional leadership may prioritize traditional approaches to safe, traditional topics. A best practice emerges with a nudge for principled transformation of these traditionalisms—in a both/and dialogue toward the enrichment of the traditions and the structures and strategies that give rise to them. Diverse collaborations are a vital resource toward realizing this best practice. One limitation of the current project that speaks to a best practice for the future is the engaged leadership and participations of youth reflected in the development, design, engagement, and outcomes of said project.

From Chapter 3, requiring the public privacies of critical reflection in dialogues across differences is a beneficial best practice of faith-health, community-engaged pedagogy. More specifically, to realize improved quality-of-life outcomes and a broader justice of a project like CoCHY, these difference dialogues are best informed by a variety of foci and intended outcomes. Regarding the more macro and communal scale, the CoCHY SLI succeeded when university researchers enhanced the ease with which equitable exchanges take place with diverse community partners. Having and sustaining diverse voices at the leadership table and prioritizing the partnering of that diversity with equity when mediating tensions that arise are essential. When violations of that equity occur, as happened in the larger CoCHY project (e.g., when an insensitive "joke" was made by a university project leader that offended community partners), a means toward healing from the toxicity the said violation brought about had to be engaged. And as a best practice, the means toward healing must itself be collaborative. A feeble apology shared among a limited leadership proved woefully incomplete. Its distance from the very community-engaged pedagogy the project attempted to nurture was apparent to all except the person who attempted to apologize. Collaborative healings in various forms will likely be necessary across any longitudinal project, especially one marked by race, ethnic, denominational, class, and other group differences.

On the much more micro scale, a dialogue of differences can be furthered through the use of critical reflection as a required aspect of the research before, during, and after the direct participation of those who are conducting it, as was the case in the CoCHY SLI. These difference dialogues led students to engage with their community SLI workshop collaborators, their small group student peers, and the youth participants of the SLI events themselves. Future best practice can expand access to feedback of critical reflection from among those on a project's community side. Follow-up interviews were completed with the church leadership of SLI projects, and focus group feedback sessions were also completed at both a secular venue (i.e., health department) and a religious venue (i.e., one of the SLI project churches). As in the SLI project, voices and experiences of youth can be recorded in critical reflections, office hours, and in-class comments of service-learning students and in the informal, post-event exchanges I had with select youth. Adapting an "exit interview" approach complete with a follow-up some months later could improve the assessment and refinement mechanism for future effectiveness.

Best Practices in the Tensions of Faith

The erotics of faith were analyzed through the parent and pastor focus group perceptions of how they socialize church-affiliated teens. In Chapter 4, intergenerational and intragenerational dialogues were central. These included former teen parents, most of whom had left church for some time when they were near the beginning of their teen parenting. From the large, near-suburb commuter churches, to the much smaller, storefront community churches and others in between them, the parent focus groups included a "best practice" of multiple diversities in religious leadership, church size, denomination, areas of the city, and probable class predominances among the church members. (This is exemplified in two collaborating churches, one of which is a very large, nondenominational church adjacent to an outer suburb of the city, where members are asked to submit W-2 tax reports of income. Another is a very small, storefront church near one of the concentrated poverty neighborhoods of the city, where a sizeable portion of their child members qualify for the school meal program.) This best practice of rich diversity is reflected across the ethnographic moments and emergent themes in the findings throughout. Across these differences, the challenges of the erotic socialization of young persons were very much shared, and the "What Works?" section of Chapter 4 provides the best practice strategies of action that were most highly valued by parents and pastors.

In Chapter 5, with generations understood as perhaps the most fundamental reciprocity that exists in the process and practice of faith, suspended judgment, open access to leadership, and diverse means of meeting youth where they are were among the aspects of communication valued most. Also among the best practices to emerge were the multimethod framework of the research project itself and the analytic approach I used among the data sources. This allowed for a synthetic set of intergenerational exchanges (e.g., between SLI workshop youth and focus group participating pastors) to be triangulated with the actual intergenerational exchanges that did take place (e.g., young adults who joined the focus groups for parents of teenagers). The fact that those actual dialogues were unintended speaks to the utility of flexibility in both data collection and analyses as an essential best practice. While this violated the intent of the focus group, it improved the quality of dialogue that took place, as in the case of another two former teen parents now in their early 20s who thought the group was for them, that is, those who had been faith-socialized teens who were also sexually active during their teenage years. Though their kids were only in first and second grade, their misunderstanding again improved the quality of data that emerged from the focus group. For young adults, exploring their sustained engagement and the churches most successful in their retention is both a future research focus and a best practice extension of the "What Works?" section of Chapter 4. This is also for the teen parents in their early to mid-20s who have returned to religious affiliation and are raising their children in church. Future best practices can emerge from these unanticipated focus group adaptations and subsequent successes of focusing on these two subgroups.

Toward Transformative Collaborations and a Broader Justice?

Pedagogy, Erotics, and Generations are collaborative in service of faith. This book has explored how each of these is an expression of, and expressed through, the contemporary faith of African American church-affiliated Christians in a Midwestern city. Any congregation is much more than simply the systematic analyses of patterns and means of information exchange guided by a Sacred curriculum (pedagogy), the passion-centered motives and actions that inform individual and collective well-being (erotics) and exchanges among persons from distinct periods of socialization (generations). Churches participating in the CoCHY project nurtured the means "in service of a broader mission, a praxis toward transformative collaborations."[15] These collaborations were toward a richer, deeper faith, and improved health-wellness outcomes for African American youth and across the life course. The SLI workshops were an important, if not essential, aspect of it. The SLI project was education "saturated with service," true to the call of John Dewey, toward the practice of freedom Paulo Freire emphasized. Both of these progressive researchers of teaching and learning were in a triangulated dialogue with W. E. B. Du Bois's analysis of "The Negro Church" from more than a century ago.[16] May this book contribute to the continuing momentum toward a greater appreciation and understanding of the reciprocity between faith and health and many other related reciprocities of a capacity-building present and future.

To enrich that future, pedagogically, next research steps from within the CoCHY project include exploring the youth panel survey results of the 400 youth who shared their lives across three and a half of their teen years. By doing so we can understand information they value most, secular and otherwise, how they engage that information, and how both of these inform the contexts of faith, family, health, and well-being. Beyond the CoCHY project and data, what patterns of information exchange and class contexts shape utilities of faith in health-related civic participation? Too often African American middle class community members may misdiagnose community challenges and means toward community change.[17] Future research can help us better understand how faith informs the information sharing about these civic differences and their related health and health disparity consequences.

Regarding tensions of faith, from within the CoCHY project next research steps include exploring the 55 other in-depth interviews of teenage women and men not available to be analyzed for this book, those who are sexually active and have been for multiple years, those who have maintained their virginity who recently turned, and the many youth in between these subgroup patterns. Like many others in the full spectrum of faith tensions, the erotic is "a resource within each of us that lies in a deeply female and spiritual plane, firmly rooted in the power of our unexpressed or unrecognized feeling [as a] source within the culture of the oppressed that can provide energy for change."[18] Knowing what—if any—gender, age, church size, and other narrative differences emerged in how African American young women and men understand their experiences of faith, health, race, and place would be helpful. And within and beyond CoCHY, recent work has demonstrated the utilities of a social justice-based intervention helpful in fostering the resilience of "street life-oriented" African American men.[19] It would be helpful to systematically explore broader applications of this intervention for women and men in other environments where the interdependence of faith and health are nurtured.

Generationally, a beneficial next step would be a deeper exploration of how different types of trauma inform the "how" of faith from uncommon voices that matter. Consistent with research on pastoral care, more detailed analyses of stigma, resilience, and faith would expand our familiarity with triumph over tragedy and the reciprocity between them in the process of community capacity building. For example, the role of faith among African American survivors of sexual assault has not been explored in detail. And in what is coming to be known as a "feminization of faith," exploring the uncommon voices of young, church-affiliated African American males in an increasingly secular age could prove helpful. Within and beyond CoCHY, the spiritual dissonance regarding Hip Hop was among the most salient, pregnant pauses of the entire project. In one of the pastor focus groups, a young pastor referred to his congregation as a "crunk" church. Crunk is "a form of Hip-Hop music that fuses Southern rap and electronic dance music of the early 1990s. [It] most likely comes from the melding of the words 'crazy' and 'drunk' and signifies, according to Lil' Jon, a 'heightened state of excitement' redefined to refer to the spiritual high felt through Christ."[20] From gender and gender identity dynamics, to relationships between trauma and resilience, to the patterns of a crunk church, these and other themes of future research can help maximize beneficial ways of faith that are nurturing sanctuary in contemporary African American churches.

EPILOGUE—A CONVERSATION WITH PASTOR ORINDA HAWKINS BRINKLEY

During the three and a half years of the CoCHY research project, I had the opportunity to interact with a diverse group of health professionals and faith leaders: women and men, older and young, those from large and small churches and many sizes in between, those from traditional denominations extending back generations into African American religious history, and many from the contemporary nondenominational churches that seek to broaden their market base by removing distinctions toward being "one in the body of Christ." Some of the CoCHY project pastors had been child evangelists in contemporary versions of the "streetcorner caller for Christ" urban tradition, while others had maintained a career and life into adulthood outside of faith leadership, and had then come to their pastor role. And there were many mixtures of these and other characteristics among those I was fortunate to share time with during the project.

I came to know Pastor Orinda Hawkins Brinkley due to her leadership of St. Peter's Evangelical Lutheran Church. I have kept in touch with Pastor "O" over the now eight years since CoCHY ended. She is an African American woman of great depth and caring, a passionate, resilient, and thoughtful survivor who has experienced much in her life within and beyond faith leadership. Like my late mother, Dr. Lois Price Spratlen, Pastor O was first trained and worked as a nurse. While raising her children, she returned to school and changed careers. And like my mother, all the while, she continued to live her life within, and enact, the Calling to care, heal, and engage renewal in the lives of others, as she nurtures the same in her own.

St. Peter's closed its doors in 2011 as the result of a variety of forces in the contemporary religious marketplace: a lack of denominational familiarity, changing racial predominance of the neighborhood, a split at the congregational core with the appointment of an African American woman pastor, especially as she exhibited her cultural humanist sensibility more freely, along with a quick wit and willingness to share it with others—her hair in (dread) locks, and having a rather complicated personal "backstory" that was not in convenient keeping with many of the more traditional powers that be within the Lutheran tradition. Perhaps most striking was the surrounding neighborhood's increasingly concentrated poverty, leading to increases in real and perceived risk, along with the current era of secularization, with its apparent decline of the community church, as commuter churches increase. As I was completing this book, I met with Pastor O to reflect on ways of faith, the CoCHY project, and how it continues to inform our lives. A portion of our conversation follows:

TPS: I jotted some themes down, but not questions.

OHB: Oh, good. Good. Because you didn't say I was going to be interviewed. You said we were going to have a conversation. (shared laughter) And if you had a list of questions, then that would be an interview.

TPS: Sounds good. As I've reviewed with you, there are three themes of the book: (1) Pedagogy, the systematic exploration of information exchange across the Sacred-secular bridge; (2) Erotics, passion-centered sensibility of self in fellowship with others that may or may not be sexual in nature. The Uses of the Erotic are true to what Audre Lorde suggested. "We must find that place of passion, our sense of deepest knowing as women—she was talking to women when she first made this speech-turned-essay—"so that we can manifest that, because, we can be more conveniently oppressed when we are distant from that sense within ourselves. And that oppression cannot happen. It must be resisted from that place of deepest knowing as impassioned living in various forms toward true change"; and, 3) Generations, interactions between era-specific groups. And within this text, as you'll recall from the second focus group follow-up event, we had a dialogue regarding Hip Hop. And, that tension-filled dialogue may be different eight years later. But, we were where we were at that time, and it was worthwhile to explore the intergenerational tensions and the role faith plays in using that [tension] as a resource toward capacity building change.

So, all of this to say, the larger idea of the CoCHY project and my book is that faith is a good thing that can beneficially manifest through religious community. When it does so within the African American tradition, Sacred-secular partnership can make both a research contribution that also, ideally, makes a contribution that improves the quality of those congregational lives, family lives, and individual lives among and beyond those who are participants in the project. So, the quality of life for all was improved through participating in the project. It brought faith and health together as the beneficial Sacred-secular dialogue they are. As you look back, what was useful for you about participating in the CoCHY project?

OHB: I think the most beneficial aspect of participating was to have my hypotheses about church youth being assailed by, involved with, and victimized by the same things as the kids who don't go to church. That the things you would choose to talk to, and develop relationships over with youth in the church, pre-teens, teens, need to be as "ground floor," and as transparent, as if you were talking to kids out on a street corner. Hoochie mamas come to church on Sunday mornin.' Acolytes, boys who serve in church and the choir, still have hickies. So the church cannot delude itself into thinking that we have reincarnated Holy angels in our children, who are not going to do the same things YOU did when you were their ages. Because, now, you got religion, and you think that you're getting religion and telling them is going to change what they saw when they were three and four, before you got saved. And some pastors who have large numbers of kids in their congregations are more sensitive to the fact that they may not have any children who have not been exposed, 'cause they can see how they come to church dressed. They try to have programmatic things to keep them busy. But you need to talk about other things too.

TPS: Was there anything about the CoCHY project that was disappointing in some way?

OHB: It ended. It ended. And we had not developed a cohesive enough relationship to build something out of it. There was enough information. I mean, just knowing about the amount of anal sex among our little church chil'ren (9% of Wave I surveyed youth). The amount of oral sex going on with them (26%). The amount of kids who were in the church, but didn't really feel like they had someone to talk to (approximately 55%). So that meant outside [the church] and inside, these children had nobody they could really talk to. The fact that we had information like that and, it wasn't compelling enough for people to put aside other things. [i.e., being doctrinally obstinate by] Exhibiting a "Think like I think always, or you're wrong" type attitude. (chuckles) To do something for the group we had just got through studying. (long pause). That's my biggest disappointment.

TPS: One paradox is the research model. The project is funded within a particular period of time. We design the project and generate the data. Then we begin the analyses of it and conference papers and on to the next steps. But I'm absolutely with you. In view of the earlier part of our conversation, I use this metaphor with great care. This is often referenced as the "rape model." Where a project gains what it seeks to gain, and then from the secular side, really doesn't maintain Sacred fellowship.

OHB: Well, I don't. I appreciate that. But I don't think we should have expected any more than that. The [church, collaborative] expectations should not have been more than that. This is the way I'm lookin' at it. I may be lookin' at it kinda skewed. You take advantage of the resources that are available to you, to get information that you need in order to perform the job you need to perform, at its highest level, to affect the most people, in the most positive way. CoCHY, all y'all [academics], y'all were doing research! You came together, collaborated, thought about what you want, wrote the grant, and got the grant. Connected with the CDC [Centers for Disease Control and Prevention]. Great! Can you imagine a model for sexual health that five churches could have created based on CoCHY? A model for really attaching itself to the fact that we got young girls out there, and young boys, and… You can tell the boys more easily than you can the girls. But their androgyny. What's that about? [As if speaking with an androgynous youth] "Is this your protection?" Right after CoCHY, in my area, I kept seeing all these little girls who seemed to be trying to hide the fact they were girls, or something.

        And, I believe, truly, I believe that people are born homosexual. They're born like that. And everybody that practices [engages in same-sex sexual activity] ain't like that though. E'rybody that does it, ain't! You know. And our lack of being able to really look at abuse, and how young people live out the abuse of that, and seek normalcy whichever way they can get it. Perhaps have been abused over a certain period of time, in a homosexual way. And then that's the lifestyle that they fit into more easily for them. But that doesn't mean they were born that way. The church needs to get over tryin' to decide who the sinner is. 'Cause you don't know. You don't know. You just know that, if you hurt somebody, without knowing how you're hurting them, then you a sinner. And, so while you're tryin' to find out who the sinner is, and you go 'round callin' e'rybody a sinner, and somebody's woke up and looked in the mirror at ten and said, "Who am I? Who is this?" We could have created a healthy model, based on empirical data. Not a doctrine of sin. We could have done that, and we didn't do it. And we had everything we needed in the findings to support what we could have done.

TPS: Very helpful. Thank you. Toward that end, one of the phrases regarding the beneficial emergence out of a research project such as this is "best practices."

OHB: YES! That's the therapeutic model too.

TPS: With you. With you. Toward that end, if you were to specify best practices to emerge out of CoCHY. Now, of course, there are multiple strands here. Because there's the research strand. The congregational strand. There's the community strand of outreach, because many of the youths who took the survey were friends of the church-affiliated youth, more than being affiliates of that church themselves. So there was a whole outreach piece, to the larger community. And, because it included everything from the commuter churches, to the storefronts CoCHY engaged distinctions between them [OHB: Yes. They are different.] So, amidst these strands, what might be best practices emerging from the project as a whole? (after a brief break) What is heartening to hear is the impact the research process and output made on you. It's a reminder that there was a communal utility to the process and the project as a whole.

OHB: Well, I would not have done it if I couldn't see beyond the process. See, every process leads to something. And if it leads to nothing, then what's the purpose? I have to have a purpose in doing things. I'm not going to just do something for the sake of doing it. I would not have subjected kids to rape [referencing the rape model research comment made earlier]. But because I knew that out of that it would present some definitive information. 'Cause churches have been failing children forever.

TPS: One of the things that was surprising to me was that, in none of the [7] parent or [3] pastor focus groups, and I co-facilitated all ten… I was surprised. That when we speak of faith and health, yes, it's centered in youth. But it's also an exploration of intergenerational wellness.

OHB: But I think that was one of the places of disconnect. Because, the focus group I was in, as I recall, it was a "them" and "us" mentality. You know. "WE the grownups, and THEM the children" kind of thing. And this level of having arrived at a superiority as an adult versus the kids, the children. That kind of thing, as I recall. That group was still having a hard time even accepting risky behavior as normal for the kids they dealt with. They just could not accept it.

And they seemed to be disconnected from their own past. That was then, and this is now. And I would say, "Ya, but you the same person that was then, that is now. And everything you were then you brought with you now." And so, it was. It was. (voice trails) Ya.

TPS: It was powerful that in the focus groups over and over again, within the parent groups in particular, "Ya, I remember myself at 17, once upon a time." Their use of that phrase was often connected to their comfort with the idea of groups. As if risk is about isolation. So if youth are in groups, then two individuals within that, who seek to have sex with one another, are in the safety of a group. And parents might even say, "But I remember what I would do," acknowledging that they used groups as a cover to go out with whomever, and then hook up with the person they wanted to hook up with. And yet, when putting together the ["What Works?" in the "Erotics of Faith" socialization] strategies of action parents consistently vested confidence in was groups. Chaperoned, or unchaperoned. And then as now, I thought, there's a dissonance here. They recognize what they themselves did. And I interpreted that not as, "Oh you short- sighted parents. How could you be so naïve?" My view then as now is, there is this very strong desire for something that they themselves usurped [to work]. By way of faith, they want to believe there's protection from risk in the collective that their children are experiencing that they themselves were willing to violate. It was clearly a struggle for many parents.

If you were to specify emergent best practices extending from your CoCHY experience, what might they be? Considering all of your project experiences. Your shepherding those youths who came to St. Peter's to participate. You participated in one of the pastor focus groups. You par- ticipated in the second focus group feedback session. You were among our longest-tenured Steering Committee member pastors, and were with us through all those monthly meetings. And you co-facilitated the commu- nity meeting in which the findings of the CoCHY project were presented.

OHB: And I went to the CDC in Atlanta with Kenny [Kenneth Steinman, principal investigator of the CoCHY project] to do that RFP project re- port. [TPS: That's right. How was that?] It was awesome, because we saw, I saw where CoCHY fit in the wider expectation in terms of the RFP for the grant. We were CoCHY. But others who were also responding to that same RFP with different projects from other places were doing other things. Those projects were about youth and reproductivity. Reproducing themselves before they are able to take care of themselves. So we came in underneath that heading. The CDC wanted to know how many babies they are having. How many repeat pregnancies are they having? What is the incidence of infant mortality among this age group? What is their quality of prenatal care? At which gestation period is prenatal care initi- ated in repeat pregnancies? So I had an opportunity to see us and what other grantees were doing. I saw how we were a microcosm within the macrocosm of getting information to the CDC to develop best practices in relationship to birth control for teens.

TPS: I'm with you. We MUST honor those CoCHY children who gave of their private information. I hope this book does somewhat. But this is just the start, even these years later. These are extraordinarily rich data, and we must do more than this book.

OHB: For CoCHY, whenever you have a pastor that gets mad because he doesn't want you to expose the fact that the youth of his church are having sex, and some of it "unnatural" sex. Didn't want it exposed. "What are you going to say?" "People are going to think…," and so forth. What?! That's information that [too many] people didn't want to get out.

TPS: Yes. Any other emergent best practices from your CoCHY experiences?

OHB: (Long pause) Enter into the relationship with the knowledge that nothing is off base. That everything, EVERYthing is within the realm of being alright to talk about. Because that immediately takes away barriers, secrets, hiding, delusion. We aren't going to entertain any of that. So that we're willing to talk about everything. You've opened the doors and turned the light on. Raise the shades. Create no hiding places.

TPS: Did CoCHY do that?

OHB: CoCHY had potential for that. I treated it like it did. But some people like to hide. And I've learned I can't do that.

TPS: This is a parenthetical. To be honest, I believe that many people on the project were unsure how to respond to you. [OHB: I know] (shared laughter) Because you are a striking, commanding, Black woman. You are an Evangelical Lutheran. And that leads us, back to your earlier point, to go through our historical rolodex. Others could not then place you in a convenient denominational, historical lineage that is conveniently "Black" as we understand it. Then you had that beautiful building and a small church, which many were aware of. So there was this dissonance regarding what is the meaning of leadership and resources, when it's that physical space, housing such a small critical mass. And given the association of size and power, people just weren't sure how to respond to you. And that whole thing at the focus group follow up, and your reasoned perspective regarding Hip Hop. It was just fascinating to watch how others were responding to you. Back to your earlier comment, and the reading that began this conversation, what is the meaning of trust when leadership differences are present? So, your first point: At the project's point-of-origin, nothing is off base. All is alright to learn and speak about as a best practice. Are there others?

OHB: (Long pause) There is now no condemnation for them who are in Christ Jesus (Romans 8:1). 'Cause that's one of the reasons we get so little information. 'Cause no one wants to be condemned. That was the easiest way to get it. The fact that it was anonymous no names, and that we would not have access to anything.

TPS: Helpful. Openness in the sharing of information. And sustaining the complete absence of condemnation or shaming of any kind as a shared ethic. Any other best practice?

OHB: Someway, think in terms of permission rather than restriction. [TPS: Would you be willing to say a bit more?] A lot of times we base our acts on what we feel like we can't do as opposed to what we can do. And community, Sacred community, believes that with God, all things are possible. Nothing is impossible with God. Third thing says, "I'm the God of all flesh. Nothing is too hard for me." So, when you think outside of human limitation to guide possibility, then you have to think in terms of permission rather than restriction.

TPS: Strategically, how might that have informed the "how" of CoCHY?

OHB: See, there's a difference between saying the stuff in the Bible, and living the stuff in the Bible. So, at the place where strategy and intention would come together with CoCHY, those truths that I hold to be for me, I don't know whether they would have worked, because the church was such a big portion of that. And a big portion of the churches that I was involved with have a duality. "The Word says this, but—" So, where do you get a but after the Word? That IS the final word. But in livin' it, they preach a lot of stuff they don't live. You know. God will forgive, but you can't forgive. God died for a sinner. But you don't want to sit beside one. But YOU'RE one. How do you sit with yourself? It's like you become sanctiFIED, as opposed to being in the process of being sanctified day by day. The –ed is dead. When you put an –ed on the sanctified, that means that you done breathed your last.

TPS: This has been so helpful. I'm very grateful for your willingness. Thanks so much.

OHB: You're surely welcome. Did you get what you wanted?

TPS: Yes. And so much more. Thanks again.

NOTES

Chapter 1

1. MacMullan (2005).
2. Du Bois (1903/2003).
3. Pew Research Center (2012).
4. Gruber and Hungerman (2008, p. 831).
5. Leavey and King (2007, pp. 97–98).
6. Bearman and Bruckner (2001); Ku et al. (1998).
7. Steinman et al. (2006).
8. Regnerus (2007).
9. Steinman et al. (2006).
10. Regnerus (2007).
11. Steinman et al. (2006).
12. Centers for Disease Control and Prevention (2012).
13. Centers for Disease Control and Prevention (2012).
14. Smith (2005, p. 4).
15. Smith (2005, p. 266).
16. Smith (2005, p. 267).
17. Ginwright and Cammarota (2002, p. 90).
18. Smith (2005, pp. 267, 269).
19. Smith (2005, p. 268).
20. Pew Research Center (2012).

21. Blanchard, Bartkowski, Matthews, and Kerley (2008); Blasi (2011); Marks (2005).
22. Lincoln and Mamiya (1990, p. 2).
23. Festinger (1957).
24. Fisher and Brumley (2006, p. 53).
25. Smith (2005, p. 398).
26. Mattis et al. (2004).
27. *Holy Bible*, Hebrews 11:1 (KJV).
28. World Council of Churches (WCC, 1990, p. 6).
29. Plante and Sherman (2001, p. 1); see also Mitchem and Townes (2008).
30. Miles (2009, p. 946); see also Ramsdell (1943).
31. Price-Spratlen (1998, 1999, 2008).
32. Freire (1970, p. 15).
33. Price-Spratlen and Goldsby (2012, pp. xvii–xviii); see also Chaskin, Brown, Venkatesh, and Vidal (2001); Goodman et al. (1998); Kretzmann and McKnight (1993).
34. Saegert (2006, p. 276).
35. Gray (2011).
36. Andrews (2002); Du Bois (1903/2003); Taylor, Chatters, and Levin (2004).
37. Smith (2005, p. 2).
38. Adamo (2011); ben-Jochannan (1991).
39. Smith (2005, p. 5).
40. Smith (2005, pp. 4–5).
41. Atchley (1997); Koenig, Kvale, and Ferrel (1988).
42. Ingersoll-Dayton, Krause, and Morgan (2002).
43. Steinman et al. (2005).
44. Eke, Wilkes, and Gaiter (2010, p. 55); see also Chatters, Levin, and Ellison (1998).
45. Barnes (2004, 2008); Billingsley (1992); Du Bois (1903/2003); Mays and Nicholson (1933); Smith (2005).
46. Cotton, Zebracki, Rosenthal, Tsevat, and Drotar (2006); Wallace and Forman (1998).
47. Chiswick and Mirtcheva (2013).
48. Price-Spratlen and Goldsby (2012).
49. Dewey (1900, p. 29).
50. Dewey (1900, p. 44).
51. Freire (1970, p. 34).
52. hooks (1994).
53. Giles and Eyler (1994, pp. 81–82).
54. Myers and Jackson (2008, p. 336).
55. Minkler and Wallerstein (2010).

Chapter 2

1. Names, churches, and other private information in this chapter and throughout the book are pseudonyms. This was done to protect the confidentiality of the research participants.
2. Dewey (1900, pp. 29, 44).

3. *Holy Bible*, 2 Corinthians 9:6.
4. Cattell (2001, p. 1505).
5. Warren (2006, p. 19); see also Dohmen, Falk, Huffman, and Sunde (2008).
6. Rubin et al. (2012, p. 481); see also Hawes and Berkley-Patton (2014).
7. Adamo (2011); ben-Jochannan (1991).
8. Campbell et al. (2007).
9. Kampf (2009, p. 2257).
10. Steinman, Price-Spratlen, Cooksey, and Myers (2003).
11. Price-Spratlen, Love, and Steinman (2004a).
12. Price-Spratlen and Goldsby (2012, pp. xvii–xviii); see also Chaskin et al. (2001); Goodman et al. (1998); Honadle (1981).
13. Hironimus-Wendt and Lovell-Troy (1999, p. 361).
14. Du Bois (1899/1967, p. 147).
15. Mechanic (1972, p. 146).
16. Institute of Medicine (1988, p. 78).
17. Mechanic (1972, p. 146).
18. Institute of Medicine (1988, p. 78).
19. Eng et al. (2005, p. 80).
20. Flanagan (2002); Langton and Kammerer (2005).
21. Minkler (2000, p. 191).
22. Regnerus (2007, p. 19).
23. Regnerus (2007, p. 21).
24. Rubin et al. (2012, p. 481); see also Hawes and Berkley-Patton (2014).
25. Vangen and Huxham (2003, p. 6); see also Lewis and Weigert (1985).
26. Strauss (2000).
27. Whitt-Glover, Hogan, Lang, and Heil (2008, p. 1).
28. Petrosino, Turpin-Petrosino, and Finckenauer (2000).
29. "Revirgination" is a largely Evangelical approach to apply a form of the resurrection and/or redemption narrative and religious premise to the sexual activity of (largely female) religious youth. The number of participating denominations and churches may be declining (see http://www.beliefnet.com/Faiths/Catholic/2006/11/You-Can-Become-Avirgin-Again.aspx).
30. Nelkin (2004, p. 144).
31. Centers for Disease Control and Prevention (2014).
32. Finkelhor, Turner, Ormrod, and Hamby (2009).
33. Campbell, Dworkin, and Cabral (2009).
34. Department of Health and Human Services' Administration for Children and Families (1998); Finkelhor (1979).
35. Pinwheels for Prevention (n.d.).
36. Parkinson (2002).
37. Vangen and Huxham (2003).
38. Lorde (1984b, p. 42).
39. Freire (1970, p. 34).
40. Minkler (2000, p. 191).

41. Simons and Cleary (2006, p. 308).
42. Simons and Cleary (2006, p. 309).

Chapter 3

1. Eyler (2002, p. 520).
2. Bringle and Hatcher (1999, p. 182).
3. Campbell et al. (2007); Israel et al. (2010).
4. Freire (1970, p. 15).
5. Terry and Bohnenberger (2003).
6. Mills (1959/2000, p. 226).
7. Petray and Halbert (2013, p. 452).
8. Bradley (1995); see also Terry and Bohnenberger (2004).
9. Dewey (1927, p. 213).
10. Hsieh and Shannon (2005); see also Garrison, Cleveland-Innes, Koole, and Kappelman (2006).
11. Altheide and Johnson (1994); Creswell and Miller (2000); Patton (1980).
12. Welch (2010, p. 1).
13. Welch (2010, p. 3).
14. U.S. Department of Health and Human Services (2010).
15. Substance Abuse and Mental Health Services Administration (2011).
16. Gruenwald (2003); Haymes (1995); Stevenson (2008).
17. Dash, Jackson, and Rasor (1997); Jones and Wijeyesinghe (2011); Williams, Tolan, Durkee, Francois, and Anderson (2012).
18. Green (2003).
19. McIntosh (1988); Vaught and Castagno (2008).
20. Russell-Brown (2008).
21. McAllister and Irvine (2002, p. 433); Noddings (1984).
22. Goffman (1967).
23. Lewis (2000, p. 16).
24. Kezar (1998); Litke (2002).
25. Freire (1985, pp. 84–85); see also Dewey (1927); Freire (1970); Gruenwald (2003); Haymes (1995); Lewis (2000); Stevenson (2008).
26. Simons and Cleary (2006, p. 308).

Chapter 4

1. Pollard (2004, p. 317).
2. Regnerus (2007).
3. Lorde (1984c).
4. Lorde (1984c).
5. Clark, Zabin, and Hardy (1984).

6. Pollard (2004, p. 317).
7. Finlay (2006, p. 2).
8. Lorde (1984a, p. 111).
9. King and Furrow (2008, p. 43).
10. Durkheim (1912/1965, pp. 463–464).
11. Regnerus (2007, p. 18).
12. Festinger, Riecken, and Schachter (1956).
13. Dawson (1999, pp. 60–61).
14. Spencer, Fegley, and Harpalani (2003, p. 181).
15. Brown and Brown (2003, p. 618); see also McRoberts (2003); Pattillo-McCoy (1998).
16. Brown and Brown (2003, p. 620).
17. Pollard (2004, p. 317).
18. Bearman and Bruckner (2001); Regnerus (2007).
19. Bearman and Bruckner (2001); Regnerus (2007).
20. *Holy Bible*, Romans 13:14 (KJV).
21. Pollard (2004, p. 317).
22. Douglas (2004, p. 349); see also Lockwood (2010).
23. Denizet-Lewis (2003).
24. Donahue and Benson (1995); see also Sherkat and Ellison (1999); Taylor, Chatters, and Levin (2004).
25. Pinn (2004, p. 7).

Chapter 5

1. Kirk-Duggan and Hall (2011, pp. 74–75).
2. Price-Spratlen and Goldsby (2012, pp. xvii–xviii); see also Chaskin et al. (2001); Goodman et al. (1998).
3. Kirk-Duggan and Hall (2011, pp. 74–75); see also Barnes (2008, p. 99).
4. Kirk-Duggan and Hall (2011, pp. 74–75); see also Barnes (2008, p. 99).
5. Mays and Nicholson (1933); see also Barnes (2004); Billingsley (1992).
6. Spencer et al. (2003, p. 181).
7. Festinger (1957); see also Du Bois (1903/1969).
8. Du Bois (1903/1969, p. 45).
9. Dillard (2006, p. 99); see also Allen (2003); Black (2012).
10. Burris, Harmon-Jones, and Tarpley (1997); Lincoln and Mamiya (1990); Prus (1976).
11. Uecker et al. (2007).
12. *Holy Bible*, Hebrews 11:1 (KJV).
13. Lincoln and Mamiya (1990).
14. Hiltner (1959, pp. 49, 52).
15. White (2011, pp. 3–4); see also Miller (2012).
16. Howard (2012, p. 41); see also Akom (2009); Hopkins, Olson, Pain, & Vincett (2011).
17. Howard (2012); see also Akom (2009); Hopkins et al. (2011).
18. Andrews (2002, p. 24); see also Wimberly (1982).

Chapter 6

1. Martel (2003, p. 17).
2. Fanon (1968, pp. 17, 132).
3. Andrews (2002); Du Bois (1903/2003); Haight (2001); Lincoln and Mamiya (1990); Mattis, and Jagers (2001); Taylor et al. (2004).
4. Price-Spratlen and Goldsby (2012, pp. xvii–xviii); see also Chaskin et al. (2001); Goodman et al. (1998).
5. Walker (1995, p. 111); see also Hild (2007).
6. Johnston and Benitez (2003).
7. *Holy Bible*, 2 Corinthians 9:6 (KJV).
8. Warren (2006, p. 19).
9. Hild (2007, p. 12).
10. Lorde (1984c, pp. 54–55).
11. Lumpkins, Greiner, Daley, Mabachi, and Neuhaus (2013); Sinha, Cnaan, and Gelles (2007).
12. Mueller, Plevak, and Rummans (2001); see also Koenig, King, and Carson (2012).
13. Mueller et al. (2001, p. 1225).
14. Taylor et al. (2004).
15. Taylor et al. (2004, note 3, p. 218).
16. Dewey (1900, 1937); Du Bois (1903/2003, p. 97); Freire (1970, 1985).
17. Ginwright (2002).
18. Lorde (1984c, pp. 54–55).
19. Brown et al. (2010).
20. Tatum (2010, p. 101).

BIBLIOGRAPHY

Adamo, D. T. (2011). Christianity and the African traditional religion(s): The post-colonial-round of engagement. *Verbum et Ecclesia, 32*:1–10.

Akom, A. A. (2009). Critical hip hop pedagogy as a form of liberatory praxis. *Equity and Excellence in Education, 42*, 52–66.

Allen, E., Jr. (2003). Du Boisian double consciousness: The unsustainable argument. *The Black Scholar, 33*(2), 25–43.

Altheide, D. L., & Johnson, J. M. (1994). Criteria for assessing interpretive validity in qualitative research. In N. K. Denzin & Y. S. Lincoln (Eds.), *Handbook of qualitative research* (pp. 485–499). Thousand Oaks, CA: SageAGE.

Andrews, D. P. (2002). *Practical theology for black churches.* Louisville, KY: Westminster John Knox Press.

Atchley, R. C. (1997). The subjective importance of being religious and its effect on health and morale 14 years later. *Journal of Aging Studies, 11*, 131–141.

Barnes, S. (2004). Priestly and prophetic influences on black social services. *Social Problems, 51*, 202–221.

Barnes, S. (2008). The least of these: Black church children's and youth outreach efforts." *Journal of African American Studies, 12*, 97–119.

Bearman, P. S., & Bruckner, H. (2001). Promising the future: Virginity pledges and first intercourse. *American Journal of Sociology, 106*, 859–912.

ben-Jochannan, Y. A. A. (1991). *African origins of major "western religions."* New York, NY: Black Classic Press.

Billingsley, A. (1992). *Climbing Jacob's ladder: The enduring legacy of African-American families*. New York, NY: Simon & Schuster.

Black, M. E. (2012). *Meanings and typologies of Du Boisian double consciousness within 20th century United States racial dynamics* (Unpublished master's thesis). University of Massachusetts, Boston.

Blanchard, T. C., Bartkowski, J. P., Matthews, T. L., & Kerley, K. R. (2008). Faith, morality and mortality: The ecological impact of religion on population health. *Social Forces, 86*, 1591–1620.

Blasi, A. J. (2011). *Toward a sociological theory of religion and health*. Leiden, The Netherlands: Brill.

Bradley, J. (1995). A model for evaluating student learning in academically based service. In M. Troppe (Ed.), *Connecting cognition and action: Evaluation of student performance in service learning courses* (pp. 13–26). Providence, RI: Campus Compact.

Bringle, R. G., & Hatcher, J. A. (1999). Reflection in service learning: Making meaning of experience. *Educational Horizons, 77*, 179–185.

Brown, A. L., Payne, Y. A., Dresner, L., & Green, A. G. (2010.). A social justice based intervention for fostering resilience in street life oriented black men. *Journal of Systematic Therapies 29*, 44–64.

Brown, R. K., & Brown, R. E. (2003). Faith and works: Church-based social capital resources and African American political activism." *Social Forces, 82*, 617–641.

Burris, C. T., Harmon-Jones, E., & Tarpley, W. R. (1997). "By faith alone": Religious agitation and cognitive dissonance. *Basic and Applied Social Psychology, 19*, 17–31.

Campbell, M. K., Hudson, M. A., Resnicow, K., Blakeney, N., Paxton, A., & Baskin, M. (2007). Church-based health promotion interventions: Evidence and lessons learned. *Annual Review of Public Health, 28*, 213–234.

Campbell, R., Dworkin, E., & Cabral, G. (2009). An ecological model of the impact of sexual assault on women's mental health. *Trauma, Violence, & Abuse, 10*, 225–246.

Cattell, V. (2001). Poor people, poor places, and poor health: The mediating role of social networks and social capital. *Social Science & Medicine, 52*, 1501–1516.

Centers for Disease Control and Prevention. (2014). Report on child maltreatment: Facts at a glance. Retrieved from http://www.cdc.gov/violenceprevention/pdf/childmaltreatment-facts-at-a-glance.pdf.

Centers for Disease Control and Prevention. (2012). Youth risk behavior surveillance—United States, 2011 (*Morbidity and Mortality Weekly Report*, Vol. 61, No. 4). Retrieved from http://www.cdc.gov/mmwr/pdf/ss/ss6104.pdf

Chaskin, R. J., Brown, P., Venkatesh, S., & Vidal, A. (2001). *Building community capacity*. New York, NY: Aldine de Gruyter.

Chatters, L. M., Levin, J. S., & Ellison, C. G. (1998). Public health and health education in faith communities. *Health Education & Behavior, 25*, 689–699.

Chiswick, B. R., & Mirtcheva, D. M. (2013). Religion and child health: Religious affiliation, importance, and attendance and health status among American youth. *Journal of Family and Economic Issues, 34*, 120–140.

Clark, S. D., Jr., Zabin, L. S., & Hardy, J. B. (1984). Sex, contraception and parenthood: Experience and attitudes among urban black young men. *Family Planning Perspectives, 16*, 77–82.

Cotton, S., Zebracki, K., Rosenthal, S. L., Tsevat, J., & Drotar, D. (2006). Religion/spirituality and adolescent health outcomes: A review. *Journal of Adolescent Health, 38*, 472–480.

Creswell, J. W., & Miller, D. L. (2000). Determining validity in qualitative inquiry. *Theory Into Practice, 39*, 124–130.

Dash, M. I. N., Jackson, J., & Rasor, S. C. (1997). *Hidden wholeness: An African American spirituality for individuals and communities*. Cleveland, OH: United Church Press.

Dawson, L. L. (1999). When prophecy fails and faith persists: A theoretical overview. *Nova Religio: The Journal of Alternative and Emergent Religions, 3*, 60–82.

Denizet-Lewis, B. (2003, August 3). Double lives on the down low. *The New York Times Magazine, 128*, 28–36.

Department of Health and Human Services' Administration for Children and Families. (1998). Retrieved from https://www.childwelfare.gov/pubs/usermanuals/sexabuse/sexabuseb.cfm

Dewey, J. (1900). *School and society* (2nd ed.). Chicago, IL: The University of Chicago Press.

Dewey, J. (1927). *The public and its problems*. Chicago, IL: Gateway.

Dewey, J. (1937). Education and social change. In Jo Ann Boydston (Ed.), *The later works of John Dewey* (pp. 408–417, Vol. 11). New Haven, CT: Yale University Press.

Dillard, C. B. (2006). *On spiritual strivings*. Albany: State University of New York Press.

Dohmen, T., Falk, A., Huffman, D., & Sunde, U. (2008). Representative trust and reciprocity: Prevalence and determinants. *Economic Inquiry, 46*, 84–90.

Donahue, M. J., & Benson, P. L. (1995). Religion and the well-being of adolescents. *Journal of Social Issues, 51*, 145–160.

Douglas, K. B. (2004). The black church and the politics of sexuality. In A. B. Pinn & D. N. Hopkins (Eds.), *Loving the body: Black religious studies and the erotic* (pp. 347–362). New York, NY: Palgrave-MacmillancMillan.

Du Bois, W. E. B. (1967). *The Philadelphia Negro* (p. 147). New York, NY: Schocken Books. (Original work published 1899)

Du Bois, W. E. B. (1969). *The souls of black folk*. New York, NY: Signet. (Original work published 1903)

Du Bois, W. E. B. (2003). *The Negro church*. Walnut Creek, CA: AltaMira Press. (Original work published 1903)

Durkheim, E. (1965). *The elementary forms of the religious life*. New York, NY: The Free Press. (Original work published 1912)

Eke, A. N., Wilkes, A. L., & Gaiter, J. (2010). Organized religion and the fight against HIV/AIDS in the black community: The role of the black church. In D. H. McCree, K. T. Jones, & A. O'Leary (Eds.), *African Americans and HIV/AIDS* (pp. 53–68). New York, NY: Springer.

Eng, E., Moore, K. S., Rhodes, S. D., Griffith, D. M., Allison, L. L., Shirah, K., & Mebane, E. M. (2005). Insiders and outsiders assess who is "the community." In B. A. Israel, E. Eng, A. J. Schulz, & E. A. Parker (Eds.), *Methods in community-based participatory research for health* (pp. 77–100). San Francisco, CA: Jossey-Bass.

Eyler, J. (2002). Reflection: Linking service and learning—Linking students and communities. *Journal of Social Issues, 58,* 517–534.

Fanon, F. (1968). *The wretched of the earth.* New York, NY: Grove Press.

Festinger, L. (1957). *A theory of cognitive dissonance.* Stanford, CA: Stanford University Press.

Festinger, L., Riecken, H. W., & Schachter. S. (1956). *When prophecy fails: A social and psychological study of a modern group that predicted the destruction of the world.* New York, NY: Harper & Row.

Finkelhor, D. (1979). *Sexually victimized children.* New York, NY: Free Press.

Finkelhor, D., Turner, H., Ormrod, R., & Hamby, S. L. (2009). Violence, abuse, and crime exposure in a national sample of children and youth. *Pediatrics, 124,* 1411–1423.

Finlay, L. (2006). Dancing between embodied empathy and phenomenological reflection. *The Indo-Pacific Journal of Phenomenology, 6,* 1–11.

Fisher, J., & Brimley, D. (2006). Nurses' and carers' spiritual well-being in the workplace. *Australian Journal of Advanced Nursing, 25,* 49–57.

Flanagan, W. (2002). *Urban sociology: Images and structure.* New York, NY: Pearson.

Freire, P. (1970). *The pedagogy of the oppressed.* New York, NY: Seabury.

Freire, P. (1985). *The politics of education.* South Hadley, MA: Bergin & Garvey.

Garrison, D. R., Cleveland-Innes, M., Koole, M., & Kappelman, J. (2006). Revisiting methodological issues in transcript analysis: Negotiating coding and reliability. *The Internet and Higher Education, 9,* 1–8.

Giles, D. E., & Eyler, J. (1994). The theoretical roots of service-learning in John Dewey: Toward a theory of service-learning. *Michigan Journal of Community Service Learning, 1,* 77–85.

Ginwright, S. (2002). Classed out: The challenges of social class in black community change. *Social Problems, 49,* 544–562.

Ginwright, S., and Cammarota, J. 2002. "New Terrain in Youth Development: The Promise of a Social Justice Approach." *Social Justice 29,* 82–95.

Goffman, E. (1967). *Interaction ritual.* New York, NY: Pantheon Books.

Goodman, R. M., Speers, M. A. McLeroy, K., Fawcett, S., Kegler, M., Parker, E., Wallerstein, N. (1998). Identifying and defining the dimensions of community capacity to provide a basis for measurement. *Health Education & Behavior, 25,* 258–278.

Gray, M. (2011). Back to basics: A critique of the strengths perspective in social work. *Families in Society: The Journal of Contemporary Social Services, 92,* 5–11.

Green, A. E. (2003). Difficult stories: Service-Learning, race, class, and whiteness. *College Composition and Communication, 55,* 276–301.

Gruber, J., & Hungerman, D. M. (2008). The church versus the mall: What happens when religion faces increased secular competition? *The Quarterly Journal of Economics, 123,* 831–862.

Gruenwald, D. A. (2003). The best of both worlds: A critical reflection of place. *Educational Researcher, 32,* 3–12.

Haight, W. L. (2001). *African-American children at church: A sociocultural perspective.* Cambridge, UK: Cambridge University Press.

Hawes, S. M., & Berkley-Patton, J. Y. (2014). Religiosity and risky sexual behaviors among an African American church-based population. *Journal of Religion and Health, 53*, 469–482.

Haymes, S. N. (1995). *Race, culture, and the city: A pedagogy for black urban struggle*. Albany: State University of New York Press.

Hild, C. M. (2007). Places and states of mind for healing. *ReVision, 29*, 12–19.

Hiltner, S. (1959). The Christian shepherd. *Pastoral Psychology, 10*, 47–54.

Hironimus-Wendt, R. J., & Lovell-Troy, L. (1999). Grounding service learning in social theory. *Teaching Sociology, 27*, 360–372.

Honadle, B. W. (1981). A capacity-building framework: A search for concept and purpose. *Public Administration Review, 41*, 575–580.

hooks, b. (1994). *Teaching to transgress: Education as the practice of freedom*. New York, NY: Routledge.

Hopkins, P., Olson, E., Pain, R., & Vincett, G. (2011). Mapping intergenerationalities: The formation of youthful religiosities. *Transactions of the Institute of British Geographers, 36*, 314–327.

Howard, C. L. (2012). Dialogue between the black church and hip hop. In E. G. Price III (Ed.), *The black church and hip hop culture: Toward bridging the generational divide*. (pp. 33–42). Lanham, MD: Scarecrow Press.

Hsieh, H., & Shannon, S. E. (2005). Three approaches to qualitative context analysis. *Qualitative Health Research, 16*, 1277–1288.

Ingersoll-Dayton, B., Krause, N., & Morgan, D. (2002). Religious trajectories and transitions over the life course. *The International Journal of Aging and Human Development, 55*, 51–70.

Institute of Medicine. (1988). *The future of public health*. Washington, DC: National Academy Press.

Israel, B. A., Coombe, C. M., Cheezum, R. R., Schulz, A. J., McGranaghan, R. J., Lichtenstein, R.,... Burris, A. (2010). Community-based participatory research: A capacity-building approach for policy advocacy aimed at eliminating health disparities. *American Journal of Public Health, 100*, 2094–2102.

Johnston, G. N., & Benitez, B. (2003). Faith: A project in building community capacity. *American Journal of Health Studies, 18*, 138–145.

Jones, S. R., & Wijeyesinghe, C. L. (2011). The promises and challenges of teaching from an intersectional perspective: Core components and applied strategies. *New Directions for Teaching and Learning, 125*, 11–20.

Kampf, Z. (2009). Public (non-)apologies: The discourse of minimizing responsibility. *Journal of Pragmatics, 41*, 2257–2270.

Kezar, A. (1998). Exploring new avenues for leading community colleges in the 21st century: The paradox of participatory models. *Community College Review, 25*, 73–88.

King, P. E., & Furrow, J. L. (2008). Religion as a resource for positive youth development: Religion, social capital, and moral outcomes. *Psychology of Religion and Spirituality, S(1)*, 34–49.

Kirk-Duggan, C., & Hall, M. (2011). *Wake up! Hip-hop Christianity and the black church*. Nashville, TN: Abingdon Press.

Koenig, H., King, D., & Carson, V. B. (2012). *Handbook of religion and health*. Oxford, UK: Oxford University Press.

Koenig, H. G., Kvale, J. N., & Ferrel, C. (1988). Religion and well-being in later life. *The Gerontologist, 28*, 18–28.

Kretzmann, J. P., & McKnight, J. L. (1993). *A path toward finding and mobilizing a community's assets*. Chicago, IL: ACTA Publishing.

Ku, L., Sonenstein, F., Lindberg, L. D., Bradner, C. H., Boggess, S., & Pleck, J. H. (1998). Understanding changes in sexual activity among young metropolitan men: 1979–1995. *Family Planning Perspectives, 30*, 256–262.

Langton, P., & Kammerer, D. A. (2005). *Practicing sociology in the community: A student's guide*. Upper Saddle River, NJ: Pearson/Prentice-Hall.

Leavey, G., & King, M. (2007). The devil is in the detail: Partnerships between psychiatry and faith-based organizations. *British Journal of Psychiatry, 191*, 97–98.

Lewis, D. J., & Weigert, A. (1985). Trust as a social reality. *Social Forces, 63*, 967–985.

Lewis, D. L. (2000). *W. E. B. Du Bois: The fight for equality and the American century, 1919–1963*. New York, NY: Henry Holt.

Lincoln, C. E., & Mamiya, L. M. (1990). *The black church in the African American experience*. Durham, NC: Duke University Press.

Litke, R. A. (2002). Do all students "get it?" Comparing students' reflections to course performance. *Michigan Journal of Community Service Learning, 8*, 27–34.

Lockwood, K. (2010). Creating an identity and protecting inclusivity: The challenge facing progressive Christianity. *The International Journal of Diversity in Organizations, Communities and Nations, 10*, 39–48.

Lorde, A. (1984a). The master's tools will never dismantle the master's house. In Audre Lorde (Ed.), *Sister outsider: Essays and speeches*. (pp. 110–123). Freedom, CA: Crossing Press.

Lorde, A. (1984b). The transformation of silence into language and action. In Audre Lorde (Ed.), *Sister outsider: Essays and speeches*. (pp. 39–44). Freedom, CA: Crossing Press.

Lorde, A. (1984c). The uses of the erotic: The erotic as power. In Audre Lorde (Ed.), *Sister outsider: Essays and speeches*. (pp. 53–59). Freedom, CA: Crossing Press.

Lumpkins, C., Greiner, K., Daley, C., Mabachi, N., & Neuhaus, K. (2013). Promoting healthy behavior from the pulpit: Clergy share their perspectives on effective health communication in the African American church. *Journal of Religion and Health, 52*, 1093–1107.

MacMullan, T. (2005). Beyond the pale: A pragmatist approach to whiteness studies. *Philosophy & Social Criticism, 31*, 267–292.

Marks, L. (2005). Religion and bio-psycho-social health: A review and conceptual model. *Journal of Religion and Health, 44*, 173–185.

Martel, Y. (2003). *Life of Pi*. New York, NY: Mariner Books.

Mattis, J. S., Eubanks, K., Zapata, A. A., Grayman, N., Belkin, M., Mitchell, N. K., & Cooper, S. (2004). Factors influencing religious non-attendance among African American men: A multimethod analysis. *Review of Religious Research, 45*, 386–403.

Mattis, J. S., & Jagers, R. J. (2001). A relational framework for the study of religiosity and spirituality in the lives of African Americans. *Journal of Community Psychology, 29*, 519–539.

Mays, B. E., & Nicholson, J. W. (1933). *The Negro's church*. New York, NY: Institute of Social and Religious Research.

McAllister, G., & Irvine, J. J. (2002). The role of empathy in teaching culturally diverse students: A qualitative study of teachers' beliefs. *Journal of Teacher Education, 53*, 433–443.

McIntosh, P. (1988). White privilege and male privilege: A personal account of coming to see correspondences through work in women's studies. In R. Delgado & J. Stefancic (Eds.), *Critical white studies: Looking behind the mirror* (pp. 291–299). Philadelphia, PA: Temple University Press.

McRoberts, O. (2003). *Streets of glory: Church and community in a black urban neighborhood*. Chicago, IL: University of Chicago Press.

Mechanic, D. (1972). Sociology and public health: Perspectives for application. *American Journal of Public Health, 62*, 146–151.

Miles, A. (2009). On a medicine of the whole person: Away from scientific reductionism and towards the embrace of the complex in clinical practice. *Journal of Evaluation in Clinical Practice, 15*, 941–949.

Miller, M. R. (2012). *Religion and hip hop*. New York, NY: Routledge.

Mills, C. W. (1959/2000). *The sociological imagination*. Oxford, UK: Oxford University Press.

Minkler, M. (2000). Using participatory action research to build healthy communities. *Public Health Reports, 115*, 191–197.

Minkler, M., & Wallerstein, N. (2010). *Community-based participatory research for health: From process to outcomes*. San Francisco, CA: Jossey-Bass.

Mitchem, S. Y., & Townes, E. M. (Eds.). (2008). *Faith, health, and healing in African American life*. New York, NY: Praeger.

Mueller, P. S., Plevak, D. J., & Rummans, T. A. (2001). Religious involvement, spirituality, and medicine: Implications for clinical practice. *Mayo Clinic Proceedings, 76*, 1225–1235.

Myers, J., & Jackson, M. (2008). The freedom of a teenager: Vocation and service learning as the future of youth ministry. *Dialog, 47*, 327–338.

Nelkin, D. (2004). God talk: Confusion between science and religion: A posthumous essay. *Science, Technology & Human Values, 29*, 139–152.

Noddings, N. (1984). *Caring: A feminist approach to ethics and moral education*. Berkeley: University of California Press.

Parkinson, P. 2002. "What does the Lord require of Us? Child sexual abuse in the churches." *Journal of Religion & Abuse* 4: 3–31.

Pattillo-McCoy, M. (1998). Church culture as a strategy of action in the black community. *American Sociological Review, 63*, 767–784.

Patton, M. Q. (1980). *Qualitative evaluation methods*. Newbury Park, CA: Sage.

Petray, T., & Halbert, K. (2013). Teaching engagement: Reflections on sociological praxis. *Journal of Sociology, 49*, 441–455.

Petrosino, A., Turpin-Petrosino, C., & Finckenauer, J. O. (2000). Well-meaning program can have harmful effects! Lessons from experiments of programs such as scared straight. *Crime & Delinquency, 46*, 34–379.

Pew Research Center. (2012). *"Nones" on the rise: One-in-five adults have no religious affiliation*. Washington, DC: Author.

Pinn, A. B. (2004). Introduction. In A. B. Pinn & D. N. Hopkins (Eds.), *Loving the body: Black religious studies and the erotic*. (pp. 1–10). New York, NY: Palgrave Macmillan.

Pinwheels for Prevention. (n.d.). Retrieved from http://www.pinwheelsforprevention.org/

Plante, T. G., & Sherman, A. C. (2001). *Faith and health: Psychological perspectives*. New York, NY: Guilford Press.

Pollard, A. B. (2004). Teaching the body: Sexuality and the black church. In A. B. Pinn & D. N. Hopkins (Eds.), *Loving the body: Black religious studies and the erotic* (pp. 315–346). New York, NY: Palgrave Macmillan.

Price, E. G., III (Ed.). *The black church and hip hop culture: Toward bridging the generational divide*. Lanham, MD: Scarecrow Press.

Price-Spratlen, T. (1998). Between depression and prosperity? Changes in the community context of historical African American migration. *Social Forces, 77*, 515–539.

Price-Spratlen, T. (1999). Livin' for the city: African American ethnogenesis and depression era migration. *Demography, 36*, 553–568.

Price-Spratlen, T. (2008). Urban destination selection among African Americans during the 1950s great migration. *Social Science History, 32*, 437–469.

Price-Spratlen, T., & Goldsby, W. (2012.) *Reconstructing rage: Transformative reentry in the era of mass incarceration*. New York, NY: Peter Lang.

Price-Spratlen, T., Love, R., & Steinman, K. (2004a). *Service learning initiative grant, Columbus congregations for healthy youth*. Columbus, OH: The Ohio State University, Service Learning Initiative.

Price-Spratlen, T., Love, R., & Steinman, K. (2004b). *Update of the Columbus congregations for healthy youth service learning initiative (Final report)*. The Ohio State University, Service Learning Initiative.

Prus, R. (1976). Religious recruitment and the management of dissonance: A sociological perspective. *Sociological Inquiry, 46*, 127–134.

Ramsdell, E. T. (1943.). "Concerning the nature of religious faith." *The Journal of Religion 23*: 186–193.

Regnerus, M. (2007). *Forbidden fruit: Sex & religion in the lives of American teenagers*. Oxford, UK: Oxford University Press.

Rubin, C. L., Martinez, L. S., Chu, J., Hacker, K., Brugge, D., Pirie, A.,… Leslie. L. K. (2012). Community-engaged pedagogy: A strengths-based approach to involving diverse stakeholders in research partnerships. *Progress in Community Health Partnerships: Research, Education, and Action, 6*, 481–490.

Russell-Brown, K. (2008). *The color of crime: Racial hoaxes, white fear, black protectionism, police harassment, and other macroaggressions*. New York: New York University Press.

Saegert, S. (2006). Building civic capacity in urban neighborhoods: An empirically grounded anatomy. *Journal of Urban Affairs, 28*, 275–294.

Sherkat, D. E., & Ellison, C. G. (1999). Recent developments and current controversies in the sociology of religion. *Annual Review of Sociology, 25*, 363–394.

Simons, L., & Cleary, B. (2006). The influence of service learning on students' personal and social development. *College Teaching, 54*, 307–319.

Sinha, J. W., Cnaan, R. A., & Gelles, R. W. (2007). Adolescent risk behaviors and religion: Findings from a national study. *Journal of Adolescence, 30*, 231–249.

Sinha, J. W., Hillier, A., Cnaan, R. A., & McGrew, C. C. (2007). Proximity matters: Exploring relationships among neighborhoods, congregations, and the residential patterns of members. *Journal for the Scientific Study of Religion, 46*, 245–260.

Smith, C. (2005). *Soul searching: The religious and spiritual lives of American teenagers.* Oxford, UK: Oxford University Press.

Smith, E., & Jackson, P. (2005). *The hip hop church.* Downers Grove, IL: InterVarsity Press.

Spencer, M. B., Fegley, S. G., & Harpalani, V. (2003). A theoretical and empirical examination of identity as coping: Linking coping resources to the self-processes of African American youth. *Applied Developmental Science, 7*, 181–188.

Steinman, K., David Murray, J., Kubeka, K., Cooksey, E., Price-Spratlen, T., & Edwards, K. (2006, October 19). *Congregational differences in youth outcomes: Findings from 13 African-American churches.* Paper presented at the meetings of the Society for the Scientific Study of Religion. Portland, OR.

Steinman, K. J., Price-Spratlen, T., Cooksey, E., & Myers, L. J. 2003. *Columbus congregations for healthy youth.* Atlanta, GA: Centers for Disease Control and Prevention.

Steinman, K. J., Wright, V., Cooksey, E., Myers, L. J., Price-Spratlen, T., & Ryles, R. (2005). Collaborative research in a faith-based setting: Columbus congregations for health youth. *Public Health Reports, 120*, 213–216.

Stevenson, R. B. (2008). A critical pedagogy of place and the critical place of pedagogy. *Environmental Education Research, 14*, 353–360.

Strauss, R. S. (2000). Childhood obesity and self-esteem. *Pediatrics, 105*, 1–5.

Substance Abuse and Mental Health Services Administration. (2011). Current statistics on the prevalence and characteristics of people experiencing homelessness in the United States. Retrieved from (http://homeless.samhsa.gov/ResourceFiles/hrc_factsheet.pdf)

Tatum, S. R. F. B. (2010). *Poetics with a promise: Performances of faith and gender in Christian hip hop.* (Unpublished doctoral dissertation). Ann Arbor: University of Michigan, American Culture.

Taylor, R. J., Chatters, L. M., & Levin, J. (2004). *Religion in the lives of African Americans.* Thousand Oaks, CA: Sage.

Terry, A. W., & Bohnenberger, J. E. (2003). Service learning: Fostering a cycle of caring in our gifted youth. *Journal of Advanced Academics, 15*, 23–32.

Terry, A. W., & Bohnenberger, J. E. (2004). Blueprint for incorporating service learning: A basic, developmental, K-12 service learning typology. *Journal of Experiential Education, 27*, 15–31.

U.S. Department of Health and Human Services. (2010). New challenges, new solutions, statistical overviews. Retrieved from http://ovc.ncjrs.gov/ncvrw2013/pdf/StatisticalOverviews.pdf

Uecker, J.E., M. Regnerus, and M.L. Vaaler. 2007. "Losing My Religion: The Social Sources of Religious Decline in Early Adulthood." Social Forces 85, 1667-1692.

Vangen, S., & Huxham, C. (2003). Nurturing collaborative relations: Building trust in inter-organizational collaboration. *Journal of Applied Behavioral Science, 39,* 5–31.

Vaught, S. E., & Castagno, A. E. (2008). "I don't think I'm a racist": Critical race theory, teacher attitudes, and structural racism. *Race, Ethnicity, and Education, 11,* 95–113.

Walker, D. E. (1995). Protection of American Indian sacred geography. In C. Vecsey (Ed.), *Handbook of American Indian religious freedom* (pp. 100–115). New York, NY: Crossroad.

Wallace, J. M., & Forman, T. A. (1998). Religion's role in promoting health and reducing risk among American youth. *Health Education & Behavior, 25,* 721–741.

Warren, C. L. (2006). *A quantitative analysis of the synergy among self-reported faith, health, and health care practices of black Baptists: A culturecology perspective.* (Unpublished doctoral dissertation). Pittsburgh, PA: University of Pittsburgh, School of Public Health.

Welch, M. (2010). Shedding light on the shadow-side of reflection in service learning. *Journal of College and Character, 11,* 1–6.

White, R. B. (2011). *Wholly hip-hop: A pedagogy of engagement for Christian education with African American youth.* (Doctoral dissertation). Available from ProQuest Dissertations and Theses database. (UMI No. 3464424)

Whitt-Glover, M. C., Hogan, P. E., Lang, W., & Heil, D. P. (2008). Pilot study of a faith-based physical activity program among sedentary blacks. *Preventing Chronic Disease, 5,* 1–9.

Williams, J. L., Tolan, P. H., Durkee, M. I., Francois, A. G., & Anderson, R. E. (2012). Integrating racial and ethnic identity research into developmental understanding of adolescents. *Child Development Perspectives, 6,* 304–311.

Wimberly, E. P. (1982). *Pastoral counseling and spiritual values: A black point of view.* Nashville, TN: Abingdon Press.

World Council of Churches (WCC). (1990). *Healing and wholeness. The churches' role in health* (Report of a study by the Christian Medical Commission). Geneva, Switzerland: Author.

INDEX

ROCHELLE BROCK &
RICHARD GREGGORY JOHNSON III,
Executive Editors

Black Studies and Critical Thinking is an interdisciplinary series which examines the intellectual traditions of and cultural contributions made by people of African descent throughout the world. Whether it is in literature, art, music, science, or academics, these contributions are vast and far-reaching. As we work to stretch the boundaries of knowledge and understanding of issues critical to the Black experience, this series offers a unique opportunity to study the social, economic, and political forces that have shaped the historic experience of Black America, and that continue to determine our future. Black Studies and Critical Thinking is positioned at the forefront of research on the Black experience, and is the source for dynamic, innovative, and creative exploration of the most vital issues facing African Americans. The series invites contributions from all disciplines but is specially suited for cultural studies, anthropology, history, sociology, literature, art, and music.

Subjects of interest include (but are not limited to):

- EDUCATION
- SOCIOLOGY
- HISTORY
- MEDIA/COMMUNICATION
- RELIGION/THEOLOGY
- WOMEN'S STUDIES

- POLICY STUDIES
- ADVERTISING
- AFRICAN AMERICAN STUDIES
- POLITICAL SCIENCE
- LGBT STUDIES

For additional information about this series or for the submission of manuscripts, please contact Dr. Brock (Indiana University Northwest) at brock2@iun.edu or Dr. Johnson (University of San Francisco) at rgjohnsoniii@usfca.edu.

To order other books in this series, please contact our Customer Service Department:

(800) 770-LANG (within the U.S.)
(212) 647-7706 (outside the U.S.)
(212) 647-7707 FAX

Or browse online by series at www.peterlang.com.